D0602324

lights
Camera
action!

A Century of the Cinema

☆ ☆ ☆

TONY **BILBOW** & JOHN **GAU**

PICTURE RESEARCH JAMES SMITH

LITTLE, BROWN AND COMPANY
Boston • New York • Toronto • London

A LITTLE, BROWN BOOK

First published in Great Britain in 1995 by Little, Brown and Company (UK)

A CIP catalogue record for this book is available from the British Library

ISBN 0-316-87595-3

10 9 8 7 6 5 4 3 2 1

DESIGNED BY THE BRIDGEWATER BOOK COMPANY

Printed and bound in Singapore by CS Graphics PTE Ltd

Little, Brown and Company (UK)

Brettenham House

Lancaster Place

London WC2E 7EN

CONTENTS

Foreword

People have always loved going to the cinema; and not just because of the film, although clearly the film is what gets us inside. What really captivates us is the whole movie-going experience. No other entertainment is quite like it - not books, not opera or ballet, not television, not live theatre. For a hundred years, "Going To The Pictures" has been a very special, shared, global experience, and it shows no signs of being replaced by anything else. Our grandparents were astonished by it; to our parents, it was affordable luxury and glamour at the picture palace for the whole family. Today, for our children, Friday or Saturday night at the movies is still a key experience. It is where they meet their friends, take their dates, or simply get away from their parents.

The sense of occasion is something veteran director Robert Wise remembers well. He grew up in a small town in Indiana, where the largest of three theatres was called The Auditorium. "When a road show came in, like C. B. DeMille's *The Ten Commandments*, you bought your tickets in advance, you had your reserved seats and they had the orchestra in the pit, playing the score. Those were very special events; we looked forward to them for six months before they came."

For most people, it seems, childhood memories of the cinema are ineradicable. Anthony Quinn's first visit to the cinema - or rather, a shopfront nickelodeon - was in 1918. "There had been a heavy fall of snow, so hardly anyone was there, and the pianist never showed up either. My grandmother and I sat there watching the screen; no sound, just images and titles, which my grandmother couldn't understand because she couldn't read English. I couldn't either - because I was two and a half. But I'll never forget Ramon Novarro - he was fantastic."

Director Nic Roeg also saw his first film as a small child. "I even remember the very first shot. It was Laurel and Hardy lying in bed snoring. Olly blew a feather up in the air and it came down again on

Stan's nose and then he blew it... I can see it quite clearly. Of course, going to the pictures then was a special treat... it's very unusual for kids to have treats nowadays, one gets everything."

John Schlesinger's childhood memory is of a newsreel. "There was a close-up of a dead person on the screen; it was the assassination of the King of Yugoslavia. There he was in his carriage lying face up, with a funny rictus sort of smile on his face. Very strange, and I've never forgotten it."

LIGHTS, CAMERA, ACTION! is a celebration of the first hundred years of the most vigorous popular art in the world. It is not, nor could it be in a book of this length, a comprehensive history of the cinema. We have treated the story of the movies thematically, each chapter devoted to a different aspect of film-making down the years. In this way, each chapter may be read on its own without reference to the others, but taken together they provide a considered portrait of a century of the cinema. The book is easy to dip into, an invitation to browse and to take in the broader picture at leisure.

Cinema's one hundred-year journey is clearly sign-posted at all its cross-roads - the everyday scenes captured by the hand-cranked camera of the Lumière brothers, Edwin S. Porter's first narrative film, *The Great Train Robbery*, Al Jolson's audience-stopping ad-lib, "You ain't heard nothing yet!" that ushered in sound, the lush wonders of Technicolor - just some of the breakthroughs that have fuelled the cinema's irresistible progress.

In the beginning there were visionaries like Edison, who invented the technology of film; the early and innovative film-makers G.A. Smith, James Williamson, Porter, D.W. Griffith and his eccentric pupil, Mack Sennett, whose work helped form the now familiar language of film; Eisenstein and Gance, who invented new and dazzling film techniques. Later there was Walt Disney, whose feature-length *Snow White* changed for ever the audience's view of animation; and the masters of today, Lucas and Spielberg, who saved Hollywood from decline and turned it into the supreme entertainment phenomenon it is today.

LIGHTS, CAMERA, ACTION! is intended for the general reader; nevertheless, the movie buff should not be disappointed, and may even encounter a few arcane facets of film history and legend.

Tony Bilbow and John Gau, October 1995

C H A P T E R

The Sweet Smell of Success

Sitting behind the wheel of a becalmed Range Rover is Bob Peck, the great white hunter employed by Lord Attenborough of Clones. With him are publicity man Sam Neill and two fearless palaeontologists from Central Stereotyping, Jeff Goldblum and Laura Dern.

So far so unexceptional; for, in the last decade or so, we've become blasé and cynical, taking spectacle for granted and media hype for what it is. Nevertheless, our sense of wonder is still there, simply waiting for a master film-maker to appear and astonish us with his *own* sense of wonder...

And we are about to be shamelessly manipulated. In a reaction shot we see that Goldblum is stunned by what we know is there, but haven't seen yet. Dern is too busy with fossil-speak to look, but when at last she - and *we* - see those heart-stopping dinosaurs, the helmet and goggles of virtual reality couldn't do what Steven Spielberg has done for us in *Jurassic Park* (1993). Suspension of disbelief is total - his creatures are *alive*.

Once in a while a film comes along which so captures the public imagination that it becomes part of our culture. It is that rare event that perfectly encapsulates cinema's awesome power - the power to bring a new entertainment experience to a world-wide audience, introduce new words into the language, new toys into the market place, a new excitement into our culture and, of course, generate fabulous riches for the people involved in its making. Spielberg's film is the perfect and most successful example of what movies are always striving for - but only occasionally achieve - an irresistible appeal to the human spirit, a call that is answered by millions of us. Today we call this movie phenomenon "the blockbuster".

Every film that has ever been made is beholden to the Kinetograph (camera) and Kinetoscope (projector) invented by Thomas Alva Edison.

In the days of the silents, movie hits were as much the work of the cameraman as the director.

Now in 70 mm. wide screen and full stereophonic sound!

DAVID O. SELZNICK'S PRODUCTION OF MARGARET MITCHELL'S

"GONE WITH THE WIND"

STARRING

CLARK GABLE
VIVIEN LEIGH
LESLIE HOWARD
OLIVIA de HAVILLAND

Winner
of Ten
Academy
Awards

A SELZNICK INTERNATIONAL PICTURE · VICTOR FLEMING · SIDNEY HOWARD · METRO-GOLDWYN-MAYER INC.

Music by MAX STEINER · IN 70mm. WIDE SCREEN · STEREOPHONIC SOUND · METROCOLOR   MGM

Call it irresistible. Selznick's 1939 blockbuster remains at the top of the (inflation-adjusted) box-office hits list.

The century-old movie-going habit hasn't had to depend on the blockbuster for its longevity, but *only* the blockbuster can bring together millions of different people to produce the vast shared excitement and emotion that makes the movie-going experience unique. *The Birth of a Nation* (1915) had it in spades, *Gone With the Wind* (1939) has become legend, *The Sound of Music* (1965) reached out to embrace us and still refuses to let some of us go; and then, surpassing all of them came.... *Jurassic Park* (1993).

Almost eight decades earlier, the cinema's first blockbuster - and the most successful silent film ever made - was premiered at Clune's Auditorium in Los Angeles in 1915. It was, of course, D.W. Griffith's *The Birth of a Nation*. It's difficult now to imagine the impact it had on that first night audience, but the atmosphere of anticipation in the theatre must have been almost tactile. The music, specially composed for the film and conducted by Joseph Carl Breil, was played by scores of musicians, most of whom were moonlighting from the Los Angeles Symphony Orchestra.

At the end of the film, three hours later, people stood up and cheered, yelling and stamping their feet until Griffith finally made an appearance. According to one eye-witness (Griffith's assistant cameraman, Karl Brown, author of *Adventures With D.W. Griffith*), "He did not bow or wave his hands or do anything but just stand there and let wave after wave of cheers and applause wash over him like great waves breaking over a rock."

In a highly unstable business, David Wark Griffith took enormous risks to make his Civil War epic, not least among them being the budget of $100,000 - an improvidently high figure 80 years ago.

Griffith didn't set out to make a blockbuster - neither the word nor the concept existed, of course - but he did everything possible to ensure that his film would be financially successful. He was no businessman, but in some respects he was as shrewd as any of the commercial film-makers who came after him. Griffith tempered his creative vision with a disarming modesty, holding sneak previews - not just one or two, but as many as he deemed necessary to obtain his audiences' seal of approval. The previews were held in great secrecy so that no professionals - in particular, no partisan professionals from his own studio - could upset the balance of grass roots reaction. Other film-makers might refer, patronisingly, to the hicks in the sticks, but if Griffith's hicks didn't laugh and cry in the right places then he knew

The
MONEY MAKERS

It is very hard to come up with a definitive list of history's most successful films (TABLE 1) because inflation constantly distorts the figures. However, adjusting box-office returns to 1994 prices does create an interesting new version (TABLE 2) — even if only using North American revenues. As for the flops, they are harder still to pin down, but these (TABLE 3) are genuine turkeys.

1 • ALL-TIME INTERNATIONAL CHAMPS

1. *Jurassic Park* (1993)
2. *The Lion King* (1994)
3. *E.T. – The Extra-Terrestrial* (1982)
4. *Forrest Gump* (1994)
5. *Ghost* (1990)
6. *Star Wars* (1977)
7. *The Bodyguard* (1992)
8. *Home Alone* (1990)
9. *Indiana Jones and the Temple of Doom* (1989)
10. *Aladdin* (1992)

2 • MOST SUCCESSFUL FILMS OF ALL TIME

1. *Gone With the Wind* (1939)
2. *Star Wars* (1977)
3. *The Ten Commandments* (1956)
4. *The Sound of Music* (1965)
5. *Jaws* (1975)
6. *E.T.* (1982)
7. *Doctor Zhivago* (1965)
8. *The Jungle Book* (1967)
9. *Snow White and the Seven Dwarfs* (1937)
10. *101 Dalmatians* (1961)

3 • GREATEST FLOPS OF ALL TIME

1. *Hudson Hawk* (1991)
2. *Heaven's Gate* (1980)
3. *The Adventures of Baron Munchausen* (1988)
4. *Ishtar* (1987)
5. *Inchon* (1981)
6. *The Cotton Club* (1984)
7. *Santa Claus: The Movie* (1985)
8. *Pirates* (1986)
9. *Rambo III* (1988)
10. *Raise the Titanic* (1980)

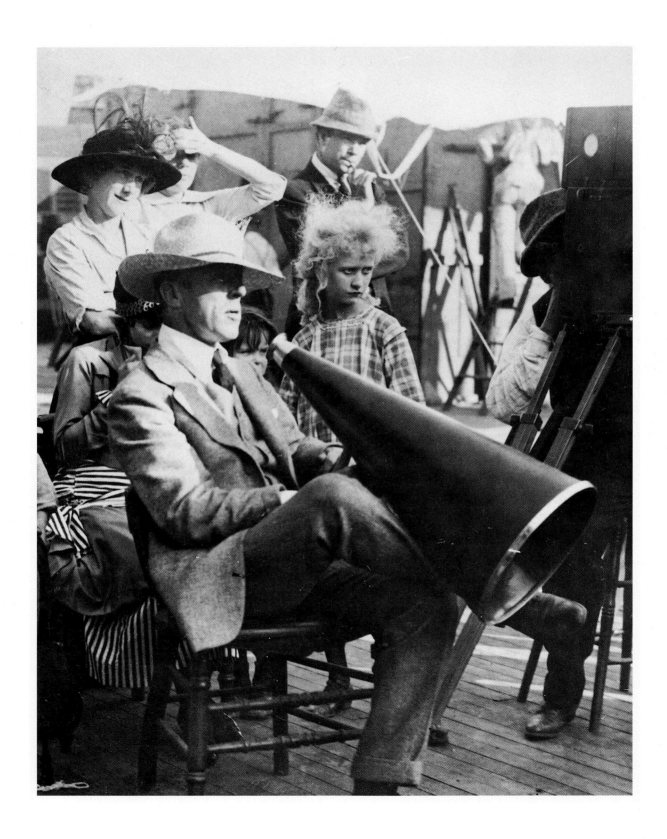

he was wrong - and not his loyal public. *The Birth of a Nation* was previewed several times and, as a result, honed and fine-tuned until DW's *audiences* were satisfied.

But before his masterpiece was finished, Griffith was fast running out of money. One of the people who helped him out was his cameraman, Billy Bitzer, who lent his hard-up boss $10,000. Not counting world-wide sales, which are difficult to calculate now, *The Birth of a Nation* made a *hundred times its original investment* in North America alone - and that's something no film since then has achieved, not even *Jurassic Park*. The sum of $10 million *then* would be about $133 million today. Billy Bitzer, who prudently didn't give up the day job, rapidly became a millionaire. Griffith, on the other hand, didn't.

As a general rule, artists aren't good with money. Even so, it's hard to see by what perverse genius Griffith managed to keep so little of the total profits. Louis B. Mayer, one of the people who merely *showed* the film, made a cool million. The answer lies in the money Griffith poured into his next - and financially disastrous - film, *Intolerance* (1916). *The Birth of a Nation* retained its position as the biggest movie of all time - until, 24 years later, David O. Selznick nudged it out of the way with *Gone With the Wind*.

Released in 1939, *Gone With the Wind* grossed $1million in its first week, and went on to make well over $76 million in North America alone. World-wide, the figure reached at least $152 million. Judged by the currency of today – that was phenomenal. As every year boasts a new "biggest-grossing film ever", it is worth remembering what a dollar or pound bought in those pre-war days. In Britain in 1939 on average it cost 5d (not even sixpence) to go to the cinema, although in the West End you could pay two shillings. Today the average ticket price is £3.11. And an American cinema-goer would have paid 23 cents to see *Gone With the Wind*. Today it would be $4.15. So, taking into account what inflation has done over the last 50 or so years, *Gone With the Wind* has grossed $1.8 *billion* - and it's still earning. In cinema's extreme youth, the mostly unsophisticated audiences didn't take much persuading to fill the shopfront theatres. The only couch potatoes in those days were the people who read books, and there weren't too many of them in the early 1900s. Film, on the other hand, was universally accessible. As for publicity, a few posters and word of mouth kept the takings nicely topped up.

Most directors, in the early days, called "Camera" and "Cut". D.W. Griffith, director of *The Birth of a Nation* (opposite), never did. For him, it was always "Fade in" and "Fade out".

Selznick's memos would have filled a book, and did. *Memo from David O. Selznick* ran to 475 (edited) pages.

But by the Twenties and Thirties, audiences had become choosy, and huge financial successes didn't, on the whole, happen by accident. This was the heyday of the studio star system and, crucially, of studio publicity and professional ballyhoo - the forerunner of the sophisticated hype we see today.

David O. Selznick chalked up two-and-a-half years of free publicity with his famous search for Scarlett O'Hara. Indeed, he spent all those two-and-a-half years working on this, his pet project - and during that time he never doubted that he was on to a winner. And if there is a recipe for a blockbuster, consider the ingredients. The screenplay was based on the best-selling novel by Margaret Mitchell and therefore had an enormous potential audience breathlessly waiting. This audience had already decided that it wanted Clark Gable, and no other, to play Rhett Butler, and it was further delighted and vastly entertained by the never-ending search for Scarlett O'Hara. The film eventually won eight Oscars, and Oscars bring in more audiences. The recipe for a blockbuster was complete.

However, not everyone thought as Selznick did. Before he died in 1936, Irving Thalberg, head of production at MGM, had already turned down Margaret Mitchell's book. It is a measure of the boy-wonder's reputation that his boss, Louis B. Mayer, who had made a fortune out of *The Birth of a Nation*, took it on the chin when his protégé told him, "No Civil War picture ever made a nickel".

It was Selznick who went ahead and bought the rights to Margaret Mitchell's book - although, in true mogul style, he'd only read a synopsis. The price of $55,000 was high in those days for a novel as yet unpublished but, had Selznick waited to see how phenomenally well the book would do, the price would have been much higher.

In an age of hands-on moguls, Selznick stuck more fingers into production pies than any of them, and when he wasn't actually on the set, he was firing off longwinded memos to everyone. A deadpan Bob Hope said, "Last year, I received a memo from David Selznick.... I've just finished reading it."

In the case of *Gone With the Wind*, Selznick was into everything - casting, wardrobe, publicity, set design, editing, directing - and especially the screenplay, which is credited on screen to Sidney Howard but which has a huge Selznick input.

To direct, the great George Cukor was hired, fired, and replaced by Victor Fleming who received sole screen credit as director, even

though a good deal of Cukor's work remains in the film. Also uncredited is the additional work of director Sam Wood.

But the biggest come-on to the public was the nation-wide search for Scarlett O'Hara. It was more than a publicity stunt - although it was that too: Selznick's agents saw over 2000 young women, and some of them actually got to stand in front of the camera. In fact, the amount of film shot on tests could have made several feature films.

For the part of Rhett Butler, Clark Gable was the people's choice, but he was under contract to MGM. The only way Selznick could get him was to give MGM 50% of the film's profits. Oddly enough, Clark Gable wasn't at all keen on being loaned out to Louis B. Mayer's son-in-law. The readers

Memo from Selznick: "Gable's clothes. There is no excuse for their fitting him so badly, especially round the collar."

His women (and some of the men) fans would have given anything to be kissed by the King of Hollywood; but Leigh hated the idea. Gable had false teeth "and they smell."

of the book had scores of different Rhetts in their heads, so Gable reckoned he'd be on a hiding to nothing. But... he was in the middle of an expensive divorce, and wanted to marry Carole Lombard at the end of it, and a handy increase in his salary finally convinced the King of Hollywood that the part of Rhett Butler was, after all, tailor-made for him - "....but you can forget the Southern accent, Selznick, and I sure as hell ain't gonna play the cissy and cry when Scarlett has that miscarriage." Cut to Gable on set, weeping. Selznick was seldom to be denied; and, to be fair, Gable was too much the professional not to recognise the dramatic force of the scene.

Gable was in, but Scarlett wasn't even on the horizon. As well as the unknowns who were interviewed and occasionally tested, the "Stars" and "Also Starrings" and "Introducings" were tested and short-listed. Among them were Bette Davis, Katharine Hepburn, Loretta Young, Ann Sheridan, Norma Shearer and Tallulah Bankhead, but in the end it came down to a short-list of four - Joan Bennett, Jean Arthur, Paulette Goddard and Vivien Leigh.

Selznick had always said he wasn't going to be rushed but, after over two years, he could delay no longer, and shooting started on *Gone With the Wind* before the female lead had been cast.

The burning of Atlanta was the first scene to be shot. Old film sets on the back lot at MGM had been repainted and then set alight, with party-pooping fire brigades standing by in case things got out of hand. Rhett and Scarlett appear in the scene, but they're played by doubles. Standing, Nero-like, on top of his observation platform, watching Atlanta burn, Selznick was tapped on the shoulder by his tardy and well-oiled theatrical agent brother, Myron, who had brought a young actress from England to meet him. As Selznick turned round, there - pause, gulp, recover, take a memo - stood Scarlett O'Hara. Well, yes... but in fact, Selznick had already seen Vivien Leigh in *Fire Over England* (1937), a film she'd made with her lover, Laurence Olivier; but the dramatic meeting, stagily staged by the Selznicks or not, made, and still makes, a pretty story.

But, right up to the last minute, Paulette Goddard had been in with considerably more than a chance. In one of his memos, Selznick said, "I have looked at the new Goddard test practically daily since it arrived, to see whether my first impression of the great improvement in her remained; and I must say that each time I see it I am more and more impressed."

The signing of Scarlett. Left to right: Selznick, reluctant Leslie Howard, cats-with-cream Vivien Leigh and Olivia de Havilland.

In the end of course, it was Vivien Leigh who got the part. But why? Was Vivien Leigh really better than Goddard?... Or even as good? The truth is - if truth can ever be discovered 50-odd years later - that Paulette Goddard was regarded as a loose woman. She was, at that time, living openly with Charlie Chaplin, and, in the moral climate of 1939, this simply would not do. The irony of it is that Vivien Leigh and Laurence Olivier were having an affair (they were respectably married, but to other people), as were Clark Gable and Carole Lombard. Unlike Paulette Goddard, the fruity foursome kept quiet about it. If they'd *all* been caught with their knickers down, who would have played Scarlett and Rhett? And would *Gone With the Wind* still have been a blockbuster?

Once the film was under way, Selznick and director George Cukor had differences of opinion. Selznick listened carefully, and then settled the matter in his own democratic style: Cukor was sacked. Gable was delighted when Victor Fleming took over, because he considered Cukor to be a "woman's director". But Cukor remained a shadowy presence; after each day's shooting, Vivien Leigh and Olivia de Havilland sneaked off to Cukor's home for tea, sympathy and direction by stealth.

One key scene in the film gave David Selznick momentary pause. The censor, Will H. Hays, wanted Rhett to say "Frankly my dear, I don't give a darn." Selznick didn't put his trust in memos this time. He flew to New York to try to persuade Hays that the word "damn" was essential. Selznick got his way, and craftily didn't tell Hays that he'd already had the scene shot both ways - belt and braces - just in case.

In the nation's cinemas, *Gone With the Wind* had a running time of three hours and forty minutes. Selznick demanded an intermission because he was afraid his blockbuster would turn into a bladder-buster. But his promotions manager - a brave man indeed - disagreed. Selznick then insisted on a tryout intermission during one of the screenings, and then counted the number of people who headed for blessed relief. Selznick had got it right once again.

Gone With the Wind remained unchallenged as the most successful sound film until 26 years later, when the hills of Hollywood were alive with the sound of Julie Andrews. *Gone With the Wind* and *The Sound of Music* represent the Holy Grail that movie-makers dream about; and they've tried all sorts of ways of getting their hands on it. One of the ways is to sneak up on it unawares. Don't try for it in one; instead, go for built-in safety with a production line of small, or at least *smaller*, attempts - in other words, apply the blockbuster principle to series and serials.

The "Star Wars" trilogy returned, in spirit, to Flash Gordon's stamping ground, the Saturday Morning Pictures; while the adventures of Indiana Jones (not to mention his Dad's), with their endless procession of cliff-hangers, harks back even further, to *The Perils of Pauline* and the beginnings of cinema. It is one of those "I Could Kick Myself" stories that Universal turned down young George Lucas's treatment of *Star Wars*, even though he'd recently made a fortune for them with *American Graffiti* (1973). Universal's loss was 20th Century-Fox's lip-smacking profit, although they would have turned Lucas down, too, it if hadn't been for the enthusiasm of Alan Ladd Jnr who persuaded the Fox board to back his faith in the project.

In 1977, Steven Spielberg and George Lucas were on holiday in Hawaii. This in itself sounds like fiction, since it's hard to imagine either of them taking a holiday. In fact, they used the time to worry about their respective films. *Close Encounters of the Third Kind* (1977) wouldn't be seen for another six months, and Lucas was still waiting for *Star Wars* (1977) to open. So they decided to worry about something else. "Listen," one of them must have said, "How about we..." (pause) "You mean......yes! Of *course!*" And there it was - the idea for a film which, as Lucas really did say, should be "....based on the serials I loved when I was a kid: action movies set in exotic locales with a cliffhanger every second. I wondered why they didn't make movies like that any more. I still wanted to see them." Ditto Steven. So four years later, Spielberg the Big Spender and Lucas the Tightwad joined forces to make *Raiders of the Lost Ark* (1981). It was an ideal partnership. Lucas kept Spielberg on a tight rein, and Spielberg shot the film in not much more than two months, his fastest time since his days with that nice television doctor, Marcus Welby, and Columbo.

The series, or serial, has always held out the promise of financial safety - a promise frequently broken, of course... but if a formula has worked once, why not again? In the late Thirties and Forties, there were the popular "Andy Hardy" films starring a teenage Mickey Rooney and his screen father Lewis Stone; and in their "Road" movies, Bing (Crosby) and Bob (Hope) scored points off each other, with the help of their incomparable straight-person, Dorothy Lamour.

☛ page 22

THE GOLD RUSH
UNITED ARTISTS 1925

Producer/Director: Charlie Chaplin

Stars: Charlie Chaplin, Georgia Hale, Mack Swain, Tom Murray

"What I have done in *The Gold Rush* is exactly what I want to do. I have no excuses, no alibis." And Charlie Chaplin didn't need any. Completed in 1925, *The Gold Rush* was the biggest grosser at the box-office since D.W. Griffith's *The Birth of a Nation* (1915), and regarded by many as Chaplin's masterpiece.

> " In the Gold Rush ...
> I got into a single
> situation: hunger...
> starving to death...
> eating shoe strings...
> And I thought
> ' Oh yes, there's
> something funny in
> that'. "
> **CHARLIE CHAPLIN**

Inspiration

The idea for *The Gold Rush* came to Chaplin in the nick of time. Having lost money at the box office with his previous film, the social drama, *A Woman of Paris* (1923), Chaplin was under pressure to hit back with an ambitious comedy. He was also not unaware of increasing competition from comedians of the stature of Buster Keaton and Harold Lloyd.

One Sunday morning, while staying at Douglas Fairbanks' house, Chaplin happened to pick up a stereoscope to look out at the view. What he saw was a band of prospectors working their way up a snowy Klondike mountain. The image started ideas flooding into his mind, "..and although I had no story, the image of one began to grow..." remembers Chaplin in his autobiography.

This first impression obviously did take hold. *The Gold Rush* opens with a dramatic image of of a long line of men scaling a snow-covered mountain slope, black against the white snow.

Chaplin with Georgia Hale, who replaced the pregnant Lita Grey as female lead and became Charlie's loyal friend.

With Mack Swain who plays a hungry and hallucinating prospector.

THESE BOOTS WERE MADE FOR EATING

Perhaps the most famous scene in *The Gold Rush* is the one in which Chaplin eats his own shoe. Introduced by the title "Thanksgiving Dinner", Chaplin is seen turning his shoe-laces like spaghetti, sucking at nails like juicy bones and ending the evening asleep with his foot in the oven.
The inspiration behind this gag was the grisly story of the Donner Party. Shooting in Northern California - not far from where the Donner Party had met it's end over 70 years before - Chaplin became intrigued by the sad fate of these snow-bound pioneers, forced to eat the flesh of their comrades to survive.
In case you were wondering, Chaplin's laces were made of liquorice.

N THE MAKING

The Gold Rush took Chaplin two years to make, and brought him to the edge of a nervous breakdown - though his personal life during this period was enough to do that.
In the course of filming Chaplin married the 15-year-old girl he had hired as the film's lead, Lolita MacMurray (renamed Lita Grey). He impregnated her twice in the space of two years, and, for her pains, deprived her of her part as the dance hall girl - a role he gave to the actress Georgia Hale.

GOING FOR GOLD

The Alaskan gold rush was the dramatic backdrop of Chaplin's story, and the plight of one small man its emotional focus. Charlie was, of course, that small man, and with his baggy trousers and dark eyes, this "lone prospector" couldn't have looked more lost against the immense snowy whiteness of the landscape.
It was a powerful idea: after all, the Alaskan gold rush, with its promise of a mountain of gold, was every immigrant's dream, and, as all too many knew, things didn't always work out.
Much of the film is set inside the desolate cabin of a desperado called Black Larsen. Seeking shelter from the cold, Charlie is initially thrown out of the cabin by Larsen, but is continuously blown back in by the wind. Also blown in by the wind is the film's other main character, Big Jim McKay. The growing partnership between Charlie and Big Jim eventually results in their sharing of a mountain of gold -though Charlie gets the girl.

Shooting *The Gold Rush* spread over 15 months, with 170 days of actual filming! It took 9 weeks to edit.

Then there were: Johnny Weissmuller's Me-Tarzan-You-Jane, "The Thin Man" series with Myrna Loy and William Powell, Francis the Talking Mule - upstabling his co-star Donald O'Connor; and a nice little earner for post-war austerity Britain, "The (Incredibly Awful) Huggetts". More recently, in 1967, there was *The Planet of the Apes*, which spawned four sequels, none of them a patch on the Charlton Heston version but using its success as a financial safety net.

Although all of these films were successful, none of them - apart from the "Star Wars" and "Indiana Jones" trilogies - could be called blockbusters, either singly or expressed as series... but there's one notable exception. Its elements of super-hero star, what-happens-next-thrills, extra-special special effects and instantly recognisable style are all carefully measured - then shaken, but not stirred....

Our blockbusting hero has been with us for well over 30 years, in and out of the cold war, in and out of trouble, in and out of feminine arms with never so much as a backward glance. Indeed, James Bond's attitude to women is... now how can it be best expressed?... As a feminist he remains slightly to the right of Oliver Reed.... and yet, in spite of being politically incorrect all his life, he's never been out of fashion. Our macho man is indestructible; the more he changes, the more he remains the same.

Thirty-four years ago, in 1961, two film producers - quite separately - saw enormous box-office potential in

Bratprints. Steven Spielberg and George Lucas join the immortals outside Grauman's Chinese Theater.

THE SWEET SMELL OF SUCCESS

the James Bond character. One was Harry Saltzman, who took out an option on the Ian Fleming novels. The other was Albert R. Broccoli, aka Cubby. In *The Incredible World of 007*, by Philip Lisa and Lee Pfeiffer, Broccoli says, "I'd been reading Fleming's works and I was surprised that no one had made films of them. Wolf Mankowicz said 'I know the guy who has the rights, [Harry Saltzman] but he hasn't been able to make a deal, and there are 21 days left in his option' ". Somewhat reluctantly, Broccoli agreed to co-produce the films with Saltzman, but Columbia wouldn't put up enough money; and then, Cubby's great friend, Arthur Krim of United Artists, said come in and talk. As Cubby recalls, "In 40 minutes, we made a deal for six pictures. As we left, Harry said 'We haven't got a deal. We don't have anything on paper'. I said, "When you shake hands with Arthur Krim you *have* a deal.'" Even so, with a budget of $1 million, United Artists clearly didn't regard the first James Bond film as the studio's flagship.

But whatever the ingredients for blockbusting success might be - and we'll come to those in a moment - it was a fair bet that nothing would work unless the quintessential Bond was found.

Ian Fleming suggested either David Niven or Roger Moore. Broccoli wanted Cary Grant, who turned him down, as did Patrick McGoohan.

Other names on the list were Richard Johnson and James Stewart. But Broccoli and Saltzman saw James Bond as ruthless, sophisticated, macho and, above all, radiating sexuality. Then Mr and Mrs Broccoli went to the pictures and saw Sean Connery in *Darby O'Gill and the Little People* (1959). Husband and wife were equally impressed.

Astonishingly, Connery had the confidence - or arrogance - to refuse a screen test. His aggressive manner, thumping the table with his fists at the very idea of being put on trial, so impressed - or alarmed - the producers that they thrust the pen into his giant paw. Broccoli says, "The difference between him and the other young actors was the difference between a still and a film. We knew we had our Bond".

Connery may have been putting on an act at that meeting, because he said later that when he was offered the part, "This was like asking a boy who was crazy about cars if he'd like a Jaguar as a present. I had never actually visualised myself as playing Bond when the rights to the books were sold, but when the chance to play Bond came along, I hardly slept for days."

Over the 30 years Bond has been with us, the sum of his films adds up to a blockbuster.... so the Old Firm must have been doing something right. In fact, they were doing *everything* right, with a formula that has worked faultlessly 17 times. These are some of the carefully weighed ingredients:

A pre-titles teaser to get the adrenaline flowing - followed by the It-Could-Only-Be Bond titles and music. Stir in a principal villain - "Welcome, Mr Bond", "It is useless to struggle, Mr Bond", "Good-bye, Mr Bond" - a villain goaded or humiliated at every turn, so that, in reprisal, statues are decapitated, girls gilded, and uncomplaining reptiles licensed to be squashed.

Then we have the unfailing popularity of the Bond regulars - Miss Moneypenny, the waspish Q - "Pay attention 007!" - and curmudgeonly avuncular M. Add a dash of macho, strictly heterosexual congress, followed by a high-speed chase that becomes more elaborate with each new film. The villain's plans for world domination - which are always foiled, but only at the last possible moment - involve edge-of-the-seat count-down clocks, switches and buttons, all taking place in the preposterous set-piece sets which are themselves paragons of honesty, every last dollar visible on screen. And as an encore before the final credits, 007 must have one last close call - the most famous being Rosa Klebb's Doc Martin Specials with their poisoned, spiked toecaps in *From Russia With Love* (1963). Tot it all up, and you have an unfailing recipe for blockbusting success.

But if Bond himself is at the heart of the series and the formula, we really ought to look more closely at the actors who've played him. With *Dr No* (1962), and for five more films, Connery *was* Bond, a class act most people would have said was impossible to follow. But the act *had* to be followed, because after *You Only Live Twice* (1967), Connery left. Cubby Broccoli says, "We didn't pay him a lot of money for *Dr No* because of the budget. He complained later, but we had paid him what he was entitled to. We started his whole career."

So Connery left. Enter a brave man: George Lazenby. Comments Timothy Dalton: "Lazenby had the problem that I wouldn't go anywhere near, which is taking over from Connery. You couldn't take over from him. Sean was bloody good. As for Lazenby, *On Her Majesty's Secret Service* (1969) was a better film than most people give it credit for. Lazenby was OK, but inexperienced. I'm not going to knock him, and the film is one of the best."

BANKABLE BONDS

From the moment that Sean Connery uttered the immortal words "The name's Bond, James Bond", in 1962, the Bond films were licenced to make a killing at the box office. The first four (*Dr No, From Russia With Love, Goldfinger* and *Thunderball*) were immensely profitable, generating between 10 and 20 times what they cost to make. In recent years, due mainly to the films' greatly increased production costs, returns have been more modest. Bond films have always done better outside America. In Germany, for instance, they have received the Golden Star and Diamond Award for exceeding 30 million admissions, the only series ever to do so. And in Britain, 13 of them have been the top earners of their year.

BOX-OFFICE FIGURES - IN $ MILLIONS

Date	Title	Cost (est)	Rentals US	Rentals World	Total
1962	*Dr No*	0.95	6.4	15.9	22.0
1963	*From Russia With Love*	2.0	9.8	19.5	29.3
1964	*Goldfinger*	3.0	23.0	26.6	49.6
1965	*Thunderball*	5.5	26.9	28.0	54.9
1967	*You Only Live Twice*	9.5	19.4	24.7	44.0
1969	*On Her Majesty's Secret Service*	8.0	9.1	15.0	24.2
1971	*Diamonds Are Forever*	7.2	19.7	26.0	45.7
1973	*Live and Let Die*	7.0	15.9	32.8	48.7
1974	*The Man With the Golden Gun*	7.0	9.4	27.6	37.0
1977	*The Spy Who Loved Me*	13.0	24.4	55.6	79.9
1979	*Moonraker*	34.0	33.9	53.8	87.7
1981	*For Your Eyes Only*	28.0	26.5	53.4	79.9
1983	*Octopussy*	27.5	34.0	47.4	81.4
1985	*A View to a Kill*	30.0	25.3	40.4	65.6
1987	*The Living Daylights*	40.0	27.9	est 41.0	est 69.0
1989	*Licence to Kill*	42.0	16.6	est 25.0	est 42.0
	Totals	264.65	328.20	532.70	860.90

The Alternative Bonds

Date	Title	Cost (est)	Rentals US	Rentals World	Total
1967	*Casino Royale*	12.0	10.2	7.0	17.2
1983	*Never Say Never Again*	36.0	28.0	23.0	51.0

"You may feel a little prick, Mr Bond, but not *too* foolish, I hope." Gert Frobe as the eponymous Goldfinger and Sean Connery as Bond.

Cubby Broccoli thinks that "Lazenby could have been a good Bond but, the minute he signed up, he became impossible". And the man who directed *OHMSS*, Peter Hunt, adds, "Unfortunately he was very misled by the people he trusted, who should have known better - agents, friends and advisers."

After *OHMSS* Sean Connery came back for *Diamonds Are Forever* (1971). And then it was Roger Moore, who had no qualms about taking over from Connery. Indeed, he had his own trade-mark. Ruthlessness was out, the eyebrow was in. That eyebrow should have been knighted along with Guinness and Gielgud. Consider a mere fraction of its range; The Eyebrow Quizzical, The Eyebrow Curious, The Eyebrow Aroused, The Eyebrow At Bay. So it was inevitable that with the appearance of Roger Moore, the world was to be divided into two camps - Connery loyalists and Moore-lovers. Both Bonds established their own break-the-mould precedents.

"I didn't think I'd go beyond two", says Moore. "I figured the films would have run their course. As it went on, people would ask me 'How does it keep running?' Well, it was like a fairy tale for kids - basically the same story, and it must never change. People know what to expect when they go to see a Bond film. They pay their money, and get their money's worth. The sets are beautiful, the locations are glamorous, the ladies are lovely, the action is there - tongue in cheek, and very spectacular."

Up to and including *Goldeneye* (1995), there have been 17 Bond films made by the EON company. There were two other Bond films, the rights for which had slipped through the Saltzman-Broccoli net: *Casino Royale*, made in 1967, in which a jokey James Bond was played by David Niven; and much later, in 1983, there was *Never Say Never Again*, Sean Connery's second come-back. Roger Moore was making *Octopussy* (1983) at the same time. "Before I came on the scene I'd seen some of the early Bonds. I think Sean was terrific. Years later, when we were both doing our Bond films simultaneously, we would see each other and commiserate with the discomfort of it all - you know, what they were doing to him and what they were doing to me in terms of the stunts, and all that."

Roger Moore's last Bond film was *A View to a Kill*, made in 1985. Like Connery, he'd made seven Bond films. Timothy Dalton, the actor who said he would never have tried to replace Connery, didn't have any qualms about taking over from Roger. How did the fourth James Bond approach the character? "I just went back to the books. The early movies were really quite close in spirit to the books. They really weren't special-effects or gadget movies. They were very popular imaginative thrillers. They stretched the boundaries of believability but they were still contained within believability. Fleming made you believe this guy could do these things. Those books were the inspiration for the early movies, and the early movies were the foundation for the entire series. In them Bond seemed to me to be a much more human and real personality - kind of multi-dimensional. The way the Bond movies had gone - although they were fun and entertaining - weren't my idea of Bond movies. they had become a completely different entity. I know Roger, and think he did a fantastic job, but they were different kinds of movies. Roger is one of the only people in the world who can be fun in the midst of all that gadgetry. But in truth my favourite Bond movies were always *Dr No*, *From Russia With Love* and *Goldfinger* (1964)."

Sheltering under The Eyebrow Diplomatic, Roger Moore is quite prepared to admit that, "I never saw any of Timothy Dalton's. And for

Third Bond lucky. Roger Moore, alias The Eyebrow.

Timothy Dalton with Bond girl Carey Lowell in *Licence to Kill*.

a very good reason - I knew I would get asked what I thought. I'm always desperately honest. If I didn't like the performance, I don't know how I would answer. I do know Timothy, and he is a very, very pleasant chap and a good actor."

Now, the new super-spy is Pierce Brosnan, tried and surely true in *Goldeneye* (1995), but not yet tested over time as Connery, Dalton and Moore have been. Still, the Bond team have made few, if any, mistakes thus far - so why shouldn't the formula work yet again?

But during the lifetime of the Bond series, there's been a revolution in the film industry - a revolution that has brought us a paradox. The blockbuster movie has shrunk. It is now only part of the multi-media package, and - although it's the key to everything else - it has become the supporting player. The star names above the title are Distribution and Marketing.

Before 1975, pictures would open in one big-city cinema and stay there for a month or more, before moving to similar prestige venues in other cities until, at last, copies gradually dribbled into the rest of the country, thinly spread. And then, just when most studios thought it was still safe to dip their toes in the water in this way, they were given a nasty nip by The Big Rubber Fish.

In 1975, Universal mounted a relentless, three-day advertising campaign on television, timed to the moment when 460 prints of *Jaws* went into 460 cinemas throughout the land. The weekend the film opened, it took more than a $100 million, effortlessly overtaking *The Godfather* (1972).

Jaws had changed the pattern of big-film distribution forever. In 1981, *Raiders of the Lost Ark* saturated America, as did *Jurassic Park* 12 years later, taking over $40 million in its first weekend in the USA. Perhaps that is the true measure of the blockbuster; but if so, it's a two-sided coin. Art Linson, who produced both the star-spangled *The Untouchables* (1987) and also the less-than-successful *American Hot Wax* (1977) says that nowadays you usually know the fate of your film after the Friday opening night. "I know it's kind of shocking. Particularly if you've worked on a movie for three years and then on Saturday morning somebody calls you and says it's over. And you go, 'What do you mean it's over? It did a couple of million dollars last night', and they say, 'No, it's over - it didn't get the kind of volume we needed to sustain it'. Of course you don't get too many other calls for about three months!"

Richard Dreyfuss with Roy Scheider and friend in *Jaws*.

In the Thirties and Forties (less so in the television-dominated Fifties and Sixties), going to the pictures was something young, middle-aged and older people did all the time. The downside of the 1975 distribution breakthrough is that because studios then began to aim their product at the predominantly male, under-25s, older film-goers now look askance at the advertising hype, bide their time and wait for word of mouth. They watch fewer films than ever - and these are usually rented from the video shop. The 40-somethings (and beyond) feel that in the cinema, studio product has become, with a few honourable exceptions, perjoratively "product".

Which brings us to movie exploitation. The merchandising of all modern blockbusters is crucial, because it has become a film business axiom that *the movie makes more money from its merchandising than it takes at the box office*.

Merchandising experts would have their clients believe that all movies are equally exploitable, but some are more equal than others. As a convenient rule of thumb, cartoons - *Aladdin* (1992) and *The*

Lion King (1994), for example - lend themselves more readily to commercial tie-ins than do films with human stars. In the days when good ol' Walt was alive, merchandising meant selling a few packets of Mickey Mouse stationery in Woolworth's. But, roll on a few decades, and amateurs are out - mega-sales professionals in.

Jurassic Park isn't a cartoon, of course, nor is *The Flintstones* (1994), but the dinosaurs in both movies turned out to be pushy actors begging to be exploited. Among the *Jurassic Park* spin-offs were cuddly reptiles, furry dino-slippers, expensive computer games for parents to grumble about, jolly Jurassic socks, toothbrushes, sweatshirts, T-shirts, trousers, pyjamas, chocolate eggs lunch boxes, and dinosaur rugs. Spielberg, like his friend, George Lucas, is a jealous guardian of licences, and he was furious when unapproved manufacturers produced toys with the name "Jurassic" stamped on them. Poised to sue, he was advised by his army of lawyers that even he could hardly claim copyright to the second period of the Mesozoic era.... "But it's mine, damn you, mine!"

Over here, we narrowly escaped the Rocdonalds of America, but in the high street, Marks and Spencer, W.H. Smith, Mothercare, Tesco, Tie Rack and Debenhams were full of Fred and Wilma clothing, tinned food, cereals, chewing gum, ice cream, jewellery and tableware. Then there were the Talking Freds and wrist watches (but happily no condoms) all shouting, "Yabba Dabba Doo!" More than a hundred marketing licences were issued for *The Flintstones*.

The 35-year-old Hanna-Barbera cartoons which inspired the live-action Flintstones have themselves been given a new lease of television life by their monstrous child. This circularity is like a marketing conjuring trick. One can see how it's done, but the astonishment remains as we clamour, "Show us again!"

And for the benefit of any innocent who still believes that a commercial blockbuster's impact at the box office can be reduced by bad art or bad reviews - forget it. *The Flintstones* was almost universally panned - but $40 million spent on "awareness" rendered the critics impotent. Any competition between Fred Flintstone's dinosaurs and those to be found in *Jurassic Park* is fairly academic, of course, since both films enjoy the Spielberg Connection.

But in the world of merchandising saturation, the crowning glory for the blockbuster as living legend must be the theme park. What started as a random thought on the back of an envelope, a handful of actors playing Let's Pretend; what progressed to a few months on location, can now end up as a daily, month in month out, decade in decade out, entertainment with a life of its own, bringing in millions of dollars for its organisers. *Jurassic Park* has now achieved immortality in a Spielberg-approved theme ride at Universal's parks in Florida and Los Angeles.

No film is too old to be given the kiss of life. A *Gone With the Wind* theme park is planned 32 miles outside Atlanta, where visitors will walk through replica film sets of Tara and Twelve Oaks. It's more Vivien Leigh and Clark Gable than Civil War history but, even so, perhaps especially so, Disney must be green with envy after their defeat at the battle of Virginia.

Cinema-based theme parks go back 80-odd years. Rubber-necking members of the public loved to watch what they could of the filming going on behind the walls of Carl Laemmle's Universal City. Never missing a trick, kindly Uncle Carl invited them inside the gates of the biggest studio in the world - "Oh, and by the way, that'll be 25 cents.... Thank you!"

The place never looked back. Today, the shark from *Jaws* rears up at the studio bus-load on the Universal Studios tour. True, some of the visitors are too young to remember the 20-year-old film; but it doesn't matter, because *Jaws* is now the stuff of legend - or in the case of poor old Robert Shaw, leg end.

But first make your blockbuster. At the back-of-an-envelope stage, most film professionals are whistling in the dark. William Goldman, the man who wrote *Butch Cassidy and the Sundance Kid* (1969), *Marathon Man* (1976), and who more recently brought back *Maverick* (1994) from its television grave, says there is only one lesson to be learned, "Nobody knows anything".

And if you don't believe him, try this impeccably bred bread-winner. Take a couple of star actors, Dustin Hoffman and Warren Beatty, a star writer/director, Elaine May, and a budget of $50 million - and you've *got* to be first past the post. The trouble is... your dead cert may be impeccably well-bred - and yet still end up as a camel instead of a horse. This one was called *Ishtar* (1987).... But *Ishtar* doesn't quite head the list of Greatest Flops (see chart on page 11).

So it's true - nobody knows anything.... But then what about Steven Spielberg, who sprang, fully formed, from TV. He was still only 23 when he directed *Duel* (1971) his first major TV-movie (then

☞ page 34

Steven Spielberg

Steven Spielberg is certainly the most successful director in the history of Hollywood. *Jaws* (1975), *Raiders of the Lost Ark* (1981) and its two "*Indiana Jones*" sequels, *E.T. - The Extra-Terrestrial* (1982) and *Jurassic Park* (1993) are six of the most lucrative films ever released, and *Close Encounters of the Third Kind* (1977) collected a bundle too. They have made him one of the wealthiest men in moviedom. For a period of two weeks in 1982, he was banking $1 million a day in personal profits from *E.T.* and *Poltergeist* (1983), which he wrote and co-produced. Finally, in 1993, he won the Oscar that had eluded him for so long - for *Schindler's List*.

LIFE IN THE BURBS

Steven Spielberg was born in Cincinnati on 18th December 1947, but grew up in the American suburbs of Haddonfield, New Jersey, and Scottsdale, Arizona. Accused at various stages of his career of having "a love affair with the suburban middle class", the inspiration for the setting of such films as *Poltergeist* or *Close Encounters* undoubtedly sprang from a childhood spent in condo-land in front of the TV.

Above left: *Close Encounters of the Third Kind.*
Above right: **Harrison Ford in Raiders of the Lost Ark.**

CALIFORNIA DREAMING

After his parents' divorce, Spielberg moved with his mother and sisters to California. Although television and making his own 8mm movies were Spielberg's two great passions, poor school grades prevented him getting into the University of Southern California's film school; he had to make do with a film course at California State College. But, at 21, on the strength of *Amblin'* (1969) - a short movie he'd made with the help of a backer - he landed a seven-year contract with Universal and became the youngest director ever to be signed up with a major Hollywood studio. Later on he would name his phenomenally successful production company "Amblin Entertainment" after the film that got him started.

MAGIC FORMULA

After *Jaws*, Spielberg's future was secured, despite the fact that early praise for his work was short-lived. "Profound as a cow pat" and "it made the child in me throw up" were the kind of comments his films started to provoke - and, in fact, have done so ever since, from *E.T.* to *Schindler's List*. But despite this lack of critical acclaim, the audiences going to his films have grown ever bigger. It is clear that Spielberg's strength lies in his films' unabashed sentimentality. In the Spielberg universe, extra-terrestrials have cute eyes and delicate sensibilities, children are the harbingers of goodness, and home is where both humans and extra-terrestrials are heading. Spielberg films make a bee-line to the heart, and that, it seems, is where a lot of us want to be taken.

SHORT CUTS

Spielberg's first job at Universal was directing Joan Crawford in a TV movie. More TV work followed, including a full length episode of *Columbo* and the made-for-TV movie *Duel* (1971), which was so stylishly made that it reached the cinema screen. But it was *The Sugarland Express* (1974), starring Goldie Hawn as a mother on the run, that first brought him to the attention of the critics; Pauline Kael of the *New Yorker* hailed the film as "the most phenomenal directorial debut in the history of the movies". But by the time *Sugarland* was released, he was already hard at work on *Jaws*.

Above: Laura Dern and Sam Neill in ***Jurassic Park,*** **the highest-grossing film of all time. Below: Spielberg on the set of** ***Empire of the Sun.***

released in cinemas) followed, at 26, by *The Sugarland Express* (1974). A year later he mad his first blockbuster, *Jaws*. If William Goldman is right, Spielberg doesn't know anything *either*; but in that case - how does one explain his astonishing track record?

Perhaps it's because Spielberg has somehow kept the child inside him alive. His approach is so unpatronisingly open that he disarms us. Spielberg's films also have more than a touch of Hollywood's Golden Age about them. Even his use of favourite actors reflects this. Richard Dreyfuss, star of *Jaws, Close Encounters, Always* (1989), is no Redford or Newman, let alone Schwarzenegger. Spielberg's Dreyfuss is Spencer Tracy, the no-nonsense, down-to-earth, common-sense common man - shamelessly radiating the kind of star quality that involves all of us in the elabarate and deeply satisfying deceit that is art.

Spielberg says he makes the kind of films that he, as one of the audience, would want to see; he doesn't set out to change the way in which people think, although, with *Schindler's List* (1993), he was attempting much more than a record of one man's crusade against the holocaust.

Jaws was Steven Spielberg's first blockbuster. *E.T. - The Extra-Terrestrial* (1982), *Raiders of the Lost Ark*, and *Close Encounters of the Third Kind* were similarly huge successes, of course; and one tends to forget that the maturing Spielberg didn't exactly hit the jackpot with *Hook* (1991), *The Color Purple* (1985), *Empire of the Sun* (1987) or *Always*.

Jurassic Park took two years to make and, depending on which sources you believe, cost between £60 million and $80 million. Even at the highest estimate, it was cheap at the price. And when it arrived in the cinema, the film captured our imagination in a way that isn't entirely explained by those miraculous computer-generated images.

Where did the fantasy that is *Jurassic Park* come from? No film is made by one man, of course, and Spielberg couldn't have set up the first shot without Michael Crichton's book. This has its roots partly in Crichton's own previous story of a robot takeover in *Westworld* (1973), and partly in the terrifying imaginings of others - among them, Fritz Lang's evil robot Maria in *Metropolis* (1927), and the Hollywood versions of Mary Shelley's *Frankenstein*. To say that *Jurassic Park* derives, in part, from Robert Louis Stevenson sounds a little fanciful, perhaps; nevertheless, Stevenson's death, in 1894, is a

close chronological link with the birth of the cinema and with its development. Over the next 100 years, there were to be adaptations of his stories (*Treasure Island, Kidnapped*) including many re-workings of *The Strange Case of Dr Jekyll and Mr Hyde*. The metamorphosis of good into evil, with terrifying forces out of control, is the mirror image of *Jurassic Park*.

There's a Disney connection, too, in the way Spielberg puts the children in *Jurassic Park* into only-just-acceptably scary situations; nevertheless, the film was given a PG certificate in Britain, but not before it had been tried out on 200 squealing guinea pigs, children between the ages of eight and eleven. It was a bold experiment in zero-protected exposure to the sudden shocks of *Jurassic Park*; but in the end, The British Board of Film Classification came to the unanimous conclusion that, in spite of some evidence of eyes peeping through fingers, and knicker-wetting among the under-eight-and-a-halfs, not one child had been seriously scared. For all of us, from children to young adults and the not so young, going to the pictures is still part of our culture: thrilling, terrifying, entertaining. On Friday or Saturday night at the movies everthing comes together, as we surrender to the marvellous, quintessential, popular experience that embraces us all in the velvet dark.

Three feature films behind him and still barely a Thirty Something. Steven Spielberg working on *Close Encounters of the Third Kind*.

CHAPTER 2

Hooray for Hollywood

The parents, midwives and guardians of cinema were the pioneering inventors, technicians and early film-makers, and the entrepreneurs who later became the flamboyant moguls who built the dream factories of Twenties and Thirties Hollywood.

Before the twentieth century had even begun, What The Butler Saw machines, based on an 1868 invention called the Mutoscope, showed flickering pictures of saucy ladies to saucy customers in penny arcades. But it could hardly be called cinema. The very first motion picture camera, the Kinetograph, was invented by William Kennedy Laurie Dickson, who was working under the direction of Thomas Alva Edison at his plant in New Jersey. Edison himself went on to invent a peep-show projector to go with it - the Kinetoscope.

Kinetoscopes on parade. Edison's new attraction made available a one-minute show for one.

Older readers - or younger ones addicted to old movie re-runs on television - will instantly conjure up a picture of Spencer Tracy in a 1940 biopic, *Edison, The Man*, intoning 'Mary Had a Little Lamb' into his new-fangled phonograph and being gosh-shucks modest all over the place. The phonograph reference is accurate, the second unlikely, but then the function of dream factories is to render heroes heroic and not show them as miserable old curmudgeons. But to return to Edison's Kinetoscope - it showed one-minute loops of

Home of The Marx Brothers, Mary Pickford and Maurice Chevalier. The Crosby-Hope "Road" films were made here, too.

Poster advertising the Lumière brothers, fathers of the cinema: Auguste (1862-1954) and Louis (1864-1948).

moving pictures, photographed on celluloid rolls supplied by another pioneer, George Eastman. When Edison demonstrated his new invention, it went over so well that in 1894 he expanded his Kinetoscope market to Europe.

Unfortunately, Edison, who was slightly contemptuous of his invention, regarding it as not much more than an expensive toy, had neglected to take the next logical step.

But in France, two enterprising young men did. The moment they saw Edison's glorified peep-show, the Lumière brothers - Auguste and Louis - were inspired to make a crucial imaginative leap. Inside a year they had developed and patented a projector which they called the Cinématographe. Moving pictures could now be thrown onto a screen and viewed by almost any number of people at once.

On December 28th, 1895, in an old billiard hall below the Grand Café on the Boulevard des Capucines, the Lumière Brothers showed a programme of ten short films before a paying audience. When they found themselves miraculously transported to the Gare de Lyons, and saw a train rushing towards them, several people ran for their lives. But they came sneaking back to see a baby, the first child film star, being fed.

And the baby had a companion, because on that winter's day a hundred years ago, the cinema was born.

Back at the ranch, though, a chastened Edison set about doing what he should have done in the first place - getting himself a projector. He arranged with a fellow-inventor called Thomas Armat to take over Armat's Vitascope projector - which thereafter was known as the Edison Vitascope - and then joined the rush to make films. In West

Orange, New Jersey, he opened America's first film studio - in his back garden. It was not so much a dream factory, more a cottage industry, but the middle-aged inventor's hand had lost none of its cunning. The Black Maria, as his studio became known, was built on a mechanical revolve, so that the studio sets were flooded with sunlight all day.

One of Edison's first productions was the prize-fight between James J. Corbett and Peter Courtenay - or, at least, a reconstruction of the fight's dramatic moments. He also starred a human nose - his assistant's - in a little number entitled *Fred Ott's Sneeze* (1893). By the early 1900s Edison's short films, along with all the others being made - or hired out by independent distributors, were being shown in nickelodeons - viewing theatres born out of converted shops. Soon there were thousands of them all over the USA, playing for the most part to poor immigrants who got their first lessons in English from the captions. One distinguished pioneer film-maker, who worked for

Proposal or proposition? Unidentified actors on an early film set.

Early
PICTURE PALACES

The world's very first cinema was the Cinématograph Lumière at the Salon Indien, a billiard hall below the Grand Café, 14 Boulevard des Capucines. Only 35 people turned up on 28th December, 1895, to see the cinema's first show. Soon 2,500 were passing through the cinema's doors daily. Admission: 1 franc.

★

America's first cinema was the Vitascope Hall in New Orleans. It opened on 26 June, 1896. Admission: 10 cents.

★

The first cinema in Britain was the Kineopticon opened at the junction of Piccadilly Circus and Shaftesbury Avenue on 21 March, 1896. A few weeks later the cinema was burnt down. Admission: 6d.

★

The first British cinema of any permanence was Mohawk's Hall in Upper Street, Islington. Opened in 1901, it was forced to close down after a few months, but reopened in 1908. It finally stopped being a cinema in 1962. Admission: 6d, 1s, 2s and 3s.

★

The first purpose-built luxury cinema was built in Paris. The Cinéma Omnia Pathé opened in 1906 on Boulevard Montmartre. It had a sloping floor so that people could see over each other's heads. Admission: 50 centimes to 3 francs.

★

The first purpose-built cinema in Britain was Joshua Duckworth's Central Hall in Colne, Lancashire. Opened in 1907, it remained a cinema until 1924 when it became a spiritualist chapel.

★

The earliest open-air cinema in Britain was the Garden Cinema in Hull. It opened for business in the July of 1912; it closed with the coming of winter and never re-opened.

★

The oldest cinema in Britain to survive with its original fabric largely intact is the Electric Cinema, Portobello Road, in London. It opened in 1911.

Edison, was Edwin S. Porter. Porter had been much impressed by some British films he'd seen; in particular, one called *A Daring Daylight Robbery* (1903), made by Frank Mottershaw. What attracted Porter to it was Mottershaw's simple story-line. In the early days of cinema, for a film to have a story *at all* represented an enormous advance, and Porter was inspired to build on the technique by telling an exciting story in an exciting way. The resulting movie was, in fact, the third narrative film ever to be made. He made it in 1903 and the title says it all - *The Great Train Robbery*.

When Porter edited the film, he cross-cut the action between the train and the victim - and back again. This dramatic effect had an equally dramatic effect on audiences, who had never seen the technique before, and the big-finish close-up of a man firing a gun at the audience caused a sensation. *The Great Train Robbery* became a runaway success in nickelodeons all over the country. In passing, it is of historic interest to note that Porter sometimes employed a very bad actor who finally became so embarrassed by his screen appearances that he decided to go away and tell other people how to act. His name was D. W. Griffith.

Like *The Great Train Robbery*, all movies at this time were very short; almost everyone involved in making, distributing or showing films, was convinced that audiences would be bored by anything that ran longer than a few minutes (a patronising view shared by some television programme-makers today). But several of the early pioneers had other ideas - or, rather, they had the *same* other idea: to make film stories that were as long, and as entertaining, as stage plays. But converting the unbelievers wasn't easy. Even D.W. Griffith met resistance. When he made a two-reeler in 1911 called *Enoch Arden*, the reels were shown separately - until audiences complained.

In New York, Sam Goldwyn, still an unselfconscious Sam Goldfish in 1913, sold the idea of longer films to his partners, Jesse Lasky and Arthur Friend. They bought the rights to a stage play called *The Squaw Man* (1914) - a romantic Western. Sam and Jesse went straight to the top - D.W. Griffith - but he wanted too much money up front. So they went from the sublime to the illiterate - and offered the job to a young man who'd never made a film in his life. He was keen to learn, though, and after spending *almost a whole day* watching one of Edison's directors at work, he announced that he'd cracked it. The name of this one-day film graduate was Cecil Blount DeMille.

"Heap ready when you are, Mr DeMille." Cast and director of *The Squaw Man*, Hollywood's first feature film.

DeMille headed west, partly because *The Squaw Man* was a Western, but largely to escape the bad guys employed by the prohibitive Trust set up by Edison and his fellow film-makers to stop jumped-up independents muscling in on their lucrative business.

Sam and Jesse told DeMille to shoot the film in Arizona, but when he stepped off the train at Flagstaff, young Cecil didn't think much of it - and climbed back on, perhaps anticipating that "Hooray for Flagstaff!" lacked rather more than alliteration. If he had stayed in Arizona, though, what sort of films might he have made? Stories of the Foreign Legion, perhaps, or nature films about the scorpion. But he didn't stay; he and his company journeyed on until the train reached Los Angeles. There DeMille found a cornucopia of movie locations, all under clear blue skies. There for the picking, or shooting, were palm trees, snow-capped mountains, desert - and views to the Pacific Ocean. In this place you could make a film about anything. And on top of all this, young Cecil found a studio. He sent a telegram to the Jesse L. Lasky Feature Play Company back in New York:

... "FLAGSTAFF NO GOOD FOR OUR PURPOSE. HAVE PROCEEDED TO CALIFORNIA. WANT AUTHORITY TO RENT BARN IN PLACE CALLED HOLLYWOOD FOR $75 A MONTH. REGARDS TO SAM"...

Although this was in the days before Goldwynisms had become part of the language, poor Sam very nearly had a cadillac arrest. But *The Squaw Man*, which eventually made a tidy sum for the partners, was the first full-length feature film ever to be made in Hollywood. It was completed and previewed in 1914. Cecil B. DeMille's first effort may not look too exciting today but, after the screening, eager buyers crowded round Sam - who in his new high-profile role was probably already thinking. "Well, OK, so Gold-*something*."

One of the buyers was Louis B. Mayer, who later co-founded the MGM studios. He said he'd pay $4000 to show the film in his theatres, but when Goldfish became Goldwyn he always told anyone who would listen - and everyone listened to Goldwyn - that Louis never coughed up in full.

Meanwhile, the broader picture showed that in Britain, all over Europe, in Australia and Japan, with more countries joining in - almost daily, it seemed - film production was expanding to world-wide proportions, with film techniques developing all the time - often faster than in America. Everyone was influenced by everyone else. A 1914 Italian epic, Giovanni Pastrone's *Cabiria*, was shown, with full orchestral accompaniment, at the Astor theatre in New York. Much of D.W. Griffith's subsequent work can be seen as having ben influenced by *Cabiria*.

In 1914, World War I engulfed Europe, while America was still unaffected. A side effect of the war was that film-making in Britain and the rest of Europe was wiped out. Then, in 1915, D.W.Griffith's *The Birth of a Nation* took America by storm. Hollywood was now the film capital of the world.

It is an irony that if film production in Europe hadn't stopped in 1914, Hollywood - its equivalent, anyway - might have been built here. Imagine it.... Alfred Hitchcock and Chaplin would have remained ours, and the first British film-makers, such as Cecil

Hepworth, James Williamson, George Albert Smith and Robert Paul - and all of them were shouting "Action!" a hundred years ago - might now be, if not as famous and revered as D.W. Griffith, substantially more than footnotes in cinema history.

In the century's Teens and early Twenties, Hollywood came into its own. The silent film was perfected by such giants as Chaplin, Edwin Porter, Lewis Milestone and, of course, D. W. Griffith.

Griffith has always been credited with inventing the basic grammar of film but, in France, Abel Gance was at the very least his equal in developing and creating new ways of film storytelling. Gance didn't look for ways to use technical skills; instead, he used whatever he needed to realise his vision, and if that vision demanded something that had never quite been achieved before, he developed an existing technique or invented a new tool. In *Napoléon*, his masterwork, completed in 1927, he shows Napoleon as a boy, having a snowball fight with his peers. This short sequence is edited in a way that is as astonishing today as it must have been nearly 70 years ago; the whole is exhilaratingly greater than the sum of its fleeting parts, and one is unaware at first viewing that some of the cuts are so short as to be almost subliminal (a technique employed to vacuously flashy effect in the Sixties and beyond). And for the great battle scenes, Abel Gance wanted to show panoramic views of the action, as well as three separate but simultaneous pictures, all on the same screen. This should have been an impossible dream in 1927, but not to Gance, who simply invented the forerunner of Cinerama, using three synchronised cameras and projectors. Gance's extraordinary film was virtually lost when sound came in; but happily, many years later, the British film-maker and historian, Kevin

Above: Genius meets genius. French director Abel Gance with D.W. Griffith.

Opposite: Mack Sennett, king of slapstick. At the foot of the tripod, a furry comic appears to have mistimed a pratfall.

Brownlow, laboured with love - and with Abel Gance himself, who was still alive - to restore *Napoléon* very nearly to its original glory.

Gance, who was 15 years younger than Griffith, certainly admired and was influenced by the great American film-maker. Griffith was held in awe by many directors, of course, among them a young film-maker in Russia, Sergei Eisenstein, whose theory of editing was directly influenced by his study of Griffith's work. But the unlikeliest disciple must surely be Mack Sennett, he of the Keystone Kops, who turned his old boss's brilliant film techniques on their head to make comedies. In a way, he could be said to have developed Griffith's close-up into the double-take and slow burn exemplified by comedians and comic actors over the next 80 years - from Ben Turpin and Laurel and Hardy, to the Three Stooges, Sylvestor - the cat, not Stallone - Walter Matthau and Steve Martin.

Mack Sennett was also the man who discovered Charlie Chaplin - although it would be more accurate to say that Chaplin discovered himself. The comic had already made one short for Sennett, and wasn't really much more than the new kid on the lot. And then, for a six-minute film called *Kid Auto Races at Venice* (1914), Sennett asked Chaplin to liven up an otherwise pretty dull length of footage with something funny, and if possible... a bit different. Enter the most famous icon the world has ever known.

Chaplin was among the stars and studio heads who resisted the arrival of sound in 1927, having proved that he, above all, didn't need it. Sound, of course, goes back to Edison's phonograph, invented before the turn of the century. Edison later tried to link the system to film, the biggest problems for him (and for the others who followed) being to make the sound loud enough to fill a theatre, and - even more important - to marry sound to picture. D. W. Griffith said, loftily, "Music - fine music - will always be the voice of silent drama." But beware of great men when they pontificate, because he also said, "It will never be possible to synchronise the voice with the pictures. There will never be speaking pictures."

In 1927, a small studio, facing bankruptcy, took a gamble on a new-fangled sound system called Vitaphone. As a result, the Broadway entertainer, Al Jolson, became the world's first pop star, simply because he was seen - and, much more importantly, *heard* - in *The Jazz Singer*. For the Warner brothers - there were four of them, Sam, Harry, Albert and Jack - the film turned their terminally broke

studio into one of the majors overnight. But it did rather more than that. *The Jazz Singer* changed the movie industry for ever.

Surprisingly, Vitaphone was only one of several sound systems going the rounds. The competing systems worked perfectly well - and at least one of them was more advanced than Vitaphone - but the films they were supposed to bring to life had no life at all. Vitaphone, on the other hand, was attached to *The Jazz Singer*; and that over-flowed with life - sentimental, tear-jerking life - with Al Jolson talking directly to his audience, standing in front of them larger than life. When the star improvised his lines, Jolson was irresistible. People stood up - some of them climbed onto their seats - and cheered.

In fact, *The Jazz Singer* wasn't really a sound picture at all. It was a silent film with musical numbers and *bits* of dialogue: amazingly,

Al Jolson, in *The Jazz Singer*, uttered the first words in movie history: "Wait a minute, wait a minute, you ain't heard nothin' yet!"

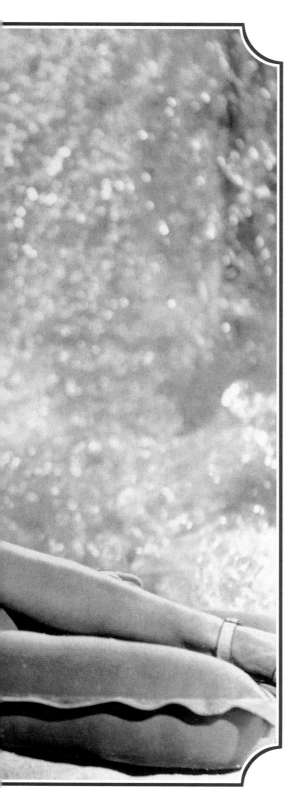

there were only 354 words altogether. What actually turned the trick was that *it was the first time synchronised sound had been used to tell a story*. The result was a staggering box-office success.

The effect on the industry was immediate. After the premiere, one Hollywood producer rang his studio to say, "Stop shooting. I have seen the future." The ripples spread wider and wider - all the way to Chaplin's birthplace. Chili Bouchier, today a vigorous 86, was, in 1927, Britain's answer to the American "It" Girl and silent film star, Clara Bow. Ms Bouchier remembers, "We got back from Paris where we'd been filming *City of Play* (1929) - it was a silent film of course - and found that *The Jazz Singer* had arrived and was playing in London. So everyone was in a mad panic. The company I was working for said 'Take two weeks off, Chili, we're going to make this into a talkie.' By the time we came back into the studio, they'd written a script - and a song. So I talked *and* sang, just like Jolson. We'd become a talkie half-way through."

At the very first Academy Awards ceremony, in May 1929, *The Jazz Singer* won a special Oscar. Three hundred guests were sung at by the star of the film. Jolson belonged to the shouting school of singing, so when *he* sang at you, you *stayed* sung at. He brought the proceedings to a close by saying, "I noticed they gave *The Jazz Singer* a statuette, but they didn't give me one. For the life of me I can't see what Jack Warner can do with it. It can't say yes"

British siren of the Twenties, Chili Bouchier, later blacklisted by Warner Bros. for being homesick.

The Jazz Singer wasn't, in fact, the first sound picture. Warner Brothers had used Vitaphone before, to record a synchronised music score for a John Barrymore silent, *Don Juan* (1926); and they saw it merely as a way to stake their claim to original music, and to pick up a few dollars more by selling the equipment to movie theatres. And it turned out that the Vitaphone sound system wasn't really the best system because it depended on synchronising a huge recorded disc with the film projector. In the early Twenties, a man called Lee De Forest had already developed a much more practical sound-on-film process called Phonofilm. This was pirated by one of De Forest's assistants and taken up, in 1927, by William Fox who used it for his Fox Movietone shorts and newsreels. Fox Movietone's sound-on-film system soon replaced Vitaphone; but there had been many other sound devices before both of them, stretching right back to the early inventions of Thomas Alva Edison.

Among the many wannabes that disappeared without trace were Photographophone, Synchroscope, Projectophone, Pallophotophone, Chronophone, Phonorama, Graphonocone, Titanifone, Madalatone, and a seven-syllable seven-day wonder - Phonocinematophone.

But for the industry - to start with, anyway - the penny hadn't quite dropped, and the other studios were reluctant to move into sound. This was hardly surprising, because it didn't make sense to exchange a sure thing that was making millions, for what might well prove to be a passing fad. All the same, *The Jazz Singer*'s triumphant arrival was very worrying.

An unlikely ally in the movie revolution was radio. Like TV in the Fifties, the new magic carpet of the Twenties was free. More importantly, it nourished its huge audiences on pure sound; and their astonished pleasure came from *listening*. So why should people leave the comfort of home - and pay to see silent movies?

By 1929, only two years after *The Jazz Singer*, all the major studios were in the sound business. Only two rebels refused to talk, Garbo and Chaplin. They held their tongues for good reasons - the first genuine all-talking feature film, *Lights of New York* (1928) being one of them. This film contained the deathless line, delivered by a gangster with perfect diction and excruciating slowness, "Take him....for....a ride." What Garbo and Chaplin saw instantly, of course, was that the new toy had brought the art of film-making to a creaking stop.

☞ page 54

PERSONAL SERVICES

When Italian cinemas first opened they were always furnished with a reading room stocked with current newspapers for the entertainment of patrons waiting for their friends.

★

Many American cinemas provided crèches, the earliest on record being The Alhambra, Milwaukee, which had a crèche from 1913.

★

In the Twenties, the Capitol Cinema in New York provided the services of a chiropodist for its patrons.

★

In the late Twenties, the 600-seat Roxy in New York could boast a permanent choir of 100 voices, a ballet troupe and a fully equipped hospital. The cinema closed in 1960.

★

Berlin's first big cinema, the Alhambra Platz, provided its clientele with tip-up trays and served beer during the performances.

★

In the Thirties, London's Cameo cinema served cups of tea and allowed ticket-holders to make free telephone calls.

★

In Australia in the Forties, cinemas provided "crying rooms" where mothers could breast-feed children behind a sound-proof glass screen.

★

Around 1960, the first automatic ticket dispenser was installed at Loew's 175th-Street Theatre, New York. It provided change, which, if it was in note form, came out wrapped in a delicate sheet of tissue paper.

THE MOGULS

The great days of Hollywood were also the era of movie moguls - the men, mainly Jewish, mostly immigrants or sons of recent immigrants from Eastern Europe, who created and ran in autocratic style America's major movie studios. Their reputations have become part of movie legend. This is how Gregory Peck described them (others were not so kind):

> " Most of them were tyrants, imposing their personalities on underlings, and overseeing every step of every picture – but they had charisma. They may have been a little short on formal education, but they were showman who created stars and built the Hollywood tradition. They did it with their guts. They got personally involved – Zanuck, Jack Warner, Sam Goldwyn, Harry Cohn, all those fellows. I liked them because they had zest and red blood in them. "

Louis B. Mayer (1885-1957)

Mayer helped found MGM and ran it for more than 20 years. He turned it into the most glamorous of all Hollywood studios, with a galaxy of stars and a roster of glossy, escapist movies promoting patriotism and family life. His maxim was: "I will only make pictures that I won't be ashamed to have my children see." Mayer was, for years, the industry's most powerful magnate . Indeed, during the Thirties, he was the highest-paid executive in the USA.

Jack Warner (1892-1978)

Jack was one of the four brothers who founded Warner Bros. - and he went on to run it for almost 50 years. He managed his studio with a notoriously tight purse. Discipline and economy were Warner's hallmarks, so his stars had to work harder for less than those at the other studios. This led to great clashes between him and stars like Bette Davis and James Cagney. "At times he gloried in being a no-good son-of-a-bitch", his son, Jack Warner Jnr, once said.

Sir Alexander Korda (1893-1956)
➡

The only British mogul, and, even then, he was a Hungarian. Flamboyant, generous, and often only a step away from his creditors, he virtually saved the UK film industry in the Thirties, building Denham Studios and making the first British films with an international appeal. Their quality and production values set the standard for future British films.

Harry Cohn (1891-1958)
➡

Cohn founded Columbia Pictures with brother Jack and friend Joe Brandt. But it was Harry who built it up from nothing into a major studio. He was both tyrannical and crude. He gained the reputation of being the most hated tycoon in Hollywood, with the nickname "White Fang" because he spied on his employees through a network of informers and hidden microphones all over the studio.

Darryl F. Zanuck (1902-1979)
➡

Zanuck started, in the Twenties, with Warner Bros. where he wrote scripts for the Rin-Tin-Tin dog movies. But his claim to moguldom is as founder of 20th Century-Fox which he ruled for over 20 years.Tough, dynamic and a relentless womaniser, he claimed he never bullied anyone smaller than himself. Since he was 5' 2", few of his staff escaped. "Don't say yes until I've stopped talking", is the famous phrase he used on his subordinates.

Samuel Goldwyn (1882-1974)
➡

Though not a studio boss as such, no roster of Hollywood tycoons would be complete without the great showman Goldwyn and his way with the English language ("In two words, Im-Possible."). Goldwyn co-produced *The Squaw Man* as early as 1914, and went on to become Hollywood's leading independent producer, making a string of such high-quality films as *Wuthering Heights* (1939) and *The Best Years of Our Lives* (1946).

Universal City, California
"The Capital of Filmland"

Universal, the oldest studio in Hollywood, founded in 1912 by Carl Laemmle.

The technical problems were, as technical problems always are, solved; and in the case of sound they were solved quite quickly. Once established, various improvements in quality were made over the years, the most important of which came in the Sixties. Ray Dolby, an American with an unsympathetic bank manager, worked loanlessly in an old dressmaking factory in London, developing the process which eventually became known as Dolby Sound. *Star Wars* (1977) became the first stereo - optical film and since then, every Oscar for Best Sound has been won by films made using Dolby.

But returning to the early years of cinema, it has been said - notably by Neal Gabler in his social history of Hollywood, *An Empire of Their Own* - that the Jews invented Hollywood. If they did, it serves the gentiles right, because their success grew out of the pain and humiliation of rejection and a desperate need to belong. Penniless young immigrants from Eastern Europe, who became furriers and junk dealers, glove makers and adventurers in the rag trade, looked around them in the early 1900s and saw, if not a gold mine, then what just might turn out to be a living. Mind you, it couldn't be that much of a living, because nobody was trying to keep them out. Barred (by prejudice) from the professions and "respectable" businesses, these men were offered, through the film trade, not merely jobs that middle-class gentiles considered to be beneath them, but the promise of acceptance and assimilation by the country that had casually dumped them in the meanest of mean streets throughout the land.

And so, under the very noses of the respectable goyim, Hollywood started to grow. The elder statesman of Tinsel-Town was Carl Laemmle, everybody's "Uncle Carl", who built Universal in 1912. Others followed and, by the Twenties and mid-Thirties the hierarchy was clearly defined. There were the Big Five - 20th Century-Fox, MGM, Paramount, Warner Brothers and RKO; and the Little Three - Columbia, United Artists and Universal.

Metro-Goldwyn-Mayer - the greatest studio of them all - boasted that they had more stars than there were in the heavens. And in the Big Bang explosion of Hollywood there were other heavens too - at Paramount, 20th Century-Fox, Warner Brothers and the rest. This universe was known as the Studio System, whose gods, enjoying absolute power, were corrupted absolutely. The one saving grace of these extraordinary creatures was that *they loved movies.* Their approach to film-making - and to the casting couch - was strictly hands-on. These self-made gods were... the moguls. [see pages 52-53]

Hollywood could surely exist only in Hollywood. Studio life was self-contained in self-sufficient, self-satisfied cities with their own hospitals, schools, commissaries, barber-shops, even their own police and fire departments. Life here was hardly democracy at work, and the smiling paternalism of MGM was simply the acceptable face of the prison-like regime at Warner Bros., where the inmates, from the humblest messenger boy (no girls until World War II forced the studio to

A Long John Silver line-up of MGM cameramen.

invent a limited policy of Equal Opportunity) to the greatest star. For Jack L. Warner it went against the grain to loan out his artists to other studios, particularly to MGM, because he said they "came back spoiled." Psychological brutality in the Warners penitentiary made the contract artists as tough as the warders. Errol Flynn had daily rows with Jack Warner about money and lousy film parts; Bette Davis had daily rows with Jack Warner about money and lousy film parts - and about that lousy actor, Flynn, who she did not want to play Essex to her Elizabeth. Davis lost that battle, but fared better than the actor she loved to hate. As her power grew, and Flynn's diminished, she became known as the Fifth Warner Brother.

The journey of a film from factory to retail outlet was direct. The majors distributed their films to theatres they owned themselves - a vertical structure that ensured they had the movie business sewn up. In a Hollywood dream factory there was a department for everything: wardrobe, make-up, camera maintenance, fan mail, lighting and publicity - everything. Each component of film-making was to be found within the studio walls - bought-in or made on the premises. Even stars - in fact, especially stars - were made on the premises. The unwieldy was rendered super-efficient: vast sets could be recycled within hours to do double and triple duty for light comedy, mutiny on the high seas or period drama. The back lot was home to Victorian London, the Wild West, Ancient Greece, The Land of Oz or the Bronx. Enormous sums of money might be splurged on star-building, but no detail of any film was too small to be accounted for in the production budget - from the leading man's toupee to the last nail in Count Dracula's coffin.

Talent of all kinds was immediately put into seven-year straightjackets - contracts with all the options in the studio's favour: the twin spectres of suspension and the sack hovering over the heads not just of stars, but directors, writers, producers, cinematographers, designers and the disposable, ten-a-penny contract players as well. This was the Hollywood Studio System.

Within that system, and after sound, the next big pioneering development was colour. Colour processes had been around since the early 1900s; indeed, in 1902, James Williamson made a film called *Fire!* which starred the Hove Fire Brigade. The fire scenes were tinted red. Early two-colour process included Kinemacolor (1906), Cinecolorgraph (1913), two-colour Kodachrome (1915) and Prizma Color (1919).

In more recent years, George Feltenstein, vice president, MGM/UA Home Video, is the man who has restored classics like *Gone With the Wind* (1939) and *Meet Me in St Louis* (1944) to their original Technicolor glory. He recalls that Dr Herbert T. Kalmus started the Technicolor Corporation in 1915, working out of a converted trailer. By 1922, he and his partners were ready to demonstrate their first Technicolor process.

"You had," says George Feltenstein, "two strips of black-and-white film which would be hit by a prism; and as the light came in, it created either a red set of colors or a green set of colors, and when you put the two strips of film together, it gave the illusion of a more vivid spectrum of color. It was certainly a wider breadth of colors than had ever been put on the screen before."

Hollywood didn't exactly fall over itself to adopt the process because it was expensive; and the colour wasn't really "true to life." But George recalls that in the 1925 *Ben Hur*, the colour sequence was shot in Technicolor's two-colour process. "It's really quite lustrous, with a really nice broad range to it. It's got a kind of golden cast, and adds so much more majesty to the film. When it goes back to black-and-white there's kind of a let down."

Nine years later, Technicolor perfected its three-strip film, working with the three primary colours of red, green and blue. "And that", explains Feltenstein, "would also have yellow, so you really would have the full palette of colors. Each one of these black-and-white strips would go through the camera, be hit by a prism in a certain way, and create a life-like range of colors. It was perfected for live-action film-making in 1934."

But, like early sound, early Technicolor was dragged down by its own weight. The three-colour camera had to run three separate reels of black-and-white film stock. "It was very heavy", says Feltenstein, "and not at all easy to manoeuvre. Those cameras were so big and noisy they had to be blimped, adding to the weight and general awkwardness."

Two-strip Technicolor was used in *Follow Thru* (1930)
1. Red
2. Green
3. Red and green together and... voila!

It was an expensive business, too. "Trouble was," he continues, "you needed Technicolor's expertise - and their process as well. Also, you were spending three times as much money on raw stock, because every roll of film was *three* rolls of film."

Again, technical problems were gradually ironed out and, by the Forties movies in colour, although still comparatively rare, were no longer a novelty. One of Technicolor's champions was David O. Selznick, who had used the three-strip process to make *The Garden of Allah* in 1936 (it starred Marlene Dietrich and Charles Boyer), *Nothing Sacred* in 1937 (Carol Lombard and Fredric March) and *The Adventures of Tom Sawyer* in 1938. And, of course, he used Technicolor to make *Gone With the Wind* in 1939. Selznick loved the process and, more importantly, he now thoroughly understood it.

George Feltenstein tells us, "He went for a specific look in Gone With the Wind - a very pastel kind of color creation that we have brought back, or tried to anyway, in the restoration of the film. Unfortunately, in the Fifties and Sixties it was inappropriately printed in vivid colors, it had a more contemporary look - quite different to what David Selznick had wanted, his soft pastel look."

In 1939, audiences loved *Gone With the Wind*, and they loved the fact that it was in colour. George says, "Technicolor provided a huge selling point. If you look at the posters and advertising of the period, Technicolor is usually billed with more prominence than most of the cast, sometimes bigger than the title of the film."

George Feltenstein is quite certain that *Gone With the Wind* would not have made the impact it did - and does - if it had been shot in black-and-white. "The film would not be as important or as popular today if it had not been made in Technicolor. Crucially, it would not have been sold to television in the mid-Fifties, bringing it a whole new audience. In 1939, *Gone With the Wind* was set apart, unique. It was color, it was beautiful and it was a period piece, so it doesn't date."

Although MGM was slower than other studios to use Technicolor extensively, this was the dawn of the great MGM musicals. Judy Garland's first feature film in Technicolor since *The Wizard of Oz* (1939) was *Meet Me in St Louis* (1944). And George Feltenstein believes the film benefited tremendously because director Vincente Minnelli had a painter's eye. "Every frame of that film is the artist's palette. Minnelli works with the colors, the lighting, and the shading. If you look at that scene where Judy Garland is singing the end of 'The

Boy Next Door', and she's at the window - how exquisitely lit it is, the range of colors... it's one of the finest examples of Technicolor in the history of Hollywood. And it didn't hurt that the director was falling in love with the leading lady as he was making the movie. You can see how much he was falling in love with Judy. So the combination of his brilliance and his passion are what makes that movie so splendid."

And yet Technicolor died in the mid-Seventies. "Plain and simple economics," says George, "With all those theatres closing throughout the Unites States and indeed throughout the world, there weren't so many prints needed and, as a result, the Technicolor printing process became too costly. So they started printing off a single Eastman negative, and making Eastman Color prints - which we now know, of course, were subject to terrible fading. It's very sad."

The last film printed in the United States in the Technicolor process was *The Godfather Part II*. "That was in 1974. And that was it. The end. So here's hoping that the Technicolor company's current experiments in bringing the old process back are a success." Meanwhile, George Feltenstein continues his invaluable work, painstakingly restoring the Hollywood classics.

In both black-and-white and colour, the so-called Golden Age of Hollywood covered a period of about 30 years. Film fodder, and the occasional masterpiece, rolled effortlessly off the machine. Perhaps the high point was 1939. In America 80 million people were going regularly to the pictures every week and in Britain it was 20 million. Among the studio offerings they could have seen, apart from the Tara saga, were Greta Garbo in *Ninotchka*, Judy Garland in *The Wizard of Oz* (she teamed up that year too with Mickey Rooney in the musical *Babes in Arms*), James Stewart in *Mr Smith Goes to Washington*, John Wayne in *Stagecoach*, Cary Grant in *Gunga Din* (he and Douglas Fairbanks tossed each other for their parts), Laurence Olivier and Merle Oberon in *Wuthering Heights* and Robert Donat in *Goodbye, Mr Chips*.

The advent of World War II turned out to be a positive boost to the popularity and profitability of studio product. Even when the war ended, the demand for movies was insatiable.

Like the Roman Empire, Hollywood colonised the world, and, to its rulers, decline and fall was unthinkable. So in the Fifties, when they looked through the city gates of Universal and MGM and 20th Century-Fox and saw the enemy - whose name was television - the emperors of Hollywood didn't fall on their swords; instead, complaining bitterly, they suffered a long, drawn-out, undignified death.

Television in the Fifties gave the film industry a nasty jolt when audiences stayed at home to watch game shows and commercials. And yet, it may not have been entirely television's doing. The government's Anti-Trust measures had broken up the studios' vertical structure of product-straight-to-audience; they no longer had the guaranteed showcases of studio-owned theatres. Perhaps more central to the decline and fall was the fact that the old-style moguls who had hungered after respectability and prestige - and achieved both in quantity - had become deeply conservative. And this conservatism was to be seen in the films their studios produced. The emperors were out of touch with the people.

The studios' attitude to television was one of whistling-in-the-dark derision. But Sam Goldwyn had it about right when he said "Why should people go out and pay money to see bad films when they can stay at home and see bad television for nothing?"

It was panic stations all round. One of the first emergency stations was manned to resuscitate the corpse of a process first tried out in 1935 - 3-D. Apart from shock-tactic films like *House of Wax* (1953), several mainstream productions, *Kiss Me Kate* (1953), *The Charge at*

For how long can one man withstand The Curse of the Cardboard Specs?

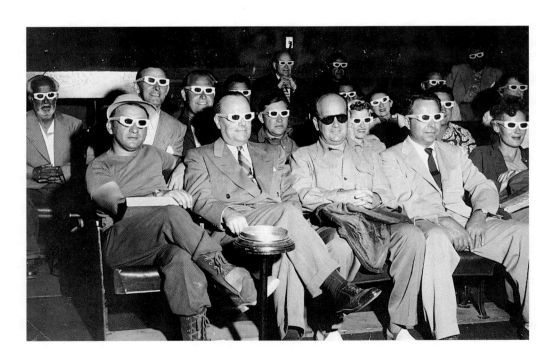

Feather River (1953), and others, were in thrall to "The Curse of the Cardboard Specs". Even Hitchcock shot *Dial M For Murder* (1954) in this cumbersome process. The industry's love affair with 3-D was short-lived - but movie-goers beware... As recently as 1994 a Son of The Curse of the Cardboard Specs appeared on the horizon; at a cinema near you they may soon be handing out Virtual Reality wraparounds at the door.

At 20th Century-Fox, Darryl Zanuck decided to make no more B pictures - concentrating on beating television with big pictures. The other studios did the same. And these pictures would also be literally bigger - or more accurately, wider. This technical demand brought forth a new crop of film pioneers.

Various wide-screen processes were developed by such studios as 20th-Century-Fox and Paramount. There were Cinerama (with its three pictures and two wobbly joins on screen), CinemaScope, VistaVision, Todd-AO, WarnerScope, SuperScope and so on. Many directors had no idea how to use these new toys. With Cinerama, in particular, the problem was how to fill the space on either side of a close-up of two stars kissing - albeit missionary-position encounters might have provided a temporary solution. In the end, most of these wide-screen processes fell by the wayside, although VistaVision was rescued many years later by another pioneer, George Lucas, for use in special effects.

Nevertheless, some exceptional work was done in wide screen, notably by David Lean when he made *Lawrence of Arabia* (1962), shot in Super Panavision 70. Like a latter-day Abel Gance, his creative vision was served by the new process.

There was also, at this time of technical change, an amiably daft pioneer working in Hollywood. William Castle made a horror film called *Macabre* (1958). He offered free insurance if anyone had a heart attack brought on by sheer fright. And during the screening of *The House on Haunted Hill* (1958), he challenged the world of special effects with an illuminated skeleton on wires which flew, rather jerkily, over the heads of the audience. But most film historians agree that William Castle's masterwork was *The Tingler* (1959). During this film, members of the audience received electric shocks from wired-up seats. George Lucas, eat your heart out.

The dream factories were still being ruled (just) by their ageing masters. When their inevitable fall came, nobody, it seemed, regretted it. It was only when the old-style moguls were long gone that some movie-makers began to feel that perhaps the hated studio system hadn't been so bad after all. The Cohns and Mayers and Goldwyns and Warners and Zanucks may have been ruthless ogres but, to their everlasting credit, they loved movies even more than they loved money. Hollywood would never see their like again. However, the greatest tragedy of all was about to be played.

At the very end of the Sixties, a distant whirlwind, no larger than a poker-player's hand, appeared on the horizon. From out of Las Vegas came a genuine, wannabe mogul - a self-made wheeler-dealer, a gambler of genius; above all a man with a dream - to make great movies in the greatest studio of them all, Metro-Goldwyn-Mayer. His name was Kirk Kerkorian.

Kerkorian's entrepreneurial career to that date would have made an excellent star vehicle for MGM's own Clark Gable, a romantic, Only-in-America hero progressing in astonishing leaps and bounds. From snapping up second-hand aeroplanes after the war, and running charter flights to Las Vegas for low-profile high rollers, Kerkorian bought two casinos at his clients' destination, before buying a real air-line - the prestigious Western Airlines. But when he gobbled up MGM, Clark Gable, no longer cast as Mr Colourful Nice Guy, would have stalked indignantly off the set, to be replaced by Vincent Price.

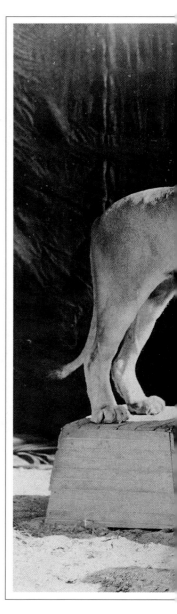

To be fair, Kerkorian started off with the best of intentions. The trouble was that, finding himself the disenchanted inheritor of huge MGM debts ($85 million, with the studio about to default on its bank loan), he tried desperately to teach Leo new tricks. These were deeply humiliating to perform, and coupled with a starvation diet, and so the poor old lion wasted away and died. But it took a succession of ring masters and 20 years to finish him off.

In 1990, Peter Bart devoted an entire book (*Fade Out*) to MGM's calamitous final days. Peter Bart is now the editor of *Variety* magazine, but was for a time a senior vice-president of MGM/UA. He says that before the Kerkorian take-over, MGM was the house of hits, the studio of Thalberg and Louis B. Mayer, the maker of quality pictures

and superlative musicals. All vestiges of greatness ended under the new stewardship. "Kerkorian starved the studio of money. They made exploitation pictures, and the level of executives he brought in was pathetic. In the two or three years I was there, I tried to start some interesting films, and then ,all of a sudden, something would happen - an important director would say, 'You know, old boy, I don't think I want to make this picture at MGM,' or a star would pull out. So for one reason or another you could never pull together a blue-ribband

☛ page 66

"I'm ready for my close-up now, Mr Mayer." The most enduring star of them all.

THE HOLLYWOOD STUDIOS

Columbia
❧

Set up by Harry Cohn in 1924, in an area of Hollyood nicknamed Poverty Row where fly-by-night producers made movies on the cheap, Columbia Pictures produced - for years - mainly B features. Unlike the major studios, it had few stars or directors of its own. It began to be noticed in the Thirties with the pictures of Frank Capra, especially when *It Happened One Night* (1934) and *You Can't Take It With You* (1938) won Oscars. It emerged as a major studio in the Forties and was the first to embrace television, setting up the very successful programme-making subsidiary Screen Gems. Its golden period of film-making was in the Fifties and Sixties, with such films as *From Here to Eternity* (1953), *On the Waterfront* (1954), *The Bridge on the River Kwai* (1957) and *Lawrence of Arabia* (1962). Britain's David Puttnam was Columbia's production chief for a short while in the mid Eighties. The company was bought by Sony in 1989 from its then owners, Coca-Cola, for an astonishing $3.4 billion.

MGM
❧

Created in 1924 by the amalgamation of three companies, MGM, under Louis B. Mayer, was for several decades the grandest studio in Hollywood. It famously boasted having "more stars than there are in the heavens", including Greta Garbo, Clark Gable, Joan Crawford, Spencer Tracey, James Stewart and Elizabeth Taylor. A combination of prestigious films with lavish production values, such as *The Wizard of Oz* (1939) and a number of low-budget highly popular series, such as the "Andy Hardy" films, made it the leading film producer of the Thirties. Then in the Forties and Fifties came a unique parade of musicals, from *On the Town* (1949) to *Singin' in the Rain* (1952). But it went into decline after the arrival of television and never recovered. By 1970, Leo the Lion had lost his roar. The studio was dismembered by a Las Vegas casino-owner, Kirk Kerkorian, and it is now a shadow of its former glory.

Paramount
❧

Paramount, in one form or another, goes back to 1912. It was then that ex-furrier Adolph Zukor founded Famous Players to present popular stage plays on screen. After a series of mergers, the company eventually emerged as Paramount. It was soon the dominant studio in Hollywood, and Zukor the most influential figure in the industry. The Twenties were a golden age for Paramount, with such stars as Rudolph Valentino, Gloria Swanson and Clara Bow, culminating in its film *Wings* (1927) winning the first best picture Oscar. Though the company went bankrupt in 1932, it emerged to become a successful studio again, the home of Cecil B. DeMille's epics and the "Road" movies with Bing Crosby and Bob Hope. The company was taken over by Gulf and Western Industries in 1966. In the Seventies and the Eighties, Paramount had a spectacular run of hits including *Love Story* (1970), *The Godfather* (1972), the "*Indiana Jones*" films and the "*Star Trek*" series. In 1994 ,Paramount was taken over by the media company Viacom.

20th Century-Fox
❧

20th Century Fox resulted from the 1935 merger of two companies, one of which was the Fox Film Corporation. Fox had pioneered Movietone, the sound-on-film process. Under the control of Darryl Zanuck for 30 years, off and on, 20th Century-Fox gained a reputation for producing technically polished films, often with gorgeous colour and visual gloss. In the Fifties, to counter the threat of television, it introduced the widescreen process, CinemaScope. Among its roster of stars were Shirley Temple, Betty Grable, Marilyn Monroe, Tyrone Power, Henry Fonda and Gregory Peck. The company hit the jackpot with *The Sound of Music* (1965), one of the most successful films ever, having lost its shirt on *Cleopatra* (1963), one of the all-time flops. Then in the Seventies it struck gold again with the "Star Wars" trilogy. It is now owned by Rupert Murdoch, as part of Fox Inc.

RKO

Between 1928 and 1953, RKO Radio Pictures Inc was one of the 5 major studios. It was taken over in 1948 by the reclusive millionaire Howard Hughes, whose eccentric management effectivelly killed its production. But in its day it was responsible for some great films - *King Kong* (1933), the Fred Astaire/Ginger Rogers musicals, Alfred Hitchcock's *Suspicion* (1941) and most famously of all, Orson Welles' *Citizen Kane* (1940).

United Artists

Never a studio, United Artists was founded in 1919 by Mary Pickford, Douglas Fairbanks, Charlie Chaplin and D.W.Griffith to make and distribute their films. "The lunatics have taken over the asylum" said one studio executive, but it prospered in the Twenties and Thirties, when it handled the films of Goldwyn and Korda. It fell on hard times in the late Forties and early Fifties before entering its golden age. With its rivals hurt by the disintegration of the studio system, UA came into its own. Among its releases were *The African Queen* (1951), *High Noon* (1952), *The Magnificent Seven* (1960), *One Flew over the Cuckoo's Nest* (1975) and of course, the "Bond" films. It was finally sold to MGM in 1981, became part of MGM/UA. And then disappeared completely in 1992.

Universal

One of the oldest studios in Hollywood, Universal was founded by cinema pioneer, German-born Carl Laemmle in 1912. He created the 230-acre Universal City in 1915 and was clever enough to open it to the public. Universal had a pretty undistinguished record for years, apart from its cycle of horror films with Boris Karloff and its Deanna Durbin musicals. In 1962 it was bought by the talent agency and entertainment company MCA Inc, and in 1995 it was taken over by the drinks' company, Seagram. Universal's greatest coup was giving Spielberg his big break with *Jaws* (1975). His production company, Amblin Entertainment, has brought such Universal blockbuster hits as *E.T. - The Extra Terrestrial* (1982), *Back to the Future 1,2 & 3* (1985, 1989 and 1990) and *Jurassic Park* (1993).

The Walt Disney Company

Created in 1923 by Walt Disney and his brother Roy, the company became famous for pioneering animated short films, especially the first sound cartoons of Mickey Mouse. In 1937 it made a spectacular success with the first ever full-length animated feature, *Snow White and the Seven Dwarfs*. The company continues the tradition to this day with equal success. Their cartoon feature *The Lion King* (1994) was the biggest-grossing film of 1994. Walt Disney moved into family, live-action and natural history features in the Forties, and entered television and theme parks in the Fifties. After Walt Disney's death in 1966, the company went into something of a decline. But with new management in the Eighties, the revitalising of Walt Disney Studios, the creation of Touchstone and Hollywood Pictures, whose films are targeted at adults, and brilliant merchandising of the Disney characters everywhere, the Walt Disney Company is among the most successful in the entertainment industry.

Warner Bros.

Founded in 1923 by the four Warner brothers, Harry, Albert, Sam and Jack, it became a major studio thanks to producing the world's first talkie *The Jazz Singer* (1927). Warner Bros. was famous for making its films on the cheap - but it still had a lot of success in the Thirties and Forties, producing gangster films, social dramas and adventure pictures, with such stars as James Cagney, Bette Davis, Humphrey Bogart, Edward G.Robinson and Errol Flynn. Sold in 1967, two years later it became part of the entertainment conglomerate, Warner Communications. For the last 20 years Warner Bros. has been among the most consistently successful studios in Hollywood, releasing the films of Clint Eastwood, the "Batman" series and the "Lethal Weapon" trilogy. In 1989 the company was acquired by Time Inc to form one of the biggest communications empires in the world, Time Warner.

picture at MGM. There was a down-draught that ultimately destroyed the studio."

Probably the most insensitive of Kirk Kerkorian's studio heads was his first, Jim Aubrey, who in his four-year tenure, became known as "The Smiling Cobra". When Aubrey, with Kerkorian's approval, cancelled 16 major films, Robert Altman was moved to call MGM "The Cowardly Lion".

Worse was to come. Jim Aubrey cut the studio workforce by half, studio assets were sold off (including overseas movie theatres and MGM Borehamwood.) Huge chunks of the studio's 187 acres were sold at knock-down prices. One desperate studio officer implored Aubrey to look at the wealth of tradition that was being squandered: the Chinese streets from *The Good Earth* 1937), the Dickensian streets from *David Copperfield* (1935), the lavish 5th Avenue set for

Selling the family jewels. One of the MGM auctions held in 1970.

Easter Parade (1948), Andy Hardy's small town square, the rolling lawns from Garbo's *Camille* (1936), and much, much more. At the end of this tour, Jim Aubrey's reaction was, "I don't want to hear any more bullshit about the old MGM. The old MGM has gone."

Peter Bart recalls that the ultimate metaphor for the life-draining process was the 13-day-long series of auctions (pre-sold to a professional auctioneer) held in 1970, during which the studio's treasures were sold to the highest bidders. The pathetic occasion was akin to a once proud dowager selling off her furnishings to pay the rent. Kerkorian aides had vastly underestimated the value of the goods, not realising that much of the furniture, chandeliers and other props, were not reproductions or fakes, but valuable antiques.

Among the clothes in a sad jumble sale were Judy Garland's dress from *Meet Me in St Louis* (1944), a gown worn by Elizabeth Taylor in *Raintree County* (1957), Garbo's 2-piece velvet suit from *Queen Christina* (1933), Susan Hayward's feather-trim chiffon dress worn in *I'll Cry Tomorrow* (1955); and for next to nothing you could buy next-to-nothing Tarzan-cod-pieces for the warmer weather.

Aubrey took a cynical view of public tastes, so new projects had to meet two criteria. They had to be cheap, and had to appeal to a clearly defined segment of the audience. Movies with sex and violence stood the best chance of getting the green light. Examples of Aubrey-approved films were *Private Parts* (1972), and the heart-warming story of a cheeky but loveable trouser snake, or smiling cobra, called *Percy* (1971). Aubrey even invited the man who made *Deep Throat* (1972) to come up with an idea for a film (abandoned after serious discussion) but inexplicably turned down *Last Tango in Paris* (11972). MGM became the studio that almost made *The Sting* (1973), *Terms of Endearment* (1983), *Dirty Dancing* (1987), *"Crocodile" Dundee* (1986) - and the fish that got away. Aubrey listened to the pitch, then said, "I don't like the story. Besides, how do you get a shark to do all those tricks?" *Jaws* (1975) went to Universal and was one of the first films whose grosses would soar past the $100-million mark.

Aubrey's artistic relationship with real film-makers was confrontational. Blake Edwards, in 1971, made a picaresque western called *Wild Rovers*, starring William Holden and Ryan O'Neal. A more appropriate title would have been "The War of The Derby Hat" - the hat worn by Ryan O'Neal in the film. To Edwards the derby represented realism - not everyone in the west wore conventional cowboy hats, as he pointed out. "Perhaps not," a truculent Aubrey countered, "but cowboys in MGM movies always wear cowboy hats." As the film was already two weeks into shooting, Edwards refused to switch hats. "Change hats or shut down!", said a now unsmiling cobra. Grimly, Edwards wrote an expository scene in which the Ryan O'Neal character explained his change of haberdashery. Thereafter he wore a cowboy hat in the film.

Peter Bart's book is a tale of studio madness, but, miraculously, one good thing did come out of the new regime. Jack Haley, Jnr, son the Tin Man in *The Wizard of Oz*, was hired by Aubrey as head of production and then, on a whim, instantly demoted to "vice-president for creative affairs". History will show that the movie-loving world owes Jack Haley a debt that can never be repaid.

Haley was distressed to find that some of the MGM classics were at death's door. The film was literally crumbling as it ran through the projector. Haley appealed to his boss for an emergency allocation to salvage the old films. True to form, Aubrey instantly turned him down. So Haley spent his lunch breaks and evenings sorting through old film clips, sensing that he might be the last man ever to see them. Some of the material was familiar, such as Fred Astaire's walls-and-ceiling dance from *A Royal Wedding* (1951, released in the UK as *Wedding Bells*); some of it was arcane, such as Judy Garland's debut in a short entitled *Every Sunday* (1936), or Jean Harlow's oddball performance in the long forgotten *Reckless* (1935). He started splicing the clips together. Almost without Haley's realising it, the body of work continued to grow. Sequences featuring Bing Crosby, Frank Sinatra, Gene Kelly and Mickey Rooney were added. When the compilation was shown to studio veterans - secretaries, film editors, lab workers, drivers, guards, commissary waitresses - the cumulative impact of the extraordinary material thrilled them. It was as though the viewers, having numbly endured the studio's recent films, were suddenly reminded of what MGM once stood for - opulence, imagination, vision. At the end, Aubrey said, "You have my okay to move ahead. What the hell - we can always sell it direct to TV" Haley's compilation of movie sequences beyond price was, of course, *That's Entertainment* (1974).

Jim Aubrey took his "The old MGM has gone" philosophy to extreme and mean-spirited lengths. The Thalberg Building - dedicated to the memory of Louis B. Mayer's boy wonder, Irving Thalberg - was bleakly re-named the Administration Building. Aubrey also had a bust of Thalberg removed, together with a commemorative plaque.

The Smiling Cobra's demise came when, after a row over policy, Kirk Kerkorian fired him. But for one studio veteran it was a double celebration. He retrieved the Thalberg bust and the plaque from where he'd hidden them and restored them to their places of honour.

By now, however, the damage done to MGM was terminal, although it took another 16 years - and four more studio heads - before the great studio died. Inevitably, perhaps, Kerkorian eventually concluded that the only way to win the game was to reinvent the rules. If he couldn't build an empire, at least he could profitably carve one up. In so doing, Kerkorian transformed corporate demolition into a high art.

The diamonds and rubies and emeralds in MGM's crown were the movies made in the great studio's prime. Jim Aubrey had had no interest in them, and Kerkorian - much later - sold them to Ted Turner, the king of cable. Turner scooped up over 3000 titles, with a bagful of RKO and Warner Brothers movies thrown in. *Casablanca* (1942) with the black-and-white heart wrenched out of it, may be heresy, but the expensive colorisation of Bogie's classic, and many others, is an investment that has made Turner's television network, TNT, a staggering success.... Television again - the old-time studio's old enemy.

Today, Peter Bart concludes, sadly, "Now, of course, MGM is simply a company that rents offices in Santa Monica and finances some pictures through the good offices of a French bank which extends them a line of credit. But it's been pillaged to such a degree that it's not really considered a major player in the entertainment business today. MGM is a great logo in search of a tradition."

Low-budget films and the threat of television may have contributed to the death of MGM, but back in the mid-Fifties there emerged an extraordinary film-maker who didn't give a damn about the threat of television, and didn't even try to make bigger movies - and yet his influence on cinema over the last 40 years is formidable. During the Fifties, Roger Corman churned out feature films on tiny budgets; he also made several screen versions of Edgar Allan Poe stories. Either by accident or design, Corman became a one-man film school. Among the unknowns who were given their start by Corman are Jack Nicholson, Francis Ford Coppola, Peter Bogdanovich, Joe

Dante, Jonathan Demme (Corman made a brief appearance in his *The Silence of the Lambs*, 1991), John Milius, and Martin Scorsese.

Unlike his students, Corman came comparatively late to films. When he started, he hoped eventually to work at the major studios. Having made a number of independent films, he looked forward to the bigger budgets, but he found that studio-based films cost more. Worse still was the studio interference. "There were people there telling me what to do that I wouldn't hire."

Low-budget means cheap but not necessarily nasty. "I tell the directors working with us that the limitations of a low budget do not involve the thinking of your mind. The intelligence, the creativity of the mind is not dependent upon the budget. As a matter of fact I say, 'You must not look down on the project - or you're finished before you start. If you're gonna make a cheap western about a monster attacking a dance hall girl, you have to go in and say I intend to make the finest western ever made about a monster attacking a dance hall girl. In other words, you give it your best shot at all times.' "

Corman once took a scalpel to the *auteur* theory of movie-making, passing on his findings to Martin Scorsese: "You need a very good first reel because people want to know what's going on; and a very good last reel because people want to know how it all turns out. Nothing else really matters."

Another Roger Corman student makes good. A scene from Francis Coppola's *The Godfather*, with James Caan, Marlon Brando, Al Pacino, John Cazale.

Corman's protégés were among the so-called "Movie Brats" of the Sixties - the young writers and directors who were destined to take over the industry. Such people as Francis Ford Coppola, Martin Scorsese, George Lucas and Brian De Palma were graduates of the film schools, but at least one of the Brats couldn't get in. Undeterred, he talked his way into Universal Studios and then took the television route to feature films. His name - Steven Spielberg.

All of these young men shared an acute awareness of the current movie scene but, perhaps more importantly, with the aid of television re-runs, they were steeped in the glorious and inglorious past. They knew every nut and bolt of movie-making, but, crucially to the Movie Brats' confident, even arrogant, advance. the studios didn't. So the kids were given the grown-ups' toys. By the mid-Seventies, the work of these newcomers dominated the industry.

All of them could be called innovators, latter-day pioneers; some were more pioneering than others, and at least three of them - Francis Ford Coppola, George Lucas and Steven Spielberg, in that order - tried to become, became, or currently intend to be, moguls. Coppola set up American Zoëtrope Studios, George Lucas built a hugely successful one-man-band empire; and Spielberg, in 1994, announced his partnership with David Geffen from the record industry, and Disgruntled of Disney, Jeffrey Katzenberg. Jaws Man, Music Man and Mouse Man are equal partners - although you can bet one of them will turn out to be more equal than the others - and they intend to produce up to 16 films a year.

Spielberg, Geffen and Katzenberg - be warned. Back in 1969, Coppola dreamed of a co-operative run by old and new pals, among them, George Lucas. "The essential objective of American Zoëtrope," Coppola announced, "is to engage in the varied fields of filmmaking, collaborating with the most gifted and youthful talent using the most contemporary techniques and equipment possible." Alas, a short time later, when seven screenplays made the journey from San Franciso to Los Angeles, they died at the hands of Warner Brothers' President, Ted Ashley, who rejected them all. Zoëtrope was badly mauled, and survived only by the skin of its toothless gums.

But George Lucas never put a foot wrong. After graduating from film school, he won a six-month scholarship sponsored by Warner Bros., which allowed a student to observe any part of the studio's operation he or she chose. On the day George Lucas walked in,

☞ page 74

KING KONG

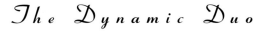

RKO RADIO PICTURES 1933

Producers/Directors:
Ernest B. Schoedsack, Merian C. Cooper

Stars:
Fay Wray, Robert Armstrong, Frank Reicher, Bruce Cabot

To see a gigantic ape scaling the Empire State Building was a spectacular vision for cinema audiences of 1933. Described in *Picture Goers Weekly* as "the mechanical marvel of this technocratic age", *King Kong* not only thrilled the public with its technical wizardry, but established monster movies as a whole new genre and crowd-pleaser. In spite of (or perhaps because of) its release in one of the worst years of the Depression, the film grossed $2,500,000 in North America - not a bad return on an original $650,000 investment.

Above: Kong's last moments. Below left: the film's human stars, Fay Wray and Bruce Cabot. Below right: the fight with the pterodactyl was a *tour de force* of early animation.

The Dynamic Duo

King Kong was the brain child of two hard-boiled documentary makers, Merian Cooper and Ernest Schoedsack. They'd collaborated together on films in the past - roaming the world in search of exotic locations - and were naturally drawn to a story of a remote tropical island inhabited by terrifying monsters.

After failing to get either MGM or Paramount interest in their project, however, Cooper finally managed to hook RKO, and in 1931 joined the studio as an executive assistant to the studio's boss, David O. Selznick (and in fact took over from Selznick a few months before *King Kong* was released).

A Strange Tale

The film was based on a story by the thriller-writer Edgar Wallace, who died before starting work on the script. It was Ruth Rose - Ernest Schoedsack's wife - along with Cooper and James Ashmore Creelman who fine-tuned the strange story of a young actress (played by Fay Wray) sent to film on a mysterious island.

This giant gorilla was actually an 18in model.

Once on Skull Island, the actress' producer (played by Robert Armstrong) and his film crew, come across a native village protected by a high wall, behind which lurks the Beast known as "Kong". Needing a human sacrifice to appease the monster, the villagers decide who better to offer up than the tasty young actress so recently arrived in their midst.

After many traumas, including being carried off by a pterodactyl, the girl is rescued, and Kong is captured and taken to New York. Kong escapes to wreak havoc on the city, and recaptures his 'lunch' - with whom he has fallen in love. He makes his last dramatic stand on top of the Empire State Building, but is finally and graphically gunned down by a circling squadron of bi-planes.

BIG
King Kong grows bigger in America. On the island he's 18ft high and in New York he's 24ft.

NOISY
His roar is the recording of a zoo at feeding time.

HAIRY
His skin is made from latex, and covered in cheap rabbit's hair.

TOUGH
The mighty Kong's victims aren't even human actors but only 6in models.

Tricks Of The Trade

There's always been speculation as to how King Kong worked. Even up until the Seventies people have claimed that it was a man in the gorilla suit. *Time* magazine went as far as to say that Kong was no more than a gigantic structure covered in bear skins and operated from the inside by a crew of six men perched in front of a battery of controls. But although a manually operated model was made of King Kong's mouth and of the giant hand in which Fay Wray famously squirms - the main Kong was a disappointing 18in high, and manipulated from the outside. How to bring this 18-in model to life was a problem solved by the talented technician and animator Willis O'Brien. Making use of the new development of stop-frame photography, he was able to make Kong move and express himself in a realistic way though having to change the position of the model 24 times per second was a long and painful process.

Bogart's old boss, Jack L. Warner, walked out, leaving only one film behind him. *Finian's Rainbow* (1976) was being directed by another ex-film student, Francis Ford Coppola, who seems not to have been told about the scholarship, because, for Chrissakes, here was this skinny kid watching every move he made, getting on his nerves if you must know, and who let him in anyway? Francis strode over to him and started both a prickly conversation and a life-long friendship.

Lucas was single-minded in his determination to make it in the industry, but on his own terms. When he went off and made *American Graffiti* for a sceptical Universal Studios, the potent soundtrack, married to visual nostalgia, became a hymn to a gone but not forgotten generation. *American Graffiti*'s huge success paved the way for *Star Wars* - the film and the trilogy that made Lucas another kind of pioneer when he kissed the dying industry of special effects back to life. Lucas founded Industrial Light and Magic for the express purpose of creating those breathtaking images in *Star Wars* (1977); but of course, up to and beyond *Jurassic Park*, ILM remains at the cutting edge of special effects.

At the start of the Fifties, Lew Wasserman of the huge agency, MCA, waved a magic wand over his client, James Stewart, showering him with sackfuls of dollars. The astonished star was to receive a percentage of the profits from a film called *Bend of the River* (1952, entitled rather poetically in Britain, *Where the River Bends*). Like an Edison who's just invented a better light bulb, Wasserman went on to create The Package: "You want the services of my star? Okay, but you also take my writer, my director, my supporting actors and my unwanted Christmas presents." In the Eighties, the Agent-Packager mutated into the Super-Agent-Packager in the shape of a man called Mike Ovitz, who pioneered the sophisticated movie exploitation - the deals, the advertising campaigns, the commerical tie-ins and the rest - that is, today, central to the film business. The address of Mike Ovitz's agency is now somewhere in the stratosphere directly above Hollywood.

Indeed the, Hollywood of the Nineties is virtually run by super-rich stars with a percentage of the gross, the ubiquitous Japanese - and above all, The Super-Agent-Packagers. What on earth would Bogie or John Wayne have said...

The cinema is a hundred years old and still growing. Pioneers and innovators emerge at all times and from all over the world. Run Run

Shaw may not have his name wrapped around an MGM lion, but in Hong Kong, the Middle East, Japan, India and China, dream factories like his are responsible for half of the world's film production. The Bollywood of India exists for a specific Asian audience, producing as many films as Hollywood did in the old days. Some of them find a world-wide audience, from Satyajit Ray's, starting with his Fifties "Apu" trilogy about a child in modern India; to Shakhar Kapur's *Bandit Queen* in 1994; while from China comes Chen Kaige's *Farewell My Concubine* (1993) and Zhang Yimou's *To Live* (1994).

The film industry has changed, developed, declined and risen many times; it will do all of these things again. The cinema is vigorously alive and well and will continue to be served by all those pioneers waiting ... just out of camera range.

Innocents cruising in *American Graffiti*, George Lucas's first success.

CHAPTER 3

A Star is Born

Stand on Hollywood Boulevard, outside Grauman's Chinese Theater, and here be ghosts - Charlie Chaplin, Rudolph Valentino, Humphrey Bogart, Shirley Temple, Marilyn Monroe, Charles Boyer, Abbott and Costello, Rex Harrison, Irene Dunne, Ava Gardner - spirits trapped in their own footprints. Some of the names are no longer familiar, others are still household words. But they all have one thing in common. They are STARS - those larger-than-life personalities who have always given movies their excitement, their glamour, their unique appeal.

Today, impressario Sid Grauman's bright idea may seem unsophisticated and corny, even vulgar, but by the early Thirties it had become a part of American culture - and a great honour for the participants. No star had truly arrived until he or she had been immortalised outside Grauman's Chinese. Even now, every year, millions of people pour out of their tour buses to stand and wonder at this mute record of Hollywood's greatest; and if you're one of today's stars, Tom Hanks, say, or Julia Roberts, or Keanu Reeves, and you're asked to "Step right in here, please", it's still an offer you'd have to be pretty churlish or pompous to refuse.

Mainstream cinema is unimaginable without stars. Indeed, stars are more important today than ever, simply because they have so much more power than their predecessors who were kept on a short rein by their studio bosses. A sobering thought is that if Jack Nicholson or Arnold Schwarzenegger or Michelle Pfeiffer pulls out of a film just before it goes into production, the chances are that the film won't happen. So if stars are so important to film-making, what exactly *is* a star? What *makes a* star?

Take "tall and good looking". Surprisingly, some vital statistics are not as vital as one might think. Dustin Hoffman is 5ft 5in. Al Pacino is only an inch taller at 5ft 6in, Danny De Vito is 5ft 0in and Dudley

There are only a few good men at the top; and Tom Cruise, 15 years in the business, is one of them.

Moore towers over him by 2½in. Mickey Rooney is 5ft 3in, and Michael J. Fox is 5ft 4in. And in 1957, when Sophia Loren starred with Alan Ladd in *Boy on a Dolphin*, her leading man had to stand on a box for his love scenes with her. "Too" tall isn't a drawback either. Kevin Peter Hall, who played the ape man in *Bigfoot and the Hendersons* is 7ft 2in, Sigourney Weaver and Margaux Hemingway are both six-footers, only 2in below the monumental summit of Christopher Lee; while Jeff Goldblum and Clint Eastwood, standing back to back in their socks, are 6ft 4in.

Male stars don't even have to have perfect features. Sample evidence - Harvey Keitel, Clark Gable, Humphrey Bogart, Nicolas Cage, Gérard Depardieu, Sammy Davis Jnr, Jack Palance, Bill Murray, Mickey Rourke, Spencer Tracy, Jim Carrey; and Lee Marvin, whose appeal survived (in 1969) even *Paint Your Wagon*'s "Aaaaah was bo-o-o-ohn under a waaaaaaandrin staaaaah." Charles Laughton was no oil painting either - unless you count his 1936 *Rembrandt*.

Arnold Schwarzenegger was told he'd never be a star because of his accent, and that a body-builder's physique was *de trop* in a leading man; In Britain, Earl St John, the *eminence grise* of the Rank Organisation, told Dirk Bogarde he could never make it above the title because his head was too small; and Oscar-winner Gene Hackman says that, when he and Dustin Hoffman were at drama school in Pasadena, their fellow students voted them the class members "least likely to succeed".

People were always telling Michael Caine that he would never make it in movies - "give it up and get a proper job". His determination never faltered, even when he auditioned for a part in *The Red Beret* (1953, retitled *The Paratrooper*). As he walked into the casting office, a voice dismissed him with an impatient "Next!"... "But I haven't said anything yet", protested Caine. The man pointed to a line drawn on the back of the door; anyone who came above it was out, because the star of *The Red Beret* was Alan Ladd. "I never got anything from auditions", Caine recalls, "And I did terrible screen tests. When I tested for *Zulu*, Cy Endfield, the producer, told me it was the worst screen test he'd ever seen. He only gave me the part because they were leaving soon and they had to find somebody quick."

As for women, perfect harmony of form seems to have little to do with stardom. Author and screenwriter Ron Base tells us, "Walk around Beverly Hills and you see some of the most incredibly gorgeous

Seduction and destruction. Marlene Dietrich in Josef von Sternberg's *The Blue Angel*.

women that have ever been put on the face of the earth, and yet they're not movie stars." The truth is that attractive imperfections will do at least as well as, and often much better than, Garbo-like beauty. Goldie Hawn was once described as a sexy Donald Duck.

We're so used to seeing stars' names above the title of a film that it's difficult to believe that there was a time when stars didn't exist at all. In very early pictures, it is impossible to identify the actors - and not just because those films were made 80 years ago; audiences had no idea who the actors were. In Westerns, the horses were far more valuable - and often better trained - than the actors, and were treated accordingly. Actors were as expendable as paper cups; if it rained while shooting was in progress, the camera was hastily sheltered, not the leading lady.

Then came a radical change, a revolution set in motion not by agents or unions, but by the filmmakers' paymasters, the audiences. The owners of nickelodeons all over the country were being asked for more of "The girl [or man] who was in that film me an' pa liked so much". Filmmakers took note and (at first) willing action.

The establishment of an international star system can be almost precisely dated, because in 1910 the name of Florence Lawrence appeared on posters advertising her films. Until then, she had been the valuable but undervalued property of her film company, and known simply as the "Biograph Girl". Then Carl Laemmle, of IMP, the man who eventually founded Universal Studios, persuaded Miss Lawrence to leave

One for the fans. A signed photo of Florence Lawrence, Biograph Girl, IMP Girl and the first film star.

Biograph to become the "Imp [IMP] Girl" instead. He then pulled off an outrageous publicity stunt. He arranged for a story to break in the St Louis papers that the actress had been killed in a street-car accident. Allowing time for the invented tragedy to sink in, Laemmle placed an advertisement in the same newspapers. It ran, "The blackest and at the same time the silliest lie yet circulated by the enemies of IMP was the story foisted on the public of St Louis last week to the effect that Miss Lawrence, 'The Imp Girl', formerly known as 'The Biograph Girl', had been killed by a street car. It was a black lie so cowardly." Then, without a blush, "We now announce our next film, *'The Broken Path'*." Within a year, the name Florence Lawrence was appearing on film posters in larger type than the title.

Then came a Canadian, Gladys Smith. The public fell in love with this innocent goldilocks, who became known as Mary Pickford, the World's Sweetheart. She was joined by a bit player, G. M. Anderson, who, after forming Essanay Productions, became the star of 376 weekly motion pictures as the American screen's first Western hero, Broncho Billy.

Coincidentally, in the same year that Florence Lawrence became a star, Urban Gad, in Denmark, starred his wife Asta Nielsen, in *The Abyss* (1910), in which she played a "fallen woman". Stars were emerging world-wide, helped by the fact that, by 1912, feature-length films were being made, a new distribution system had flowered and cinemas proper were mushrooming as places of family entertainment, augmenting, if not yet replacing, the early nickelodeons.

The silent stars of Hollywood were truly international because their films, with captions translated into the appropriate language, could be shown anywhere in the world. There were other advantages too. Many stars, such as Vilma Banky, Pola Negri and Greta Garbo, were foreign, but it didn't matter in the least that they had little or no English. American rough diamonds benefited as well, because Bronx, hill-billy, southern, or western accents could be rendered - by costume and caption - aristocratic, working-

Portrait of Margarita Carmen Dolores Cansino, later transformed into Rita Hayworth.

class or, paradoxically, foreign. The world-famous "'It' Girl", Clara Bow, was a beauty contest winner from Brooklyn, and the fact that she had a thick Brooklyn accent, and stammered badly, mattered not at all. The pre-requisites of stardom were not acting ability and the voice beautiful - they were instead youth and beauty. The line, "I can make you a star" was frequently used and genuinely meant. Valuable star material was found, literally, on the streets, in the parks, on street cars - anywhere. B.P. Schulberg was at one time general manager of Paramount Studios; his son, novelist and screenwriter Budd Schulberg, recalls that his father, while on a business trip, hi-jacked the pilot of the aeroplane he was on, thrusting contract and pen under the man's astonished nose. It was not the bizarre action of an eccentric; on the contrary, B.P. Schulberg was a practical film executive doing his job.

The extent of fame could be quite extraordinary in the days of silent films. Douglas Fairbanks Jnr recalls that his father, with Chaplin and Mary Pickford, were known in the darkest jungles of Africa and parts of China and Tibet; they were the most famous people in the world. Appearing in public was like a military operation. Mounted police held the crowds back everywhere they went. "In fact," remembers Fairbanks Jnr, "when they went over to London together, all of Piccadilly was blocked off, all round the Ritz Hotel, up and down, past Green Park, in all directions. You couldn't go down Piccadilly at all."

But where do the stars of today (and that includes the stars of yesterday who are *still* stars today) come from? How are they discovered? What were they doing before they got that big break? Part and parcel of the glamour of stardom is the myth that anyone can make it. Well... perhaps. It's true, for example, that Michelle Pfeiffer was a supermarket checkout girl, Garbo a barber-shop assistant, Oliver Reed was a strip-club bouncer, Lee Marvin a plumber's mate, and Burt Lancaster was in ladies' knickers. George Raft ran a protection racket, Sharon Stone sold hot dogs, Janet Gaynor was a cinema usherette, and Warren Beatty was a rat-catcher.

America's queen and her consort: Mary Pickford and Douglas Fairbanks.

Of course, not everyone started with those advantages. Kevin Kline studied drama in New York and made his Broadway debut in 1978. He was "discovered" in his first film, *Sophie's Choice* (1982), and Oscar-confirmed as a star actor in *A Fish Called Wanda* (1988). Katharine Hepburn, Walter Matthau, Marlon Brando and Dustin Hoffman were all on the stage before they broke into pictures.

Once discovered, how is the potential star turned into a star proper? When Betty Bacall, an 18-year-old model, made the front cover of *Harper's Bazaar*, there were several offers from Hollywood; but, after a succesful screen test, Betty signed a personal contract with Howard Hughes, a man she knew only from such films as *Barbary Coast* (1935) and *Bringing Up Baby* (1938). Shaping his protege to the fantasy image in his head, Hawks arranged for her to be dressed by Hollywood's best, to study drama and work with a music coach. He drove her to a secluded spot in the hills where he told her how he wanted her to act in the film he had not as yet chosen for her debut. She must cultivate a masculine approach. "Be insolent, give as good as you get. Never play the helpless little girl." Hawks made her read aloud to him, ordering her to lower her voice until it out-gravelled Louis Armstrong. Oh yes, and Betty had to go. From now on she would be Lauren.

At last Hawks found the ideal vehicle for Lauren Bacall's debut - *To Have and Have Not* (1944). Bacall was so terrified on set that to stop her head from trembling she kept her chin down low, almost to her chest, and only then could she look up at Bogart. Hawks approved of "the Look" even though it was not his creation.

When Bacall and Bogart fell in love during the filming, Hawks was, to put it mildly, not best pleased; he threatened to sell her contract to Monogram, the most poverty-stricken studio in Poverty Row. Bogart dried his baby's eyes and assured her that Hawks was unlikely to abort a golden goose. *To Have and Have Not* was an enormous success and the director made one more movie with the two lovers, *The Big Sleep* (1946). Hawks clung to his role as Svengali, but in the end he lost Bacall to Bogart.

Even more extraordinary was the transformation of a young Spanish dancer, Margarita Carmen Dolores Cansino, her name shortened to Rita Cansino for her early, forgettable films. In his book, *City of Nets*, Otto Friedrich tells us that, as the protégé of Winfield Sheehan of the Fox Film Corporation, she was put under contract and given

daily diction and drama classes. But when Fox merged with 20th Century, Darryl Zanuck sacked both Sheehan and Rita. The dancer, on stage since the age of 6, was 18 when she married 40-year-old Edward C. Judson, who negotiated a new studio contract with Harry Cohn at Columbia. Film roles for Spanish dancers in the Thirties were limited, even though Rita danced with a marvellous sensuality; and, if she was to be an actress, her looks were against her. Thick dark curls sprouted very low on her forehead, making her look not only very Hispanic, but somewhat primitive. It took two years of slow torture by electrolysis to deal with her hairline, each hair being removed one at a time and every single follicle on her forehead killed. The last element of her Anglicisation was flowing red hair. Margarita Carmen Dolores Cansino had become Rita Hayworth. Her big break came when Ann Sheridan walked off a 1941 Warner Brothers film called *The Strawberry Blonde*, and Rita got her first starring role in a major production with Jimmy Cagney as her co-star. When that same year she got the lead in a 20th Century-Fox film, *Blood and Sand* (1941), Darryl Zanuck had to hire back the girl he'd fired and pay five times her normal salary to Harry Cohn for the privilege of making her a major star.

Stage fright nourished "The Look". Lauren Bacall lowered her head to stop it from shaking uncontrollably.

Screenwriter William Goldman believes that stars aren't discovered at all. He says that stars *happen* - and invariably by mistake. And invariably that mistake is made by another performer who is a bigger name at the box office. When Goldman's script, *Butch Cassidy and the Sundance Kid* (1969), landed in Robert Redford's lap, it had already been dog-eared by Marlon Brando, Steve McQueen and Warren Beatty. The film, of course, made Redford a star.

Fellow screenwriter Ron Base agrees with Goldman. "In 1980, Tom Selleck was all signed and ready to play the lead in *Raiders of the Lost Ark* (1981); then, at the last moment, he couldn't get out of a commitment to a television series called *Magnum PI*. Only then did Harrison Ford get the role." For Selleck, this must have been a particularly bitter pill to swallow because the start of the television series was delayed by a writers' strike. Selleck could have been Indiana Jones after all.

When *The Graduate* (1967) was being prepared, Charles Grodin was offered both the part and a long-term contract, but very little money. Discussions became acrimonious and Grodin walked. The little-known actor who finally got the part was Dustin Hoffman. But

Hoffman thought he'd failed his screen test. "The story goes," Ron Base says, "that as he's leaving, Dustin goes round thanking people, pulls something from his pocket... and all these New York subway tokens go flying all over the place. And a member of the crew picks them up and hands them to Dustin and says 'Here, kid, you're going to need these.' So nobody thought he was going to be a star, least of all Dustin Hoffman."

Once star status is achieved, though, how to stay there? Walking a straight line on the ground, and with nobody watching you, is simple.

No chance. Dustin Hoffman trying to upstage a Bancroft leg in The Graduate.

Up on the high wire of stardom, the audience holding its breath, the next step isn't so easy to take, and if it's the wrong one, there's no safety net. Some stars, Clint Eastwood and Harrison Ford for example, have made impeccable choices. But others have made some disastrous ones. Try this for the opening scene of a Hollywood tragedy. Burt Reynolds sits in a trailer with Clint Eastwood and Burt Reynolds' manager. On the television screen Jack Nicholson gets up and accepts the Best Supporting Actor Award for his role as the washed-up astronaut in *Terms of Endearment* (1983). Cut to Burt Reynolds for a deadpan reaction shot; mercifully, there is no "I told you so" reaction from Burt Reynolds' agent. The galling fact is that not only was Burt Reynolds offered the role first, but James L. Brooks, the director, actually wrote it with Reynolds in mind. Against his agent's advice, Reynolds chose instead to make *The Man Who Loved Women* (1983) which failed at the box office. *Terms of Endearment* was a huge hit and resuscitated Jack Nicholson's whole career. Burt Reynolds never recovered from that; and he was the number one star of the Eighties at that point.

Perhaps the most astonishing collection of wrong decisions belongs to George Raft. He could have been the legend that Humphrey Bogart became. In real life he was much more interesting than Bogart in that he was a gangster who became an actor, while Bogart, Cagney and

Edward G. Robinson were actors who became nine-to-five gangsters at Warner Brothers. Unfortunately, Raft couldn't read scripts very well, and he was twitchily concerned about his image, believing that if he played a gangster, people might think he really was a gangster. So he turned down everything from *Dead End* (1937) and *High Sierra* (1941) to *The Maltese Falcon* (1941). The only reason he didn't turn down *Casablanca* (1942) was that by that time Bogie was the star Raft had unintentionally made him, and Raft was now so disliked at Warner Brothers that he was never a serious contender for the part of Rick. And, of course, the roles Raft rejected are the ones for which we remember Humphrey Bogart today. They helped to solidify his legend, whereas Raft is today all but forgotten.

George Raft - the gangster who was made offers he should never have refused.

John Travolta has a touch of the George Rafts about him. *Saturday Night Fever* (1977) and *Grease* (1978) made him a star; and then he made a bad choice with a film called *Moment by Moment* (1978). One failure is unlikely to bring a star tumbling down; indeed, Travolta could have gained all that lost ground with *American Gigolo* (1980). Thousands of dollars had been spent on his Armani suits for the part, when, at the last moment he decided to back off. Enter a lucky man, Richard Gere. Even then, Travolta might have recovered, because his next film was supposed to be *An Officer and a Gentleman* (1982). Again, at the last possible moment, he pulled out, saying that the film glorified war. Instead, it glorified Richard Gere for the second time. The George Raft connection came to a happy end when in 1994 a young film-maker, who was still at school when *Saturday Night Fever* came out, offered Travolta one of the leads in *Pulp Fiction* (1994). As a result of Quentin Tarantino's film, and the critical accolades, Travolta is regarded as something of a movie star again.

The pressures of stardom are two-fold:the internal ones - like how to avoid making the wrong career choices, the effects of which are greatly magnifed by fame - and the external pressures of the kind applied in the days of the studio system to the young, inexperienced and insecure stars-in-the-making. Both kinds of pressure are probably easier to deal with by the individual who has a stable family background and the confidence acquired through experience or professional training. The pressures for Marilyn Monroe, for example, were mostly internal. Surrounded by "experts" who held at arm's length the professionals, such as Billy Wilder and Jack lemmon, who respected her, Monroe had no belief in herself or her unique gifts; and much of her "unprofessional and irresponsible" behaviour was the unhappy manifestation of her tender fragility.

Louis B. Mayer pressured and "protected" Judy Garland with pep pills by day and sleeping pills by night, laying the foundations for her distorted life. It has to be said, however, that MGM could be self-interestedly generous. For the Judy Garland who had made *The Wizard of Oz* (1939), *Babes in Arms* (1939) and *Meet Me in St Louis* (1944), the studio bought *Annie Get Your Gun* (1950); but Garland was by now a prisoner of her drug addiction and mental instablity. In 1946, after the success of *Ziegfeld Follies* and *Till the Clouds Roll By*, the studio had increased her weekly salary from $3,000 to $5,600 in return for two pictures a year. Then, cast in *The Pirate* (1948) by her husband, the director Vincente Minnelli, she dieted almost to the point of anorexia; often she didn't show up on the set for two or three days at a time and, when she did, a psychiatrist had to be standing by. There were tantrums, unreasoning fears and a half-hearted suicide attempt. The role of Annie Oakley proved to be an impossible challenge for her, and when the part went to Betty Hutton (and although there were moments of glory still to come), the lengthening shadow of Judy Garland's professional decline lay before her.

As many stars fall as rise in every decade. In the Twenties an actor called George Bancroft became a big Hollywood star with such films as *Code of the West* (1925), *Old Ironsides* (1926) and *Underworld* (1927). By the time *Underworld* came out in 1925, George Bancroft was so famous that, when he visited London, he and his entourage couldn't get out of their hotel lobby. He was recognised everywhere, his car surrounded by people calling out his name. His salary rose from $6,000 a week to $7,500. But in the early Thirties, B.P.

Schulberg of Paramount had to explain to George, as tactfully as he could, that although he was still a star, he wasn't doing quite as well as he had been. Now that sound had arrived, rival gangsters such as Edward G. Robinson, Bogart and Cagney were overtaking him; but when Schulberg told Bancroft that he'd have to drop back to $6,000 a week, the star was insulted and walked out of the studio. Three years later, his agent was offering his client to any studio that would hire him for $250 a week.

Was Bancroft's fall the result of natural star wastage - or unfortunate film choices? Today a star may be blamed, or commiserated with, for making the wrong choice, but when the studio system was in place, the star had little say in the matter. In 1939, when MGM decided to make *The Wizard of Oz*, they wanted to borrow Shirley Temple, the biggest star in the world at that time. Unfortunately, she was under contract to 20th Century-Fox, and Darryl Zanuck refused to let her go, in spite of the fact that he had no idea how to guide her through the delicate transition from child star to adult. *The Wizard of Oz* would almost certainly have done this for her. MGM even offered to let Zanuck borrow Clark Gable to make a Fox film with Temple; the response was another stony-faced refusal. As a result, and against everybody's wishes at MGM, a young woman named Frances Gumm became Dorothy, Judy Garland, and a legend.

The studio system worked in mysterious ways. Discoveries recently put under contract could be discovered all over again. When actors were screen tested for an important role, the younger contract players would be used in the test. Ann Rutherford stood in for one of MGM's major stars, Greer Garson and, although the camera was always focussed on the actor being tested, remembers that "If you read your lines well, and memorised them, and didn't knock a light over, or any of the furniture, somebody would see that screen test and say, 'Who was that girl?' - and this is how you worked your way out of just being a contract player."

Ann Rutherford was discovered, or re-discovered, in a big way when she got the plum role as Polly Benedict, Mickey Rooney's girlfriend in the "Andy Hardy" films, an enormously popular series about a small-town kid growing up. There were 17 of these stories in all, and Ann Rutherford was in nearly every one. The plots were repetitious, if not actually interchangeable. Polly Benedict and Andy Hardy always started off together, quarrelled 20 minutes into the film, and were

ALL CHANGE

It used to be common for actors and actresses to adopt new names or for the studios to insist on new names for the performers they were grooming to be stars. So...

CHANGING NAMES

Maurice Micklewhite became **Michael Caine**
Winona Horowitz became **Winona Ryder**
Bernie Schwartz became **Tony Curtis**
Norma Jean Baker became **Marilyn Monroe**
T.C.Mapother IV became **Tom Cruise**
Diana Fluck became **Diana Dors**
Marion Morrison became **John Wayne**
Margarita Cansino became **Rita Hayworth**
Archibald Leach became **Cary Grant**
Shirley Schrift became **Shelley Winters**
Richard Jenkins became **Richard Burton**
and *Camille Javal* became **Brigitte Bardot**.
But **Arnold Schwarzenegger** *decided not to change his name.*

CHANGING PARTNERS

For some stars, getting married became a bit of a habit:

8 TIMES:
Elizabeth Taylor
Stan Laurel
Mickey Rooney

7 TIMES:
Lana Turner
Claude Rains

6 TIMES:
Rex Harrison
Johnny Weissmuller
Hedy Lamarr

5 TIMES:
Richard Burton
Judy Garland
Cary Grant
Clark Gable
Rita Hayworth

4 TIMES:
Charlie Chaplin
Peter Sellers
Frank Sinatra
Doris Day
Humphrey Bogart

reunited in time for the fade-out. In between these fixed dramatic points, young Andy strayed a little, giving a string of young actresses their first big chance in films. Among them were Lana Turner, Judy Garland, Kathryn Grayson, Esther Williams, Susan Peters, and the superb Bonita Granville, who - daringly in1946 - played a rich and randy teenager whose disgraceful advances were spurned, for the sake of middle America, by a squeaky clean Andy Hardy. It was called, not without a certain irony, *Love Laughs at Andy Hardy* .

MGM was the most paternalistic studio of them all, a mink-lined prison. Louis B. Mayer regarded his actors as talented children to be coddled. This is why, according to Ron Base, "People like June Allyson and Ann Rutherford and Jimmy Stewart look back on their days at MGM with great affection. I don't think Jimmy Cagney looked on his time at Warner Brothers as the best time of his life, though."

In Britain, the nearest thing we got to a Mayer or Warner or Cohn was Alexander Korda in the Thirties, who discovered and put several pretty young women under contract, actresses such as Vivien Leigh and Merle Oberon; and, after the war, J. Arthur Rank, whose charm school produced the likes of Margaret Lockwood, Patricia Roc and Diana Dors. Three lucky stars, or so they thought at the time, were Stewart Granger, Jean Simmons and James Mason, who escaped to Hollywood; but once outside the studio system, albeit the Rank version, they didn't do so well...

Roddy McDowell was a child actor in Britain before he became a child star at Fox with the Oscar-winning film, *How Green Was My Valley* (1941). His view of the studio system is a little less rose-tinted than Ann Rutherford's:

"They did too much for you - or else they did nothing. For me it was absolutely terrific while it lasted, but by the time I was 16½ the jig was up. The kid had grown up. It might be a phone call from your agent, but more often than not no news was bad news. And then it's like you never existed. The lack of attention is as forceful as the attention was. I was 12 when I went under contract and I was, I think, 16½ when it ended."

That kind of ruthlessness was enshrined in the standard seven-year contract. Over at Warners, Bette Davis challenged the studio system in 1936 after Jack L. Warner had offered her a longer string of bad parts than usual. A producer in London got wind of her discontent and offered her two films. Davis scurried off to England before JL could stop her. He pursued her with a charge of breach of contract and the case was tried in London. JL said, truthfully, if sanctimoniously, "If she wins, all the studio owners and executives in Hollywood will get trampled in the stampede." In court, the star was represented by Sir William Jowitt, KC, who stood before the judge to describe the Davis position as a fight against a life sentence of slavery. Sir William refused to call witnessses, thereby preventing Jack Warner's barrister, Sir Patrick Hastings, from cross-examining Miss Davis. He was so angry that he took off his wig and threw it across the courtroom. In the end, the judge ruled that a contract was a contract and that Miss Davis had freely committed herself to Warner Brothers. The decision left her with nothing but a $30,000 legal bill. Jack Warner, to his credit, paid most of it and, when Davis returned to the studio, there was in the air a new respect for this serious actress.

A few years later, Olivia de Havilland, having been loaned out to appear in *Gone With the Wind*, hoped for an improvement in her usual Warner casting. Sibling rivalry had something to do with her discontent. Joan Fontaine, Olivia's younger sister, had been made a star by David O. Selznick when he cast her in *Rebecca* (1940), and Hitchcock's *Suspicion* had won her an Academy Award in 1941. When de Havilland was put on suspension for the sixth time in her studio career, the periods of suspension were added to her contract; so she sued her employers on the grounds that under California law anything beyond seven years becomes slavery (shades of Bette Davis's trial). Jack Warner's response was to blacklist her by warning all the other studios off; so while litigation was in progress, the actress was unemployed and unemployable. Then, in March 1944, the court ruled in her favour. JL appealed and wrote to his Hollywood peers, vindictively reinforcing the blacklisting of his "ungrateful "star. He even tried to stop her entertaining the troops overseas. Olivia de Havilland was in Suva, in the Fiji Islands, when she collapsed with pneumonia. And it was here that she learned that the California Supreme Court had ruled in her favour. She was free of her contract. She had won. Jack Warner had lost, and by implication, the whole studio system had lost. It was only a crack in that system, but the cracks were spreading.

One of the unpublicised advantages of studio life was the protection they afforded their stars. Paternalistic covering up was endemic, with many an abortion not so much on demand as demanded by the studio bosses. "Fix it" was the response to any kind of scandal that threatened the respectability of star or studio. When Jean Harlow's husband, Paul Bern, shot himself, Mayer was only with difficulty persuaded not to destroy the suicide note. He would have preferred a synopsis with a happy ending. We deeply regret to announce that Paul Bern accidentally shot himself peacefully in his sleep, perhaps?

Everyone working in the sytem absorbed the "Fix It" atmosphere. Evelyn Keyes, who played one of Scarlett O'Hara's sisters in *Gone With the Wind*, remembers that being under contract was like joining a loving family, even though the family she joined was Harry Cohn's at Columbia. "You were the pet, the precious little angel they took care of. I always felt that if some terrible thing happened to me, all I'd have to do was get on the phone to Harry Cohn and say, 'Harry, I didn't mean to, but I killed this person,' and he'd say, 'Hold it, I'll be right there, just don't move!' "

That was probably what Louis B. Mayer said to Clark Gable. One night, MGM's top star got into his car - drunk - and drove off. Rounding a bend too fast, he knocked down and killed a woman. Mayer wasn't going to let a charge of manslaughter damage his studio, so he told Gable to lie low while the grown-ups looked after things. Mayer sent for a carefully chosen studio employee and made

Clark Gable and Carole Lombard on their way to the premiere of *Gone With the Wind*.

him an offer. How would he like to have his job guaranteed until retirement age? - oh, and an income for life as well, of course.... Catch? No catch. The very idea! A small... favour, perhaps.... Mayer would be *very* grateful if he could find his way to telling the police a little white lie - that Gable was in the passenger seat... Who was driving? ... Ye-e-es, *exactly!* And the time will go very quickly, almost a little holiday. ... Oh good! All settled then.

Gable went to Palm Springs; the obliging employee got 12 months - and a life sentence of financial security.

Star protection like that would not have suited everybody, of course. An actress who never had the slightest wish to go to Hollywood is 86-year-old Chili Bouchier, who began as a star in silent films. [see chapter 2, page 49] At just 17, she was absolutely certain that she would be discovered by a talent scout, if not today, then tomorrow at the latest. By 17¼ she wasn't quite so sure - until she saw something that restored her natural optimism - an advertisement in the *London Evening Standard.*:

...'WE MAKE FILM STARS

PRICE 3 GUINEAS"...

And very reasonable too. The address turned out to be a ramshackle building off Oxford Street. At the top of three flights of bare wooden stairs she announced herself to the suitably blasé young man who sat behind a desk in a tiny office. He waved her through to a larger room beyond, where several other student film stars were waiting. At the end of the room was a movie camera on a tripod. And then in walked Cecil B. DeMille.

Or, to put it another way, "This man *thought* he looked like Cecil B. DeMille – riding boots, little whip, and his cap on back to front. Then he shouted at us through a megaphone that was as phoney as his fake wooden camera. The whole set-up was phoney, of course." Time to make a grand exit, a la Garbo. "Oh *no!* I didn't walk out, because it was so much *fun*. I loved it." Chili was wiser than she knew, because when at last she did take her leave, a tall man she hadn't seen before approached her and told her to be at Hendon Airport the next day for a commercial. "Not a TV commercial, of course, a cinema commercial." Three years later, Chili made her first feature film.

Although it was never Chili's ambition to go to Hollywood, she was for a time under contract to Warner Brothers in Britain, and one day she was informed that she was being sent to Los Angeles. When she got there, Chili hated everything about Hollywood, and a few months later she bunked off back home – "to that lovely little studio at Teddington. I thought, 'We're all going to make lovely pictures together, and I'll be happy.' "Alas, the long arm of the prison governor, Jack L. Warner, reached out from Hollywood and Chili's contract was cancelled. Never mind, plenty of work around for a film star, surely? "Time went by and I thought, 'Nobody's offering me a job.' I think a year went by, and then I met somebody from Warners, and he said, 'Jack Warner has blacklisted you.' And I thought well, how can he do that? I hadn't done anything wrong, I just wanted to come home. I'd never even met Jack Warner. After that, I never went back to the big fabulous days, but I still did films, and I went into the theatre."

Of course, there are discoveries... and discoveries. Michael Caine had a 15-year acting career, including his substantial role in *Zulu* (1963), before being "discovered overnight" in *The Ipcress File* (1965). He read all the papers the morning after it opened and started to weep, because he knew he'd made it at last. Sharon Stone, who was once a model, made a calculated career move by appearing nude in *Playboy* - since when, she's never been out of bed - or work.

How times have changed. Marilyn Monroe's decision to appear nude - on a calendar - was definitely not a career move - it was something she wanted to forget. But nobody else did.

And what about discovery by camera? Bette Davis's first screen test was so appalling that she ran screaming from the Goldwyn projection room. Clark Gable failed a test for Warner Brothers in 1930 because mogul Jack called him a big-eared ape; and over at MGM, when Gable tested again, Irving Thalberg said he lacked macho appeal. It would have been cold comfort to Gable to know that a kid called Shirley Temple failed a test for the "Our Gang" series; and some limey actor called Olivier was turned down for *Queen Christina* (1933) opposite Garbo.

On the other hand, Rock Hudson's screen test for 20th Century-Fox was a great success. They kept it to show other young wannabes how *not* to perform in front of the camera.

One young woman's screen test, for a film called *The Blue Angel* (1930), was shot in Berlin in 1929. Sitting on top of the piano, elegant foot a-dangle, she lost her temper with the pianist, offfering to kick him for every wrong note - his, not hers. A free translation gives us the flavour:

☞ page 98

The Oscars

In 1927, MGM's Louis B. Mayer decided to form the Academy of Motion Picture Arts and Sciences, hoping to create an antidote to the growing influence of the film unions. Two years later came the first Academy Awards. Ever since they have been a publicist's dream, a combination of Hollywood hype, self-congratulations and controversy. A nomination increases a film's business and a win enhances a performer's status and salary. Today, the 13 art and craft branches of the Academy choose the nominations for their speciality (such as screen-writing or cinematography) and then all 6000 members vote for a winner in each category

Why Oscar?

The gold-plated trophy, a male figure standing on top of a reel of film, was designed by MGM's supervising art director, Cedric Gibbons. How the 13½ in statuette came to be called 'Oscar' has become the stuff of myth. The generally accepted version is that the Academy's librarian, Margaret Herrick, said the statuette looked like her uncle Oscar - and the name stuck. The more entertaining one is that Bette Davis named Oscar after her first husband Harmon Oscar Nelson Jnr, claiming that they shared the same backside.

Record-breaker

The picture that still holds the record for most Oscars is *Ben Hur*, with 11, in 1959. *The Last Emperor* (1987) with 9 awards is its nearest rival, with *Cabaret* (1972), *Amadeus* (1984) and *Gandhi* (1982) all getting 8. The person who has won the most statuettes is the man who designed it, Cedric Gibbons. He carried off the award for best Art Direction 11 times and received 37 nominations. But then, he had a contract with MGM which gave him a credit on all the studio's films under his control - over 1500 of them.

Left: the coveted 13in trophy. Above right: Marlon Brando and Oscar-winning Vivien Leigh in *A Streetcar Named Desire*.

Odd Man Out

No picture has ever won all four acting prizes. In fact, *A Streetcar Named Desire* (1951) is the only film to win three. Marlon Brando whose performance, first on Broadway, then on the screen, catapulted him to stardom, failed to win Best Actor. However, he later won two, for *On the Waterfront* (1954) and *The Godfather* (1972).

First Time Lucky

Barbra Streisand and Shirley Booth won Best Actress in their first-ever film performances - *Funny Girl* (1968) and *Come Back, Little Sheba* (1952).

Left: Oscar night. Below: 1959's Best Actor and Actress, Charlton Heston (*Ben Hur*) and Simone Signoret (*Room at the Top*).

No Handicap

The Academicians have a soft spot for people with handicaps, real or make-believe. Jane Wyman played the deaf mute *Johnny Belinda* (1948); Dustin Hoffman, the autistic brother in *Rain Man* (1988); Daniel Day Lewis the crippled Christy Brown in *My Left Foot* (1989), Jon Voight a paraplegic in *Coming Home* (1978) and the really deaf Marlee Matlin in the role of a deaf woman in *Children of a Lesser God* (1986). Most famous of all was Harold Russell, the war veteran with amputated hands who, in *The Best Years of Our Lives* (1946), played....a war veteran with amputated hands!

Acting Directors

Warren Beatty, Robert Redford and Kevin Costner, all top stars of their day, have never won an award for acting. But all have been named best director, the last two for the first films they ever directed: *Ordinary People* (1980) and *Dances with Wolves* (1990).

The Ones That Got Away

One of Hollywood's greatest film-makers, Alfred Hitchcock, never won an Oscar for his films. Nor, so far, has Martin Scorsese, regarded by many as among the best in the business. Of course, until *Schindler's List* (1993), Steven Spielberg, history's most successful director, was consistently snubbed by the Academy. His film *The Color Purple* (1977) shares with *The Turning Point* (1973) the record of getting the most nominations (11) and not winning a single award.

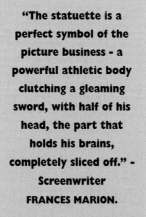

"The statuette is a perfect symbol of the picture business - a powerful athletic body clutching a gleaming sword, with half of his head, the part that holds his brains, completely sliced off." - Screenwriter **FRANCES MARION.**

British Bridesmaids

The record for most acting nominations without a win is 7. Two of the three who hold it are British - Peter O'Toole and Richard Burton. (The unlucky American, incidentally, is Thelma Ritter) Deborah Kerr, also British, holds the wooden-spoon record in the Best Actress category - 6 nominations, no awards. And a British lord shares with Spencer Tracy the honour of being the most nominated actor: Laurence Olivier - 9 nominations and one Oscar (for *Hamlet*).

Western Mystery

If one kind of film symbolises Hollywood, it is the Western. Appropriately, a Western - *Cimarron* - won Best Picture way back in 1931. Yet, 60 years elapsed before another Western won - *Dances With Wolves* in 1990, followed, two years later, by *Unforgiven*. Incredibly *Stagecoach* (1939), *High Noon* (1952), *Shane* (1952), *The Searchers* (1956) - the Golden Age of the Western - came and went unhonoured by members of the Academy.

"You call that piano playing?"

"Ouch!"

"I'm supposed to sing this junk?"

"Now look - "

"Some genius we lost in you!"

"Er, I have to go now."

The pianist was never heard of again. Marlene Dietrich was. Rather a lot.

And when all is said and done, the one thing that all stars have in common is that Dietrich Factor, the special added ingredient - Star Quality. It's a term we use almost unthinkingly, perhaps because we recognise star quality when we see it. But what exactly is it?

Ask the stars themselves, and they don't know - or if they do, they're not giving away a secret like *that*. The professionals who ought to know are the producers, the writers and the directors, such people as Robert Zemeckis, David Brown, Richard Fleischer, Art Linson or Nic Roeg. All of them are toilers in the same vineyard; but ask them to define star quality - and they lose their bearings, waffling on about "A certain indefinable magic", "It's unmistakable when you see it", "The camera loves them", "Ah, if only we knew!" and so on. Even the veteran director, Robert Wise, who juggled effortlessly with whole clusters of stars in *Executive Suite* (1964), *Somebody Up There Likes Me* (1956) and *The Sound of Music* (1965), can't really pin it down. "I call it a gene that they have. You can have all the technical knowledge of acting, but if you don't have that gene, you're not going to become a big star. It's not something you can learn. It's in your being."

A clearer definition - or explantion, perhaps - comes from Joel Schumacher. He had arranged to meet a young actress who wanted a part in his new film. She wasn't entirely unknown, indeed she was currently making a film with Richard Gere, but she was by no means a star. Schumacher had never met her until... "She came round to my house one Sunday. She had on little shorts, an old baggy T-shirt, no make-up, her hair in a rubber band, barefoot, and she was telling me why she wanted to be in *Flatliners*. (1990)" Schumacher was hardly listening, rooted to the spot. "I was watching her, and I thought, 'How have I lived without knowing this person?' And I think that's like falling in love. You see someone, and you want that person in your life. When *Pretty Woman* (1990) came out, everyone else fell in love with Julia Roberts too."

Star Quality - the ability to make millions love you? Schumacher's Law is extended by a star who isn't afraid of giving away secrets, Michael Caine. He is convinced that "People go to the cinema to see themselves on screen - even if it's Cary Grant, and they don't even *look* like Cary Grant." So perhaps movie stars are created when we fall in love with *ourselves*.

This is also the view of screenwriter Ron Base, who talks about what he calls a particular American look. For example, such stars as Paul Newman and Gary Cooper are interesting and good looking, but not downright handsome. "I think that an audience has to be able to em-pathise with that male or female up on the screen. We don't look quite as good, maybe, as Kevin Costner, but, well, you know, he's sort of one of the guys, he's one of us. Meryl Streep is not a great beauty *per se*. Bette Midler, who was a big star for a few years, is not a great beauty, nor is Jodie Foster - attractive, yes, but there's something about them that we can identify with - and I think that's the essence of movie stardom. You think to yourself, yeah, I could be Clint Eastwood."

From Clint Eastwood and Jack Nicholson to Tom Hanks and Julia Roberts, today's stars have enormous influence - because they are bankable. An innocent, or a film buff from Mars, might suppose that the most important basic ingredients of a successful movie are the screenplay, the director - and a cast made up of first-class actors. The truth is, of course, that when trying to set up a film, a bankable star name can open doors that would otherwise stay firmly shut... But which bankable star is going to do all this?

"Everyone else fell in love with Julia Roberts, too" says *Flatliners* director, Joel Schumacher.

☛ page 102

CHILD STARS

❦

Film-makers have always loved featuring children in their films, despite the practical and legal problems they pose for producers, and their widely rumoured scene-stealing habits. The box-office record explains why. Shirley Temple, at the height of her popularity, used to receive 60,000 fan letters a month. Henry Thomas, then 10 years old, was the child star of *E.T. - The Extra-Terrestrial* (1982), one of the most watched films of all time. Macaulay Culkin, at 9 years of age, starred in Hollywood's most successful comedy ever, *Home Alone* (1990). Tatum O'Neal was equally young when she won a Best Supporting Actress Oscar for *Paper Moon* (1973). In movies, kids clearly deliver. Here are some who gave up their childhood for fame, though not always for fortune.

Jackie Coogan
★

BORN: John Leslie Coogan Jnr, 24 October, 1914, in LA.
EARLY DAYS: Spotted by Charlie Chaplin at the age of 4 in a revue act.
MOST FAMOUS FILM: Co-starred with Chaplin in the *The Kid* (1921).
STAR QUALITY: His hair was styled in a cute Twenties bob.
FEE: A two-year contract with Metro earned him $1 million and a percentage of the profit.
WORST MEMORIES: Only permitted an allowance of $6.25. Jackie's mother squandered his hard-earned $4 million. In 1938 he took her to court and the resulting legislation was what came to be known as "the Coogan Act" - from then on guardians of child actors were required by law to set up trust funds for their charges.
FUTURE CAREER: Married and divorced Betty Grable. Appeared in over 1,400 TV shows, but best known for his part as Uncle Fester in "The Addams Family" television series.

Roddy McDowell
★

BORN: 17 September, 1928, in London
EARLY DAYS: A well-known child actor in Britain, he was evacuated to America during World War II.
MOVIE HITS: *How Green Was My Valley* (1941) and *Lassie Come Home* (1941) made him a star in America.
FUTURE CAREER: Grew up to play Cornelius, the masked hero of *The Planet of the Apes* (1967).

Shirley Temple
★

BORN: 23 April, 1928
EARLY DAYS: Discovered at 3 years old at a dancing school and appeared in a series called "Baby Burlesks".
STAR QUALITY: Dimples and ringlets.
CUTEST FILMS: *Bright Eyes* (1934), *Curly Top* (1935); she even triumphed over cutting off the ringlets for *Rebecca of Sunnybook Farm* (1938)
CLAIM TO FAME: She became a national institution. For four years she was the most popular film star in America and, in 1938, the highest paid. But her mother spent most of it.
HONOUR: Awarded a mini Oscar in 1934 for "bringing more happiness to millions of children and millions of grown ups than any child of her years in the history of the world"
MOST FAMOUS SONGS: "On the Good Ship Lollipop" and "What I want for Christmas"
FUTURE CAREER: US Chief of Protocol under President Ford.

Mickey Rooney
★

BORN: Joe Yule Jnr, 23 September, 1920
EARLY DAYS: At the age of 7, his hair darkened with shoe-polish, Joe was chosen for the role of Mickey McGuire - the hero of a series of comedy shorts based on a popular cartoon-strip character.
STAR QUALITY: A cocky little thing.
STRANGE ROLE: Played Puck in *A Midsummer Night's Dream* (1935).
MOST FAMOUS ROLE: Andy Hardy in the domestic drama *A Family Affair* (1937) and its 14 sequels.
CLAIM TO FAME: Managed to stay a child actor until the age of 28.
FUTURE CAREER: Continued to act, got involved in dodgey business ventures and married 8 times.

Judy Garland
★

BORN: Frances Gumm, 10 June, 1922
EARLY DAYS: Appeared with her two older sisters in "The Gumm Sisters Kiddie Act". The "little girl with the great big voice" was signed up with MGM in 1934 and, at 16, landed the role of Dorothy in *The Wizard of Oz* (1939).
BEST-KNOWN SONG: "Somewhere Over the Rainbow"
WORST MEMORIES: Made to wear a corset to conceal her developing body, given caps to wear on her teeth and put on a strict diet. She was given pills to calm her nerves, make her sleep and wake her.
FUTURE CAREER: Married 5 times and died in 1969 from an overdose.

Macaulay Culkin
★

BORN: 26 August, 1980
EARLY DAYS: Made a stage debut at 4, and appeared in commercials and a Michael Jackson video.
FILM THAT MADE HIM A STAR: *Home Alone* (1990).
CLAIM TO FAME: Has made more money than any child star in history (For *Home Alone 2: Lost in New York* (1992) he took $5 million plus a percentage.)
STAR QUALITY: Plays a mini-psychotic murderer with conviction.
FUTURE CAREER: Hopes his pocket money will go up.

Margaret O'Brien
★

BORN: 15 January, 1937
EARLY DAYS: Modelled from the age of 3 and got her first part in the film *Babes on Broadway* (1941).
CLAIM TO FAME: Said to be one of the most talented child actors ever.
BUSIEST YEAR: In 1944 she received a special Academy Award as "Outstanding Child Actor" - the year in which Margaret appeared in *Lost Angel, Jane Eyre, The Canterville Ghost, Meet Me in St Louis* and *Music for Millions*.
FUTURE CAREER: Acted on television and worked as a civilian aide for Southern California for the Secretary of the Army, Clifford Alexander.

Hayley Mills
★

BORN: 18 April, 1946, in London
EARLY DAYS: Daughter of Sir John Mills, she appeared in his film *Tiger Bay* (1959) at the age of 13. Signed up by Disney for a five-year contract.
STAR QUALITY: Sweet and innocent.
CLAIM TO FAME: Won a special Oscar for her perfomance in *Pollyanna* (1960).
FUTURE CAREER: Shocked the world by running off with producer-director Roy Boulting (33 years her senior).

Jodie Foster
★

BORN: 19 November 1962
EARLY DAYS: Performed from the age of three; appeared in many TV Disney productions.
STAR QUALITY: Could carry off sophisticated roles from a young age.
MOST FAMOUS FILMS: *Alice Doesn't Live Here Anymore* (1975) *Taxi Driver* (1976) and *The Little Girl Who Lives Down the Lane* (1977).
FUTURE CAREER: Movie star and director.

William Goldman invariably warns new writers never to describe their central character too precisely. "Six foot tall with piercing blue eyes" is dangerously specific because, on the hazardous journey to funding a movie, the screenplay may be offered to several stars, all of them bankable, and each wanting (or saying he wants) to do it. Shades of Robert Redford and the Sundance Kid.

But assuming your movie has been made, and the distribution is on stream and the television advertising has been booked, you still need your star - to promote the movie. In the old days, stars did as they were told. Promoting the product was all part and parcel of being a contract star. Press and radio interviews, whistle-stop tours all over the States were unquestioned requirements - and you were always polite to fans and press.

Ann Rutherford didn't think twice about it, because she loved every aspect of her job. Contract stars were paid 40 weeks a year, with a 12-week unpaid lay-off. At this time, the vertical studio-to-theatre structure was still in place. Loews was the parent company, MGM made the product, and Loews sold it in their theatres. Even the news-reels were made by MGM. The studio paid Ann Rutherford's salary while she spent her lay-off time promoting the "Andy Hardy" series, the good name of MGM, and herself. "Well, I couldn't think of a better way to see the United States. My mother was with me, and for three months we travelled up and down the country staying in the best hotels, and simply had the best time. And I met all the Loews theatre managers. All the theatres had a sign out in front saying, ANN RUTHERFORD APPEARING TONIGHT, and, as soon as I arrived, they'd just stop the movie wherever it was. I'd go out on stage, give my little talk and answer answer questions about Andy Hardy and Polly Benedict. And then it was off to another theatre. I loved it."

Stars pitch in today, too, of course, helping to get their latest vehicle known to as wide an audience as possible in the crucial weeks before the film opens. There's a difference, though.... Stars hardly ever allow themselves to be interviewed unless they are selling something - a fact that has become increasingly irritating to chat show hosts and their short-changed television audiences, who can't help feeling that a film star ought to do a bit more than just turn up.

On television, the same star interview pops up, accompanied by the same increasingly stale film excerpts, so it's difficult to say with certainty that we have been persuaded to visit the local cinema or pro-

The peekaboo look that was a wartime hazard, so Veronica Lake's hairdresser was soon to make the supreme sacrifice.

voked into staying away. But in a wider sense, how many of us are really neutral? The further back one goes in the history of the cinema, the bigger the direct impact stars had on our lives. During World War II, Veronica Lake was asked to cut off her peekaboo hair because long hair was killing or maiming women factory workers; and when Rudolph Valentino died, his lying-in-state and funeral triggered unprecedented scenes of hysteria. Several of his inconsolable fans committed suicide. That kind of mass involvement never really happened again, even when James Dean, Elvis Presley or Marilyn Monroe or, more recently, River Phoenix died - all of them in romantically tragic circumstances.

Stars and money and glamourous lifestyles go together. Surprisingly, the very first superstar salary was earned not by any of the Hollywood crowd, but by Asta Nielsen in Denmark in 1912.

She was getting $80,000 a year. By contrast, the World's Sweetheart, Mary Pickford, was making do with $175 a week at Biograph, but four years later, with a contract for $670,000, she was almost shoulder-to-shoulder with the highest-paid man in the world, Charlie Chaplin, whose $675,000 a year in the century's Teen years far and away outstrips, in real terms, the highest paid of today's stars.

In the silent Twenties, Fatty Arbuckle and John Gilbert were each getting $1 million a year, although both men would be tragically destroyed before the decade was out. Cowboy star Tom Mix was earning $17,500 a week, Harold Lloyd a massive $40,000. Short contracts could be very sweet, too; Douglas Fairbanks once received $37,000 a week, and John Huston's father, Walter, matched Harold Lloyd's $40,000. In Britain, it was a different story. The most popular British star of the early Twenties, Alma Taylor, was on £60 a week; and even Ivor Novello, at the height of his fame in the late Twenties, could command no more than £3000-£4000 a film.

The face that launched a thousand carbon copies. Mysterious, magical Garbo; the actress with the accent who turned down Laurence Olivier as her co-star in *Queen Christina*.

In America, sound, and the Depression, reduced salaries all round, but rich is still rich; and in the Thirties, when John Barrymore was on $30,000 a week and Garbo got $250,000 a picture, Gable was known as "the King", and not just because of his $400,000 a year. The problem for him was that he was the bought-and-paid-for property of MGM, to be packaged as his owner saw fit, with the appropriate Gable image projected at all times. Mayer and the publicity department decided that part of that image was to be the rugged man of the great outdoors, whose spare time was spent on hunting and fishing trips. To his own surprise, Gable started to enjoy his fabricated hobby; but the manipulation rankled, and it was his dream to become independent of MGM, or at least to be able occasionally to say no. The answer had to be money, of course, lots of it. Exchanging confidences over the camp fire on a hunting trip with a young and greatly flattered David Niven, Gable told him about what he called his Fuck You account. But it was James Stewart who changed all the rules when he became the first star to share in a film's profits. He would have called *his* independence money the Sorry Guys Hope You Don't Mind Too Much account.

After the stunned silence which followed Stewart's coup, star salaries in Hollywood rose almost exponentially until, in 1978, the world's highest-paid stars were Paul Newman, Robert Redford and Steve McQueen, who were getting $3 million a picture, while Brando had to rub along on a daily rate of $290,000 playing *Superman*'s dad.

Loadsamoney.
The star of
*Bend of the
River*, James
Stewart, changed
the rules of the
Hollywood game
for ever.

In 1982, Dustin Hoffman accepted $4 million for *Tootsie*; a year later Sean Connery got $5 million for *Never Say Never Again*; and in 1988, Barbra Streisand, starring in a film called *Nuts*, became the first woman to reach the $5-million plateau. In 1990, Arnold Schwarzenegger, who was paid between $10 million and $13 million for *Total Recall*, plus 15% of the net profits, went on to take $15 million, plus 15% of the gross, for *The Last Action Hero*. (1993) And, of course, multi-millionaire Macaulay Culkin makes Shirley Temple look hard-done-by.

In 1995, Jim Carrey, star of *The Mask* (1994), went from $500,000 to $7 million almost overnight; and Keanu Reeves also got $7 million to star in *Dead Drop*; the same year, Sylvester Stallone was offered $20 million by Savoy Pictures to do a picture for them. But can there really be any justification for the huge fees stars which were, and are, paid - or, for that matter, the salaries of the moguls who paid them? Louis B. Mayer, for example, earned $1,300,000 a year and was America's highest-paid executive during the Thirties. Over 27 years, when a dollar was worth a dollar, he earned more than $20 million. Small wonder that the stars, who were in thrall to the moguls, chafed a little, even though their annual salaries would have set up several ordinary citizens for life. In the early Thirties, Joan Crawford barged into Louis B. Mayer's office and demanded a $1,000 rise. As her wage packet at the end of the week was already a hefty $3,500, Mayer turned her down, so Crawford walked out of the studio. Mayer could have put her on suspension, for refusing to work, but canny Crawford had chosen the perfect moment to issue her ultimatum, the moment when her current film, *Today We Live* (1933), was almost complete. She couldn't be replaced, and the film couldn't be finished without her. Mayer finally coaxed her back with a compromise figure of $4000.

When James Cagney was under contract at Warners, he walked into the office of the most Scrooge-like of the brothers, and said, "Harry, I want $15 million tax free, or I'll never walk on this lot again." Warner refused - but then, he would probably have refused Cagney or Bogart or Davis a $5-a-week raise. Months later, no doubt congratulating himself on the money he was saving with Cagney on suspension, Harry Warner was buttonholed by one of the stockholders of the company who asked him why there hadn't been any Cagney pictures lately. "Do you know what that bum did!" said Harry, "He asked for $15 million or he'd walk off the lot." The stockholder grabbed Harry by the neck, screaming, "Give it to him, you fool! Give it to him! You're costing us £300 million dollars a year!"

Robert Zemeckis, director of *Forest Gump* (1994), confirms that a star - or the right star in the right movie, anyway - is worth his salary when his or her appearances - in television advertisements for the film, interviews and so on - ensures that the movie does well in that all-important first week-end. Director Art Linson goes further, saying that with *Last Action Hero*, Schwarzenegger justified his salary far more than the rest of the people who worked on the project could justify theirs. "When Schwarzenegger made that movie, people came. They came to see Arnie. They didn't continue to come because the movie wasn't good - but he was worth the money he was paid because even in a bad movie he sold tickets. He got people to show up." The risks involved in film-making today are so great that studio executives insist on a star-based insurance policy.

James Cagney, top-of-the-world gangster at Warner Bros. He was living proof that star quality is indefinable and unmistakable.

Worth his money or not, the Charlie Chaplin of the Nineties is Jack Nicholson. He was already way out ahead in 1989 as the Joker in *Batman*, when he took over $50 million with his profits-related deal. And more recently, when he made *A Few Good Men* (1992) - in which, mark you, his part as Colonel Jessup was not the principal role - Nicholson was paid £500,000 *a day*. Not everyone gets $9 and 50 cents a cough, of course, but there are other ways of topping up...

The star who has everything still wants a bit *more* of everything, insisting on those little extras that help to grease the already well-oiled cogs of his life. Peter Bart, editor of *Variety*, says, "Most stars start with the private jet, and go from there. A top star will demand perks worth millions of dollars. It may just be winnebagoes and dressing rooms, but it's also an entourage, the trainer the nanny, the stand-in, the cronies, incredible suites." When Sylvester Stallone was in London for the film, *Judge Dredd* (1995) he took over the whole floor of a hotel, with his entourage arrayed on other floors. "I was told that in the space of a week, Stallone went to the opening of a Planet Hollywood in, I think, Jakarta, then sped on to New York for the opening of his previous picture, *The Specialist* (1994). There he was, hopping around the world - and all during principal photography! But you have to figure it this way - if you spend, say, $10 million on a star, it's not uncommon to write into the budget another couple of million just for perks."

Some mega-buck figures and images of greed are suspect, prey to the tendency of a good story to acquire embellishments as a ship grows barnacles. But, straight from the account books of Paramount Studios, come figures never intended for publication - until a law suit liberated them. Forget the salary Eddie Murphy got for *Coming to America* (1988), forget his 15% of the gross; look instead at his gravy-train perks. During filming, Murphy received a $5,000-a-week living allowance, $4,920 for a limousine and round-the-clock chauffeur; plus $3,792 per week for a motor home that had once been cus-tomised for Sylvester Stallone, with a full-time driver to move it from place to place. Star perks also included $1,500 per week for Murphy's personal trainer; $650 per week for his valet; five production assis-tants for Eddie at $650 per week each; and $1,000 per week for his film stand-in, Charles Murphy Jnr., who just happened to be Eddie's brother. In addition to their salaries, Eddie's entourage of relatives and friends also got *per diem* pay, just like their boss. It totalled

Jack's Pot

The star who has made the real money in Hollywood is Jack Nicholson. This is how *Forbes* magazine charted his rise from zilch to zillions.

1958	**Free**	*Cry-Baby Killer* - his first film role
1960	**$700**	*The Little Shop of Horrors* - his first cameo part
1969	**$2000**	*Easy Rider* - noticed at last, but paid less than the union minimum
1970	**$2000**	*Five Easy Pieces* - with an Oscar nomination, prepare for lift-off.
1971	**$150,000**	*Carnal Knowledge* - now he's flying.
1972	**$25,000**	*The King of Marvin Gardens* - done as a favour to the *Five Easy Pieces* director Bob Rafelson. Jack is good to his friends, as the record shows.
1973	**$300,000**	*The Last Detail* - the foot's on the accelerator.
1974	**$1 million**	*Chinatown* - he's joined the millionaire club
1975	**$1 million**	*One Flew Over the Cuckoo's Nest* - his first Oscar.
1976	**$150,000**	*The Last Tycoon* - a bit part and favour for friend Robert de Niro, the film's star.
1980	**$2 million**	*The Shining* - up, up and away.
1981	**$150,000**	*Reds* - another favour to a friend, Warren Beatty.
1883	**$4 million**	*Terms of Endearment* - relaunch and another Oscar.
1985	**$1 million**	*Prizzi's Honour* - starred his then girl-friend, Anjelica Huston
1987	**$4 million**	*The Witches of Eastwick* - still soaring.
1989	**$7 million**	*Batman* - the Jackpot. As well as his fee, he gets 10% of the gross, AND 10% of the film's merchandising income. The Joker's cut is estimated at $60 million total!
1992	**$35 million**	*Batman Returns* - he doesn't appear in the film at all, but his fee and gross participation was agreed as part of his deal for the first Batman movie.
1992	**$35,000 & salary**	*Man Trouble* - another favour by the old softy in a film that reunited the team that made *Five Easy Pieces*. It didn't earn any money, though.
1992	**$7 million plus 10% of the gross**	*A Few Good Men* - a two-week job. Nice work if you can get it.

$50,400 during the two months of filming. The movie also paid their travel expenses - $68,000. In all, the limo service, food, travel, lodging, personal employees and other overheads for the movie, came to about $5 million - a $13-million-total price tag for the care and feeding of one actor in one movie. And Murphy's insistence that he be allowed to leave the set a couple of days early because he was homesick for New Jersey cost the studio $212, 800 in production delays - all of which was charged to the picture's production budget instead of being deducted from Murphy's paycheck. But the expense item that became a symbol of Paramont's profligacy was a $235.33 charge made on Eddie's petty cash account - and charged to *Coming to America*. It was for breakfast at MacDonald's.

All of which sounds like a throwback to the outrageous extravagances of the silent era. But with a puzzled shrug, Douglas Fairbanks Jnr says, "Star perks? Well, I suppose you got a better dressing room, and you got called on set maybe 15 minutes later than everybody else; and you had a chair with your name on it. But that's about all." Of course, stars of today like to give the impression that it's all very democratic and down to earth. They are presented to us as modest and unassuming and really only the rest of us writ large; which is nonsense, of course. They are nothing *like* the rest of us.

One difference is that, apart from co-stars and ex-wives with expensive lawyers, nobody ever disagrees with them. And, like George Raft, they worry and pick at their heroic image. In *Marathon Man* (1976), William Goldman wrote a scene where Dustin Hoffman, after being mugged in the park, is in bed when he hears a noise. Goldman has him grabbing a flashlight. Hoffman insisted that it wasn't in character, overriding both screenwriter and director. All very Stanislavski, but Goldman thinks it was because Hoffman was afraid his fans would think he was chicken.

Goldman swears that a scene in his novel, *Tinsel*, although written as fiction, is based on a true incident. In the book, Goldman describes the habits of a male star on location. He would snap up trifles belonging to members of the crew - a watch, a pen, a pack of gum. As Goldman puts it, "He wasn't stealing as a kleptomaniac might. It was closer to *droit du seigneur*."

The Star as Monster was perhaps less common in the old days, but no less terrifying. The novelist and screenwriter, Budd Schulberg says that his father as Paramount manager had nightmares about some of the stars. Budd remembers his dad coming home at night, then wandering about the house roundly cursing his tormenters - the likes of Gloria Swanson and Marlene Dietrich; but Maurice Chevalier was the star who filled his dreams. Chevalier was famously mean with money, and always asking for more. "One night, like three o'clock in the morning, my father was screaming out, 'Maurice, Maurice, we just can't *do* that!' And I found out that in his dream, Chevalier wanted to be paid in coins - and he wanted his limousine filled with them."

Director Richard Fleischer has battled with two monsters in three films. At the time of *20,000 Leagues Under the Sea* (1954), Kirk Douglas was only a mini-monster, his upstaging of the other actors a sign more of insecurity than anything else. But in 1958 he was both star and star producer of *The Vikings*, and for Fleischer, "Even simple scenes with him became surreal nightmares." One example conjures up the atmosphere. Fleischer was directing a short scene between Kirk Douglas and Ernest Borgnine sitting opposite each other at a table, Borgnine speaking, Douglas, his elbows on the table, arms crossed, listening. In the eventual editing, Borgnine would quite properly be featured throughout (his was a speech lasting perhaps a minute), with an occasional shot of the listening star. A few seconds would be more than enough raw material. However, since Kirk Douglas *was* the star - and producer to boot - Fleischer thought he'd keep him happy by shooting his listening close-up for the entire 60 seconds. "Cut! That's a print." and the director started to walk away. "Just a minute!" from Kirk, who wanted to know if Dick was completely happy with the take. Yes, he was. Ah, but couldn't it be better? No, it was just fine. Well, had Dick noticed how he, Kirk Douglas, was sitting there with his right arm crossed over his left? Of course, and what about it? Would it be better left over right? Fleischer thought his star was joking, but he wasn't. This artistic discussion ended with, "What the fuck do you want from me, Kirk?" and "Oh, forget the whole fucking thing!" flung over Douglas's shoulder (whether right or left is not recorded.) Nevertheless, Fleischer says that this sort of behaviour is well worth enduring when the actor has the star quality of a Kirk Douglas.

Or a Rex Harrison. This star puts Douglas into the monster pussy-cat class. On *Dr Doolittle* (1967) he was known as Tyrannosaurus Rex. Not only did he walk off the film several times - coming back several times as well - he made eccentric demands about casting.

☛ page 114

CASABLANCA
WARNER BROS. 1942

Producer: Hal B. Wallis

Director: Michael Curtiz

Stars: Humphrey Bogart, Ingrid Bergman, Paul Henreid.

O S C A R S

BEST PICTURE, DIRECTOR,
SCREEN PLAY
HAL B. WALLIS WAS AWARDED
THE THALBERG MEMORIAL PRIZE

Everyone's Favourite

I n 1977, the American Film Institute named *Casablanca* as the third best film of all time, just behind *Gone With the Wind* (1939) and *Citizen Kane* (1940). When it was first released in 1942, the film's exotic setting, tough-guy sentimentality, emotive music and memorable one-liners made it an immediate hit with wartime audiences. This bit of vintage Hollywood has remained near the top of most people's personal lists ever since.

Following the release, in 1946, of The Marx Brothers' film *A Night in Casablanca,* Warners threatened to sue. "You claim you own 'Casablanca' and that no one else can use that name without your permission," quipped Groucho, "but what about 'Brothers'? Professionally, we were brothers long before you were..."

Left: Humphrey Bogart as the cynical, soft-centred Rick and Ingrid Bergman as the loyal, love-torn Ilsa. Below: This was Sydney Greenstreet's third film with Bogart, but he was 61 before he appeared in a movie.

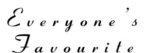

Casting Couch

Casablanca confirmed Ingrid Bergman and Humphrey Bogart as major stars, although they never pushed their luck by performing together again. The strong supporting cast was also an important ingredient in the film's success, and the fact that many of these actors were themselves refuges from Hitler's Europe - including Conrad Veidt, Peter Lorre, S.Z. "Cuddles" Sakall (Carl the Waiter), Curt Bors and Helmut Dantine - lent an authentic edge to the film. The Allied Forces did their part, too, by conveniently landing in *Casablanca* in November 1942; the film was showing in selected cinemas just 18 days later.

FILM
Facts

Left: with Claude Rains in the immortal goodbye scene.

RICK'S QUOTABLE QUOTES

Of all the gin joints in all the towns in all the world, she walks into mine.

Here's looking at you, kid.

Round up the usual suspects.

Louis, I think this is the beginning of a beautiful friendship.

Play it again, Sam. In fact this is how Woody Allen remembered the line. What Rick actually said was, "If she can stand it, I can. Play it..."

COUNTING THE COST

For Warner Brothers, *Casablanca* was a big-budget film. They paid $20,000 for the rights to the unproduced play called *Everybody Comes to Rick's*, and supporting actors and technicians were borrowed from rival studios. Ingrid Bergman was bought from David Selznick for a weekly fee of $3,125 ,and Conrad Veidt came from MGM for $5000 a week. Luckily for Warners, Bogart was already theirs. *Casablanca* cost $950,000 to make, but took $3.7 million on its intital release.

SET SECRETS

Casablanca was filmed entirely on the Warners' lot, except for one scene at L.A. Municipal Airport. None of the actors knew how the film was going to end when they started. Possibilities included: Rick being killed while Ilsa and Victor escaped, Ilsa leaving Victor for Rick or Victor being killed.

PLAYING IT AGAIN

Warners did consider making a sequel to *Casablanca* to be called "Brazzaville". The script was never written. *Casablanca* was first shown on the BBC in 1973, and has been screened 10 times since. America's TV Guide named *Casablanca* as the most frequently shown film on television.

Below: Dooley Wilson, as Sam, playing "As Time Goes By".

Sammy Davis Jnr was replaced by Sidney Poitier, who was then himself replaced. "Rex had the power at that time, and the studio gave in to him because it was a case of 'If you don't do it, then I don't do the picture' " Perhaps it would have been better to get rid of Harrison and replace *him*. Fleischer doesn't think so. For all his faults, for all his grotesque demands, "We all felt that nobody could do this part except Rex." They tried it once, though. After one of Harrison's walk-outs, they hired, at considerable expense, the excellent Christopher Plummer. While in no way denigrating Plummer, the re-casting just didn't feel right, so they sweet-talked Tyranasaurus Rex into coming back. "All those other people had to be paid off, of course - Sammy, Sidney, Christopher and the rest. Cost us a fortune. But, yes, in the end it was well worth it."

Stunt-man Loren Janes would probably find the Rex Harrison stories hard to credit, because, "I have to say that through the years, the old-time stars - the Gary Coopers, the Clark Gables and Spencer Tracys - I never saw them on set with a script, they knew their lines,

For Rex Harrison, as Dr Doolittle, eye contact was essential, but his animal co-stars tended to look shiftily away when sung at. "For God's sake, cut!" cried Rex, "It's not looking *at me!"*

ready to go. And they were respectful of everybody. But today, a lot of these modern stars don't talk to anybody, they're nasty, they put people down, and they're learning their lines on the set. Too many of them believe their own publicity, spoilt kids who think the world owes them a living."

According to producer Julian Blaustein, there is at least one star who doesn't think the world owes him a living. Perhaps this is because Charlton Heston falls somewhere between the old-time greats and the new. Blaustein was making a film called *The Wreck of the Mary Deare* (1959), and Heston, who had just won the Oscar for *Ben Hur* (1959), could have commanded serious money. "Instead, he worked for a relatively small amont up front - really just to pay expenses - and a piece of the profits. His philosophy was, 'If I'm in a picture that's a flop, why should I be the only one to come out making large sums of money when I'm supposed to contribute to the success of the picture.'. Heston's agent protested, but his client wouldn't budge. "That's really unusual," says Julian Blaustein, "You just don't get that today." Heston is undoubtedly a star in a class of his own. But, for the cynically minded, here are a few Takes One To Know One comments to savour:

Mamie Van Doren blew the whistle on Warren Beatty with,, "He's in danger of waking up one morning in his own arms", while a sweet-talking Elliott Gould says of Jerry Lewis, "He's one of the most hostile, unpleasant guys I've ever seen... an arrogant egomaniac." Bette Davis,when asked about her co-star in *Whatever Happened to Baby Jane?* (1962), replied, "The best time I ever had with Joan Crawford was when I pushed her down the stairs." Herman Mankiewicz, who resisted the impulse to do the same thing to Orson Welles, said, "There but for the grace of God, goes God." Then we have Brando on Sinatra - "He's the kind of guy that, when he dies, he's going up to heaven and give God a bad time for making him bald."

This is not the place to list every star who has made an important contribution to the history of the cinema; but, in terms of simple box-office popularity, some names come out on top. "Official" lists tend to be arbitrary and misleading, and the Quigley poll [see page 141] makes no mention of Spencer Tracy or Rita Hayworth, and, because many other stars don't "count", either, gives no indication of how public tastes have changed. Roddy McDowell, who was a child star at 20th Century-Fox, points out that each decade needs its stars for rea-

When John Wayne started to believe his own publicity, daily shooting began only when the actor had achieved a successful bowel movement. No Nonsense John Ford (the still is from *Stagecoach*) would have scared it out of him.

sons that don't apply to the previous one or the next. He cites Montgomery Clift as one of the first anti-heroes, slugging it out with John Wayne at the end of *Red River*. (1948) Clift was followed by James Dean and Marlon Brando, each representing a shift in style, each arriving at precisely the right moment in cinema history. McDowell believes that the visual statement of opulence made by a 1920s Gloria Swanson was rendered inappropriate when the Depression hit America, and that, by contrast, people like Will Rogers and Shirley Temple represented survival and hope. None of this can be expressed in a poll based purely on numbers. However, a crude barometer of star popularity over the last hundred years is better than nothing.

According to the Quigley Poll, up until 1920 the audience-pullers were William S. Hart, Mary Pickford, Douglas Fairbanks, Anita Stewart and Wallace Reid, all of whom, like others in this list, rode more than one decade. They were joined in the Twenties by Marguerite Clark, Thomas Meighan, Norma Talmadge, Rudolph Valentino, Colleen Moore, Tom Mix, Clara Bow and Lon Chaney. In the Thirties, the stars audiences most wanted to see were Joan Crawford, William Haines, Janet Gaynor, Charles Farrell, Marie Dressler, Will Rogers, Shirley Temple, Clark Gable, and Mickey Rooney. The Forties' favourites were Bette Davis, Abbott and Costello, Betty Grable, Bob Hope, Bing Crosby, Greer Garson and Ingrid Bergman.

In the Fifties the stars topping the polls were John Wayne, Dean Martin and Jerry Lewis, Doris Day, Gary Cooper, Marilyn Monroe, James Stewart, Grace Kelly, William Holden, Rock Hudson, Kim Novak, Glenn Ford and Elizabeth Taylor. The Sixties were dominated by Jack Lemmon, Sean Connery, Julie Andrews, Lee Marvin, Sidney Poitier, Paul Newman and Katharine Hepburn (Hepburn, one can't help feeling, should have appeared in Quigley from the Thirties, but then the poll is con-

Sister Act **was a plum role for erstwhile stand-up comic Whoopi Goldberg.**

cerned with popularity, not excellence). The Seventies highlighted Barbra Streisand, Ali MacGraw, Clint Eastwood, Robert Redford, Tatum O'Neal, Sylvester Stallone, Burt Reynolds, Diane Keaton and Jane Fonda. The Eighties brought us Dolly Parton, Meryl Streep, Sally Field, Tom Cruise, Bette Midler, Eddie Murphy, Glenn Close, Jack Nicholson and Kathleen Turner; and by the mid-Nineties the most popular stars shaping up for the decade are polled as Arnold Schwarzenegger, Julia Roberts, Kevin Costner and Whoopi Goldberg.

Just think, though - if it hadn't been for the audiences way back when, who wanted to know the names of the players in movies, there wouldn't be any mega-rich stars today.

So it's all our own fault. Stars - and popularity polls - are here to stay.

Burt Reynolds turned down *Terms of Endearment* **to make** *The Man Who Loved Women.* **The decision almost ruined his career.**

CHAPTER

4

Let's Make Love

Burt Lancaster and Deborah Kerr on the beach in Hawaii is one of the most famous images in the history of the cinema. Their love-making in *From Here to Eternity*, although there was no consummation - this being 1953 - was electrifying. But then, throughout the story of the movies, sex has never stopped making waves. Garbo and Gilbert in *Flesh and the Devil* (1927), Mae West and anyone she had her eye on, Harlow and Gable in *Red Dust* (1932), Basinger and Rourke in *Nine ½ Weeks* (1986), Sutherland and Christie in *Don't Look Now* (1973), Turner and Hurt in *Body Heat* (1981), Douglas and Stone in *Basic Instinct* (1992) - all of them knew, as film people have known for a hundred years, that sex sells movies. Back in the Twenties, Cecil B. DeMille said "Hit Sex Hard!", and absolutely nothing has changed since then except that fleeting flash has become frequent flesh; and sex is still the continuing story of what you can get away with.

One of the most famous images in cinema. Burt Lancaster and Deborah Kerr in *From Here to Eternity*.

Sharon Stone and Kirk Douglas's little boy getting down to basics in *Basic Instinct.*

Proof, if it were needed, that sex sells movies, is the creation, by the movie industry itself, of instantly recognisable icons of sexuality, gods and goddesses of erotic love.... sex symbols.

Of course, there are many actors, male and female - Holly Hunter, for example, or Meg Ryan, Denzel Washington, Lena Olin, Demi Moore, Angela Bassett, Harvey Keitel, Michelle Pfeiffer, Bridget Fonda, Brad Pitt, Jessica Lange, Whitney Houston, Keanu Reeves, Julia Roberts - who are desirable, the subject of private fantasy, perhaps. But when push comes to shove, they don't have that extra something that singles out Marilyn and Valentino, Bardot or James Dean; but what transforms a sexy actor into a sex symbol remains a mystery.

Hollywood has always had sex symbols, of course. The very first film star - Florence Lawrence, the Biograph Girl of 1910 - doesn't quite qualify, perhaps; but there can be no doubt about Theda Bara, who in 1915 became known as the "Vamp" after her success in *A Fool There Was*. Her real name was Theodosia Goodman, but studio publicity put it about that she was Theda Bara, the daughter of an Eastern potentate - her name being an anagram of Arab Death. Gloria Swanson started as a Mack Sennett bathing beauty and, by 1919, in *Male and Female*, she had become a lusted-after siren of the screen; while Clara Bow, the "It" Girl of the Twenties was adored and yearned for, her stammer and Bronx accent unheard. In 1916 Mae Murray stirred more than hearts when she made her debut in *To Have and to Hold*, and Pola Negri, who came to Hollywood in the Twenties, burst into flames at such low temperatures that she had to be taught how to kiss more modestly. There were Ramon Novarro and Rudolph Valentino, of course; and then, with the Thirties and sound, came *The Blue Angel* (1930) and Dietrich, whose symboldom ran and ran for an unequalled 48 years. *Grand Hotel*, in 1932, brought Garbo and Barrymore - two for the price of one - and Johnny Weissmuller reigned for nearly 20 years as king sex-pot in

Silent sex symbol speaks volumes. Theda (The Vamp) Bara.

the Hollywood jungle, first as Tarzen and then as Jungle Jim.

Sex symbols have signposted the way for a hundred years... Mae West, who, in 1933 helped to promote Cary Grant to sex symbol status in *She Done Him Wrong*; Jean Harlow, the "Blonde Bombshell", once snobbishly put down by Margot Asquith in the celebrated line "The 't' [in Margot] is silent, as in Harlow"; Jane Russell, Betty Grable, Ava Gardner, Rita Hayworth and, of course, *the* sex goddess, Marilyn.

Monroe may have been difficult to work with, but Billy Wilder knew what he was about in 1959 when he cast her in *Some Like It Hot*. Brilliant performances by Jack Lemmon and Tony Curtis may carry the story but the film's classic status owes more than a little to their co-star's presence. Curtis and Lemmon used to bet on how many takes (40 or 50 were average) before Marilyn got one simple line right. And yet sometimes, inexplicably, she sailed effortlessly through a long scene in one take - like the one in the train berth.

Monroe joined the immortals at the age of 36. Is that part of the secret - a kind of movie necrophilia? Do actors like Monroe and Valentino and James Dean have to be die young to retain their sex appeal? But then, how to explain Bardot? Roger Vadim, to whom she was once married, and who directed her in *...And God Created Woman* (1956) the film that made her an international star , said, "It was the first time on screen that a woman was shown as really free on a sexual level, with none of the guilt attached to nudity or carnal pleasure." Or to put it the same way, but in a different tone of voice - that of the Catholic Legion of Decency - her performance was, "...an open violation of conventional morality."

A character actor later in his career; but, in 1925, as the first Ben Hur, Ramon Novarro was up there with Valentino. Tragically, he was murdered in 1968.

There was a short period in the Fifties when Hollywood developed an inferiority complex about its screen sex. Female stars were the girl next door or sophisticated but not overtly sexy women of the world. Real sexuality was to be found only in Europe, expressed by Anna Magnani, Bardot, Sophia Loren or Gina Lollobrigida. But when Hollywood tried to take any of these Euro-sex goddesses to its own heaving bosom it turned them into bland, stereotypical "Oo la la"s and "Kees me darlink"s. In an act of criminal waste, Warners used Bardot as a decorative afterthought in a mid-century film called Helen of Troy. Bardot! whose European films had earned her the signal honour of being condemned by America's Legion of Decency. Seven times. And out of the whole of America, only the unique Marilyn could transcend her own pneumatic plasticity to become the world's most desirable sex symbol.

In Britain, particularly during and just after the war, stars like Patricia Roc, Phyllis Calvert and Ann Todd, trapped in the genteel RankSpeak of the period, were far too ladylike to be symbols of sex. It was impossible to imagine any of them actually having sex, let alone enjoying it. And when James Mason played Margaret Lockwood's bit of rough in *The Wicked Lady* (1945), it took a hangman's rope to suspend disbelief in her role as sexy highwayperson. But standing alone, like wartime Britain, was Diana Dors. From the screen, without the need even to wink, she shared her earthy secret with us, the secret dimly perceived by the flustered Mrs Grundys who attacked on sight. We all knew that Diana, no matter what character she half-heartedly pretended to be on screen, was celebrating the joys of sex; and that she sensed our admiring approval.

She could never be Monroe, of course - indeed, who could? Certainly not Marilyn's pale imitation, Jayne Mansfield, and even Kim Novak was not really a serious contender. Perhaps, on the whole, it was easier for men to be men than for women to be women. Errol Flynn's notoriety as a womaniser was no handicap to his popularity and sex-symbol status. Jack L. Warner, the man who made Flynn a star, said of him ""He had a mediocre talent, but to the Walter Mittys of the world he was all the heroes in one magnificent, sexy, animal package." *The Adventures of Robin Hood*, made in 1938 and still shown to appreciative audiences today, is evidence enough.

Challenging Errol as the greatest screen lover and sex symbol that year was a small, middle-aged Frenchman who breathed garlic and

Los Angeles born and bred Norma Jean Mortenson aka Norma Jean Baker aka Marilyn Monroe (1926-1962).

passion in the heroine's face. The film, *Algiers* (1938), fairly bristled with Oscar nominations, and Hedy Lamarr was never better. Interestingly, like Bogart and the "Play it again, Sam" line, Boyer never actually said "Come wiz me to ze Casbah".... but that was undoubtedly the message that came across.

The antithesis of Boyer's continental charm was the treat-'em-rough approach of James Cagney. To see him was to sense a ferocious inner energy held - just - in check; and he glowed with sexuality, even, or perhaps especially, when he shoved a grapefruit into Mae Clark's face in *The Public Enemy* (1931). A year later, in the 1932 film, *Red Dust*, Clark Gable fell in love with a prostitute, played by Jean Harlow. Publicised as the film in which "He treated her rough - and she loved it!", the film was considered daring at the time.

Certainly, every decade has promoted and paraded its new sex symbols; but very occasionally, a rebellious nominee has refused to play ball. In her first film, *The Outlaw*, produced by Howard Hughes in 1943, Jane Russell became The Sex Symbol That Never Was And Never Wanted To Be. The tacky publicity campaign sold the public what turned out to be a perfectly decent Western, hyped up with spurious claims of sizzling sex. The Sex Symbol That Never Was came provided with The Sex *Aid* That Never Was, a unique, much-publicised, cantilevered bra designed by Hughes himself. Now, Hughes didn't know this - but Jane Russell never wore it. The device was such torture to wear that the poor woman slipped into her comfortable old favourite instead. Nice, kind lady that she was, Jane Russell never let on until after Howard Hughes died.

From Hughes to DeMille and Adrian Lyne - *Nine ½ Weeks* (1986), *Fatal Attraction* (1987) and *Indecent Proposal* (1993) - film-makers clearly believed, and still do, that sex

Two sex symbols for the price of one cinema ticket. Gable and Harlow in *Red Dust*.

JANE RUSSELL MEAN...MOODY...MAGNIFICENT!

HOWARD HUGHES' DARING PRODUCTION

THE OUTLAW

ACTION! THRILLS!! SENSATIONS!!! PRIMITIVE LOVE!!!!

JACK BUETEL
THOMAS MITCHELL
WALTER HUSTON

Produced and Directed by HOWARD HUGHES
Story and Screenplay by JULES FURTHMAN

A poster for *The Outlaw*; part of Howard Hughes' huge advertising campaign.

and sex symbols get us into the cinema; but what, over the years, have audiences been seduced by?

First, there was the look, closely followed by the hesitant touch, erotic restraint being a potent force in life and on screen. Think of Chaplin and Paulette Goddard in *City Lights* (1931) - his look, her touch - Monroe, Valentino, Garbo with John Barrymore or John Gilbert; or more recently, Tom Hanks and Meg Ryan in *Sleepless in Seattle* (1993) and Geena Davis with William Hurt in *The Accidental Tourist* (1988).

Looks and touches shade into teasing. This takes many forms, from Chaplin catching sight of a nude statue in a gallery window, instantly becoming a prancing voyeur posing as art lover; to Jiri Menzel's stationmaster rubber-stamping a female bottom in *Closely Observed Trains* (1966); to Rock Hudson, at the start of the Sixties, romancing Gina Lollobrigida (one of the "Oo-la-la" transplants) in *Come September* (1961); the innocent voluptuousness of Claire's knee in *Claire's Knee* (1970), and the lip-smacking sexuality of Albert Finney and Joyce Redman in the famous eating scene in *Tom Jones* (1963). *Indecent Proposal* keeps us waiting as the prurient camera refuses to show us what we know happens to Demi Moore on Robert Redford's boat.

Teasing goes right back to the first days of cinema. In 1896, a French film, *Le Coucher de la Mariée*, shows a newly-married couple preparing for bed. The husband takes off his bride's satin slipper and presses it passionately to his lips. He watches, eyes full of desire, as she undresses. In her nightie, she performs a provocative little dance before hopping into bed. A flea hops into a lady's unmentionables in *La Puce*, a film made a year later. Based on a Paris music-hall striptease act, the girl takes off her clothes one by one to track down her invisible companion. None of the many similar productions crossed the line into pornography although, then as now, there was plenty of the hard stuff being made as well.

Frustration remembered in tranquillity is a subdivision of teasing, captured by all those rites of passage movies in which teenage girls try to cope with their hormones and teenage boys try to cop a feel. Three significant examples were made in 1971 - *Summer of '42*, *The Last Picture Show* and *Carnal Knowledge* - and then there was *American Graffiti* in 1973. As Sigmund Freud might have observed, "The adolescent libido is inflamed by the everyday process of allowing the dog to see the rabbit."

Sexual ambivalence is another subdivision, a recent (1992) example being *The Crying Game*'s surprise that lies in wait for both hero and audience when girl becomes boy. Then there were all those grown men dressing up as women - Dustin Hoffman in bed with Jessica Lange in *Tootsie* (1981), Lemmon bunking up with Monroe in *Some Like It Hot* (1959) ....As the good doctor might have added, "Charlie's Aunt this definitely ain't."

Well, quite. But from the earliest days, the mainstay of the cinema has always been the moment, often delayed but seldom withheld, when hero and heroine kiss. The first screen kiss was committed to celluloid one year after the cinema's birth. The comfortable-looking couple caught in the act in 1896 are May Irwin and John C. Rice. But the embrace generated an instant shock-horror response from the press, one newspaper calling the scene "absolutely disgusting". The free publicity guaranteed that film-makers would repeat the experiment - as they have done ever since.

Doing what comes naturally isn't always easy to do; and screen kisses are seldom as sexy as they seem. Astonishingly, Errol Flynn was embarrassed when he had to play a love-scene, and couldn't wait for it to be over. Peter Sellers found passionate kisses ridiculous

HOW WAS IT FOR THEM?
Sex on the Screen

From the moment in 1896 when May Irwin and John C. Rice exchanged the first screen kiss, in *The Kiss*, a filmed exerpt from the Broadway play *The Widow Jones*, film-makers have been exploiting sex. Pornagraphic films were soon going the rounds, but even in commercial films, producers were constantly pushing at the boundaries of what could be shown. Apart from the time when the Hays Code was in strict force in Hollywood, and for a longer period in Britain (the British Board of Film Censors was founded in 1912), the story of sex on the screen has been one of increasing explicitness.

1896: The world's first sexy film is released in Paris. Eugene Pirou's *Le Coucher de la Mariée* traces the progress of a newly married couple getting ready for bed. It stars a French music-hall actress, approriately named Mlle Willy.

1897: Georges Méliès, better known now for his special effects, is the first director to bring nudity to the screen. *Le Bain de la Parisienne* is an immediate hit with Parisians.

1902: The USA's first contribution to the new genre is less light-hearted - American Mutoscope & Biograph's *The Downward Path* warns of the perils of prostitution.

1910: Denmark leads the way with sexploitation movies, and releases the world's first full length sex drama, *The White Slave Traffic*.

1912: Fig leaves are dispensed with and the world gets its first glimpse of a full-frontal male nude in the Italian offering *Dante's Inferno*.

1913: America makes its first feature-length sex movie. *Traffic in Souls* is filmed in secret and makes $450,000 - a record for the time.

1915: The first leading ladies appear nude on screen - as artists models, pictured splashing around in rivers or waterfalls. Audrey Munson in *Inspiration* is a trailblazer, followed by Australian swimming star, Annette Kellerman, in *A Daughter of the Gods* (1916)

1933: Hedy Lamarr's nude bathing scenes in the Czech film *Extase* make such an impression that she will be forever mis-remembered as the first actress to appear naked on screen. What she should be remembered for is being the first actress to depict sexual intercourse in a film made for theatrical release.

1934: The Hays Code is introduced and nothing remotely explicit appears in Hollywood films for the next 30 years.

1951: The first film containing nude scenes to be passed by the British Board of Film Censors is the Swedish film *One Summer of Happiness*.

1958: Heather Sears makes the first open reference to the sex act in a British film in *Room at the Top*. Her partner is Laurence Harvey.

1959: The Obscene Publications Act begins to liberalise British screens.

1961: *Victim* is the first British film to deal frankly with homosexuality.

1962: A topless woman appears in the US film *The Pawnbroker* and the dismantling of the Hays Code begins.

1966: This year sees Brtain's first group sex scene in *Blow-Up*, including a hint of pubic hair.

1967: The British Board of Film Censors passes a film featuring a full-frontal female nude. Once again, the rule-breaking film, *Hugs and Kisses*, is Swedish.

1968: *.......If* is the first British film to show a full-frontal female nude.

1968: Coral Brown and Susannah York take part in Britain's first lesbian seduction scene in the *The Killing of Sister George*.

1969: Alan Bates and Oliver Reed are the first men to reveal all in the nude wrestling scene in *Women in Love*.

1974: French sexploitation film *Emmanuelle* is the first explicit commercial release to hit the box-office jackpot. Après *Emmanuelle*, le déluge.

From now on, sex on the cinema screens leaves less and less to the imagination..

because, at the exquisitely wrong moment, and in his mind's eye, he was always saw himself wearing long combinations.

As for the "King", it was every woman's dream to be kissed by Clark Gable. Mary Astor, who was one of his co-stars in *Red Dust*, described that magic moment in her book, *Bedside Hollywood*.

The film is set in the tropics. There is no air-conditioning in the studio, and the set is damp from the constant use of rain machines. The first part of the scene goes smoothly. Gable carries Astor up the veranda steps and into the bedroom. Director Victor Fleming is satisfied and calls, "Okay, let's move in on a tight two." Gable, still carrying Astor in his arms, is now required to kiss her (according to the script) "gently at first, then fiercely." Screen time, perhaps 20 seconds. Shooting time... a little longer. First, Clark can't be expected to hold Mary in his arms while they set up the shot. So a stool is found to rest the Astor bottom on. Not quite right - she's too high... so a stage carpenter saws a bit off the stool's legs. From behind the camera, Fleming says, "Clark, just before you kiss her, swing her an inch or two so we get your full face.... No, too much, back a little." "It's uncomfortable, Vic - I'll never hit it right." Meanwhile the lights, very bright in 1932, are roasting them. Never mind, the stand-ins can roast instead. When Fleming is ready once more, Gable and Astor have to be hosed down to match the first half of the shot. Everyone starts to laugh because the lights are making the actors steam like Christmas puddings on the boil. The problem is solved by heating the water; and to prevent them drying out, the prop man keeps them wet by pouring kettles of warm water over their head and shoulders. Everything is ready. "Action!"...."Cut and print!" The kiss is in the can; and that's what it's like to kiss Clark Gable.

A few years later, Gable had to kiss Vivien Leigh in *Gone With the Wind*. One day, Leigh came up to David Selznick's assistant, and said, "Marcella, you tell David he'd better not write any more kissing scenes for me with Clark Gable. He's got false teeth and they smell, and I don't like to kiss him." Selznick didn't argue and, in the completed three-and-a-half-hour film, Leigh and Gable kiss only twice. It is interesting that the actor's personal hygiene didn't seem to bother Mary Astor. True, *Red Dust* was made seven years earlier, but that couldn't have been why. Gable had had false teeth since he was 19.

And what about homosexual clinches? For heterosexual male actors, acting out a gay scene may present all sorts of nagging doubts and worries: Will their fans be shocked? Will their peers disapprove? Worst of all, will someone, or everyone, think they really are gay? In *Staircase* (1969) Rex Harrison and Richard Burton, as a couple of ageing homosexual hairdressers, copped out by proclaiming in every mincing word and gesture that they were two absolutely straight actors *acting* gay.

Thirteen years later, it was possible for heterosexuals to act out a homosexual scene truthfully. Even so, when Michael Caine and Christopher Reeve were required to kiss passionately in *Deathtrap* (1982), they had to share a bottle of brandy before they could pucker up with any conviction. After the fumes had done their work, nothing seemed to matter, and director Sidney Lumet got it in one take. Not many people know that.

In *Sunday, Bloody Sunday*, directed by John Schlesinger in 1971, Peter Finch kissed Murray Head. The embrace was tender, passionate and natural. In cinemas, the moment came as a bit of a surprise, but more in terms of character and plot than anything else; and most of the people in most of the audiences accepted the idea quite happily. Peter Finch's wife, however, couldn't. She saw

Glenda Jackson, the future Labour MP for London's Hampstead and Highgate with Murray Head in *Sunday, Bloody Sunday.*

the film several times, and John Schlesinger remembers that as soon as the kiss came up, "She would always scream. I said 'Anita please control yourself.' 'I'm sorry, John, but I can't bear it!' 'You've got to, Anita. You're ruining the moment.' Never made the slightest difference though."

The first French kiss in a Hollywood movie came in 1961. It was between Natalie Wood and Warren Beatty in *Splendour in the Grass*. The first openly sexual woman-to-woman kiss occurs in DeMille's 1922 *Manslaughter*; and eight years later, in Josef von Sternberg's *Morocco* (1930), Marlene Dietrich, provocatively dressed in a white tuxedo, kisses another woman. The highest number of kisses in a single film was notched up by John Barrymore in the 1926 *Don Juan* when Mary Astor and Estelle Taylor shared 127 Barrymore kisses.

The longest screen kiss lasted 55 seconds when Steve McQueen and Faye Dunaway kissed in *The Thomas Crown Affair* (1968.)

The acceptance of kissing - indeed, sexual expression of all kinds - varies from country to country. Iran still bans kissing on screen; and so does Turkey. The first far-eastern country to allow kissing in films was China in 1926, the first oriental screen kiss being received by Mamie Lee in *Two Women in the House*. In Japan, kissing was considered "unclean, immodest, indecorous, ungraceful and likely to spread disease", and that same year some 80,000 feet of kissing scenes were cut from movies imported from Hollywood. Japan's breaking of the taboo should have come in 1946 in the appropriately titled *A Certain Night's Kiss*, but at the last moment the director lost his nerve and a Japanese First was obscured by an open umbrella. Making up for lost time, and only four years later, the sex act itself was shown in *Picture of Madame Yuki* (1950); but perhaps they didn't kiss.

India's attitude to kissing has changed - for and against and for again - several times in the last hundred years. In the Twenties kisses were not always cut, but a note of smug approval crept into an official report in 1928 to the effect that during Western films, "when a kissing scene is shown, the ladies turn their heads away."

Nudity is something else entirely. What has been allowed on screen has depended on the country and its customs. In 1970, when Woodstock was shown in Japan, censorship was simple, practical and irreversible - all the nudes had their emulsion scraped off.

Nudity goes back a long way in the history of the cinema. The first leading lady to appear naked on screen and to face the naked wrath of our moral guardians was Audrey Munson in a 1915 silent called *Inspiration*. It was regarded, not least by its star, as "artistic and educational", Miss Munson being an artist's model in real life. She made two more films in 1916, appearing naked in both, *Purity* and *The Girl O' Dreams*. Annette Kellerman was an Olympic swimming champion who posed in the nude for one-reelers; silent starlight June Caprice also obliged. Nudity on screen had not yet been outlawed because this was in the days before censorship was institutionalised. Thus, for *Intolerance* (1916), D.W. Griffith was able to hire prostitutes to appear naked in the Belshazar's Feast sequence. But he gave the job to his assistant, Joseph Hanabery, and Hanabery - in one of the first examples of self-censorship - covered the ladies with drapery. Griffith was furious, and edited in some close shots of the women. The irony is that when *Intolerance* was re-issued 26 years later in 1942, the New York Censor Board took them all out again.

Betty Blythe went bare-breasted in *The Queen of Sheba* in 1921 and Cecil B. DeMille, in *King of Kings* (1927), had Claudette Colbert bathing nude. Fred Niblo's 1925 *Ben Hur* had one scene, cut for America, which was full of young women, all topless. Errol Flynn's first wife, Lili Damita, stripped off in a film called *Red Heels*, made in 1926; in fact, right up to the early Thirties, there were more nudes on screen than you could shake a bible at, some of them very big names indeed, one being silent star Clara Bow who went skinny-dipping in a film called *Hula* in 1927. There was no doubt at all that nudity and sex were useful aids to selling product, and many of Cecil "Hit Sex Hard" De Mille's early silents were very saucy indeed.

In Europe they were metaphorically and literally more laid back, and in Czechoslovakia in 1933 an Austrian actress, Hedwig Kiesler, appeared naked in Gustav Machaty's *Extase* (*Ecstacy*), a movie whose reputation almost destroyed her career - as Hedy Lamarr - in Hollywood. The sensation caused by *Extase* resonated so loudly down the decades that many people still believe that Hedy, or Hedwig, was the first actress to appear naked on screen. Far from it. She wasn't even the first nude in Czech movies, that distinction going to Ira Rina in Machaty's 1929 film, *Erotikon*. In America, the cut-off point came

Austrian bit-part actress Hedy Kiesler (soon to be Hedy Lamarr) in the Czech film *Extase*.

☞ page 134

Sex Symbols

The studios have always looked for ways of selling their movies - and nothing works quite so well as sex appeal. Of course opinions differ about what exactly makes someone a sex symbol. But here are a few who down the years have made cinemagoers' hearts and indeed other parts of their bodies stir.

DARK AND DANGEROUS

Rudolph Valentino
KNOWN AS: The Pink Powder Puff
SPECIALITY: Forbidden eroticism
SEXIEST FILM: *The Sheik* (1921). Women fainted in the aisles. Tragic end: Died suddenly at 31.

Marlon Brando
KNOWN AS: The Lazy Genius
TRADE MARK: Moody rebel.
SEXIEST FILMS: *A Street Car Named Desire* (1951); *On the Waterfront* (1954).
REAL-LIFE SCANDALS: Three broken marriages; a son has been arrested on a murder-charge; daughter commited suicide.

Daniel Day Lewis
KNOWN AS: Talented and Mysterious.
TRADE MARK: Long dark tresses.
SEXIEST FILMS: *The Unbearable Lightness of Being* (1988); *The Last of the Mohicans* (1992) and *The Age of Innocence* (1993).
REAL-LIFE SCANDAL: Stormy on/off relationship with the French actress Isabelle Adjani.

BLONDE BOMBSHELLS

Jean Harlow
KNOWN AS: The Blonde Bombshell
TRADE MARK: Platinum floozy with a heart of gold.
CATCH LINE: "I guess I'm not used to sleeping nights."
SEXIEST FILMS: *Red Dust* (1932); *Bombshell* (1933).
TRAGIC END: Her first husband, Paul Bern, committed suicide in 1932. She died at 26.

Marilyn Monroe
KNOWN AS: THE Sex Symbol of all time
TRADE MARK: Ultimate feminine sensuality
SEXIEST FILMS: *Gentlemen Prefer Blondes* (!953); *The Seven Year Itch* (1955); *Some Like It Hot* (1959)
CATCH PHRASE: Happy Birthday, Mr President.
REAL-LIFE SCANDAL: Found dead in 1962 from an overdose at the age of 36. Conspiracy theories implicating the Kennedy brothers abound.

Lana Turner
KNOWN AS: The Sweater Girl
TRADE MARKS: See above
SEXIEST FILMS: *Honky Tonk* (1941); *The Postman Always Rings Twice* (1946); *Peyton Place* (1957).
REAL-LIFE SCANDAL: Married 7 times, her name was linked with the mysterious Howard Hughes. In 1958, her boyfriend, the gangster Johnny Stompanato, was stabbed to death by her own daughter.

ACTION MEN

Clark Gable
KNOWN AS: The King of Hollywood
TRADE MARK: Square-jawed virility
Speciality: A man's man, and a woman's dream.
SEXIEST FILMS: *Possessed* (1931); *It Happened One Night* (1934); *China Seas* (1935); *Mutiny* on the Bounty (1935); *Gone With the Wind* (1939).
Catch line: "Dear Mr Gable - You Made Me Love You."
REAL-LIFE SCANDAL: Killed the vest/undershirt business; because he didn't wear one, sales bombed - until the T-shirt came in. His gleaming smile was not his own; it wasn't even gloriously crowned, just gloriously false. The love of his life, and third wife, Carol Lombard, was killed in a plane crash in 1942.

Errol Flynn

KNOWN AS: "One magnificent, sexy, animal package."
TRADEMARK: Dashing swashbuckler.
CATCH PHRASE: "In like Flynn"
SEXIEST FILMS: *Captain Blood* (1935); *The Adventures of Robin Hood* (1938); *The Sea Hawk* (1940).
REAL-LIFE SCANDAL: Turned to drink, drugs and sex. His autobiography, *My Wicked, Wicked Ways*, was published a few months after his death in 1959. He died aged 50.

Sean Connery

KNOWN AS: James Bond
TRADE MARK: Hunk with a twinkle in his eye.
SEXIEST FILM: *Dr No* (1962)
CATCH PHRASE: "Just call me Bond...James Bond."
REAL-LIFE SCANDAL: Not much. Lives in Marbella with his second wife and likes a good game of tennis.

Mel Gibson

KNOWN AS: The Sexiest Man Alive (at least by People magazine)
TRADE MARK: Handsome blue-eyed super-star.
BEST-KNOWN FILMS: *Mad Max* (1979); *Gallipoli* (1981); *Lethal Weapon* (1987).
REAL-LIFE SCANDAL: Lives on a ranch in Australia with his wife and five children.

SIRENS

Clara Bow

KNOWN AS: The "It" Girl
TRADE MARK: The sexy, liberated flapper of the Roaring Twenties
BEST-KNOWN FILM: *Mantrap* (1926)
REAL-LIFE SCANDAL: Her many lovers (including a football team) shocked Hollywood and she spent much of her later life in sanatoriums.

Elizabeth Taylor

KNOWN AS: The World's Most Beautiful Woman
TRADE MARK: Flashing violet eyes
MOST FAMOUS FILMS: *Cat on a Hot Tin Roof* (1958); *Suddenly Last Summer* (1959); *Cleopatra* (1963); *Who's Afraid of Viginia Woolf* (1966).
REAL-LIFE SCANDAL: Married 8 times, most famously to Eddie Fisher and Richard Burton (whom she married twice). Now married to a young construction worker, Larry Fortensky.

Sharon Stone

KNOWN AS: The Woman Who Uncrossed Her Legs
SPECIALITY: Icy femme fatales
SEXIEST FILMS: *Total Recall* (1990); *Basic Instinct* (1992); *Sliver* (1993).
REAL-LIFE SCANDAL: Highest-paid actress in Hollywood.

Rita Hayworth

KNOWN AS: The Love Goddess
TRADE MARK: Sophisticated temptress
SEXIEST FILMS: *Blood and Sand* (1941); *You'll Never Get Rich* (1941); *You Were Never Lovelier* (1942); *Cover Girl* (1944).
MEMORABLE SONG: "Put the Blame on Mame".
REAL-LIFE SCANDAL: Married 5 times, including Orson Welles and Aly Khan.

PRETTY BOYS

Paul Newman

KNOWN AS: A Classic
TRADE MARK: Chiseled good looks and stunning blue eyes
SEXIEST FILMS: *The Long Hot Summer* (1958); *Cat on a Hot Tin Roof* (1958); *The Hustler* (1961); *Hud* (1963); *Cool Hand Luke* (1967).
CATCH PHRASE: "...you're going to wake up smiling in the morning."
REAL-LIFE SCANDAL: Not much.

Warren Beatty

KNOWN AS: A Plaboy
TRADE MARK: Pretty and naughty.
SEXIEST FILMS: *Splendour in the Grass* (1961); *Bonnie and Clyde* (1967); *Reds* (1981).
REAL-LIFE SCANDAL: Plenty. Said to have slept with most of Hollywood's leading ladies. Now married to actress Annette Bening.

in 1934 with the introduction of the Hays Code; and nudity disappeared from the Hollywood screen for 30 years. But even when it returned, many actors weren't too happy. John Schlesinger, when he made *Darling....* in 1965, wanted to shoot a scene in one continuous flowing shot. Julie Christie was to walk through a large apartment, angrily undressing herself until at last she is simply a naked girl in front of a mirror. Julie Christie hated it, didn't want to do it, and it says a great deal for her trust in Schlesinger that she was finally convinced that the sequence was essential.

Male nudity on screen is commonplace today; so much so that one tends to forget how rare it was 20-odd years ago. Michael Caine was offered *Women in Love* in 1969 but turned it down because "I think men look ridiculous stark naked. Women don't, but men do. Not for $20 million would I nude wrestle a man on screen - or in real life, for that matter." For something rather less than $20 million dollars, Oliver Reed and Alan Bates took on the job. The scene was beautifully shot, an artistic cinema first - "Yes, and when I saw it in the cinema, everybody laughed. Exactly what I said they'd do."

Nudity on the British screen was banished even earlier than in America, by the British Board of Film Censors. Young ladies might be seen in bathing costumes, or even in their slips; indeed Googie Withers was once rather daringly seen wearing cami-knickers in *The Lady Vanishes* (1938), although she appears a little uncertain of the provenance today. "I'm almost *sure* it was *The Lady Vanishes* - oh yes, it must have been, because I can't think of any other film I did in which I got undressed. I came out from behind a cabin trunk on the train and I was in my cami-knicks - it was considered awfully naughty in those days." Seven years later, Margaret Lockwood's cleavage in *The Wicked Lady* (1945) was far too daring for American audiences, so the offending scenes were reshot. Some idea of the film's impact on audiences here may be gathered from the Manchester Guardian's critic, who said, "A mixture of hot passion and cold suet pudding."

In the Fifties, there emerged in Britain what might be called the respectable face of nudity, a genre with titles like *Naked as Nature Intended*; and *Take Off Your Clothes and Live*. These naturist dramas were short on both plot and whoopee, the director's principal task being to contrive a series of visual coincidences. The imagination boggled and held its breath when mixed doubles at tennis started promisingly in long shot; but in mid-shot, anything that boggled was

obscured by racquet or net. Naturists taking afternoon tea while seated on piles-inducing garden furniture would, if men, casually cross
their legs just as the shot changed, while women poured tea from
oversized teapots. Elsewhere in the film, the serendipity of rubber
rings, open car doors, ping pong bats, and flowering shrubs ensured
that we saw not one naughty bit. Like latter-day Micawbers, we were
hoping for something to turn up, but nothing ever did.

The first mainstream film that promised genuine, erotic sex was
made 21 years ago. *Emmanuelle* (1974), a French film, launched
Sylvia Kristel as a lady who really did do sexy things, most of them in
soft focus, admittedly, but even so, she gave us everything titillating
from masturbation to voyeurism; two-, three- and more-somes were
scattered like plums in the puddingy plot - and it was all very pretty,
like Sylvia Kristel herself.

In sharp-focus contrast, *Rita, Sue and Bob Too* (1986) was a film
about real people having real sex in a series of brief encounters direct
enough to make Trevor Howard's hair curl. God only knows what it
would have done to Celia Johnson.

"Oh dear, Mr
Venantini, you
must think I'm
a terrible flirt!"
Sylvia Kristel
with tattooed
ladies' man in
*Emmanuelle 2, The
Joys of a Woman.*

Perhaps cinemagoers were more innocent 60 years ago, or maybe they just kept quiet about the perpetual feast served up for dirty-minds; whatever the explanation, W.C. Fields, in his now classic 1932 short, *The Dentist*, concocted an outrageous bit of film business. In the performance of his duties, the great William Claude, his back to camera, positions himself between his female patient's legs. She slides further and further down in the chair, Fields riding her all the way. Then, as he heaves himself up to a standing position, the woman's arms go round his neck, her long and now bare legs clasping him round the waist. There is little doubt which cavity Fields is filling.

Woody Allen, in *Take the Money and Run* (1969), is walking through the park with his girl, dappled sunlight turning them into romantic figures in the landscape. Allen's voice-over says, "When I was inside, the prison psychiatrist asked me if I thought sex was dirty. I said, 'Well... it is if you're doing it right.' " Which exactly corresponds to the history of screen censorship.

In Hollywood, at the start of cinema's history, there were no set rules to be broken, so that film-makers could put almost anything on screen, always assuming the individual state concerned didn't object. But as early as 1922, alarmed by the indiscriminate use of power by

The American Censor, Will Hays, with C.B. DeMille (left) and a chorus of approval.

the State Censorship Boards and the growing number of municipal boards, all operating unilaterally to accept or to ban nice little earners, Hollywood felt that it would be better off censoring itself.

And so the Motion Picture Producers and Distributors of America was founded, with Postmaster General Will H. Hays at its head. Hays was no figurehead, and he quickly produced a list of gentlemanly "Be Carefuls" and uncompromising "Don'ts". Absolutely forbidden were - "licentious or suggestive nudity; profanity; obscenity and miscegenation; ridicule of the clergy; any inference of sex perversion; and the illegal traffic of drugs." The moral? Shoot by the book or suffer the consequences.

In the 1926 *Don Juan*, John Barrymore was one of the first actors required to keep one foot on the boudoir floor. In *The Thin Man* (1934), even though they were respectably married, Myrna Loy and William Powell were chaperoned by their dog; and by that same year, the Hays watchdog was baring its teeth, and any movie not granted a Seal of Approval stayed in the studio vaults.

Poster for *Don Juan*, with Mary Astor and "The Profile". In silent films, John Barrymore would deliver cheerful obscenities to his fellow actors. Outraged or delighted lip readers were in on the secret.

But it was impossible for the censor to exorcise the most powerful human urge in the world. The more obvious manifestations of sex might be prohibited on screen, but sexuality survived - indeed it flourished during the so-called Golden Age of Hollywood. The Hays Code may have been a moral straight-jacket for film-makers but, rather like the manufacturers of moonlight gin and whisky during Prohibition, Hollywood tackled the challenge of sexual prohibition with humour, style and infinite cunning. Imaginative film-makers and equally imaginative audiences colluded in a mischievous conspiracy; witness a quite extraordinary piece of screen eroticism which popped up in 1932.

A sultry young actress, Barbara Stanwyck, starred in a romantic drama made by Frank Capra. It was called *The Bitter Tea of General Yen*; in it, Stanwyck is captured by a Chinese war lord and then falls in love with him. Like the Rudolph Valentino films of the Twenties,

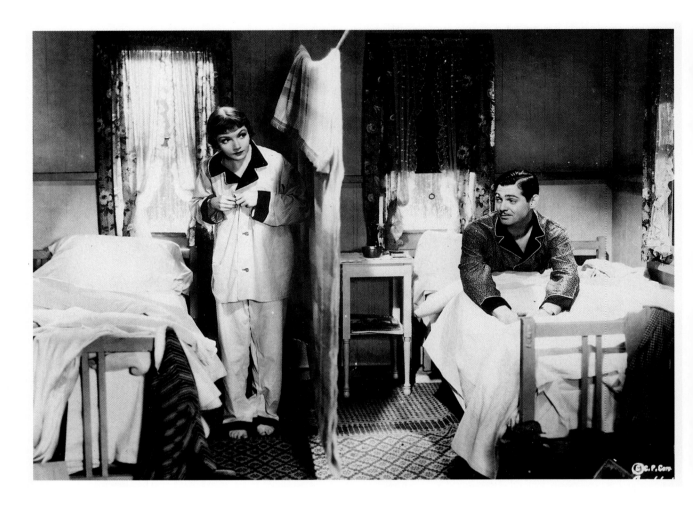

Teasing the censor. Clark Gable and Claudette Colbert in *It Happened One Night* made the separate-beds rule erotic.

the story capitalises on the twin taboos of miscegenation and exotic "perversion". The difference is that in an astonishing dream sequence, everything - and nothing - is left to the imagination. It was banned throughout the British Empire. A year later, when the Hays Office became a real force, the film would never have survived.

Of course, then as now, audiences were far more intelligent than they were given credit for. Even in the early Twenties, at the height of Valentino's 12-year reign, one might not *see* very much, but the unspoken questions were "Will they or won't they? Did they or didn't they?"... Without a grope in sight, everybody knew what Valentino got up to in the fade-outs.

But Frank Capra, who had already got away with *The Bitter Tea of General Yen*, thus breaking the "no miscegenation" rule, slipped another one past the censor in 1934. Claudette Colbert was no sex symbol, but the very law that forbade even married couples to share a bed, was turned to sizzling effect in *It Happened One Night*, when the sleeping arrangements for Colbert and Gable were made both respectable and titillating by the room-divider blanket thrown over a line. The film's five Oscars were a surprise to both Colbert and Gable - Gable had been loaned out to Harry Cohn by Louis B. Mayer as a punishment for not doing as he was told; and Colbert couldn't get away quick enough when Capra finished shooting the film.

In the 1939 film, *Intermezzo* (called, when it was shown in Britain, *Escape to Happiness*) Ingrid Bergman runs off with Leslie Howard, a married man. The sex was only hinted at, but the adulterous relationship between a famous concert violinist and his young protégé was crystal clear and, for its day, the coda of moral disapproval was surprisingly mild.

Comedy was a wonderful way of nipping past the censor. Marlene Dietrich made fun of herself in the 1939 spoof Western, *Destry Rides Again*; but send-up or not, she still radiated sexual energy when she sang "See What the Boys in the Back Room Will Have"

Screen shorthand gave us orgasmic starbursts, detumescing chimneys and towers, coded set and dress designs; special and honourable mention must be made here of the outrageous phallic bananas and superb cock hats of a fruity Carmen Miranda.

So potent were coded images that some directors, perhaps out of affection or a yearning for long-gone subtlety, went on using them. An example from 1968 is the chess game in Norman Jewison's *The Thomas Crown Affair*, in which Faye Dunaway gives Steve McQueen's bishop a good bashing.

There have been some nice jokes about sexual shorthand. Woody Allen made nostalgic fun of Thirties screen sex in *The Purple Rose of Cairo* (1985) when the hero steps out of the screen to make love to his greatest fan, Mia Farrow. He kisses her lingeringly, before breaking off, endearingly puzzled and anxious, because the scene, which he knows ought to fade to black, doesn't. Leslie Nielsen used sexual images in his *Naked Gun* films (1988 and 1991) - clay being thrown and then teased into phallic pots; opening flowers, space rockets, trains rushing through tunnels, and safe sex made safest of all by the use of all-embracing body condoms.

Censorship in the cinema is one thing; but one of the first decisions made by Will H. Hays involved the censorship not of a film but of a man's life. In 1922, Roscoe "Fatty" Arbuckle, six days after being acquitted of manslaughter, was forever banned - cast out by the film industry. Flushed with success, the censor promptly drew up a hit list of 200 people considered "morally dangerous".

Hollywood, for all its so-called glamour and sophistication, always had the soul of small-town America. People in the film industry - and stars in particular - were required in their private lives to be respectable; or, failing that, always to obey the Eleventh Commandment - Thou Shalt Not Be Found Out. Very few people have absolutely nothing to hide, skeletons large and small rattle in cupboards all over the world; but public figures have to be more careful than the rest of us. Katharine Hepburn and Spencer Tracy were lovers for many years, but not a word was said publicly about it until after Tracy's death; and if the whistle had been blown on Rock Hudson, his career would have been ruined.

Errol Flynn was accused of Statutory Rape in 1943 and eventually acquitted. No matter - he found himself ostracised by the Great, The Good and the Also Starrings. He was Fatty Arbuckle 20 years on, and only his public remained loyal. Few people knew that night after night after the trial, Flynn tried to summon up the nerve to shoot himself. Failing to do so, he very sensibly went out and bought himself a new boat instead.

More reckless souls dived from great heights into boiling water. When Ingrid Bergman, a married woman, openly admitted her affair with the Italian director Roberto Rossellini, the united voices of the blue-rinse Mothers of America almost ruined her career.

Producer William Dozier brought Diana Dors to Hollywood, announcing that he would make her an international star. She almost immediately embarked on an affair with her co-star, Rod Steiger, while she was still married to Dennis Hamilton. Dors was advised to confess her sins to the gossip columnist Louella Parsons, a clamorously devout Roman Catholic. Parsons granted Diana absolution - on the clear understanding that any updates, affair-wise or marriage-wise, would be given to kind old Auntie Lou, and not to her rival, Hedda Hopper. Three Hail Marys and an Exclusive.

The glass houses whose inhabitants should never have thrown stones were the Hollywood studios. Here the men who controlled the studio system were dictators, sultans who had instant access to an inexhaustible supply of casting-couch partners.

THE BRIGHTEST OF THEM ALL

Each year since 1933, Quigley Publishing has polled cinema-owners across America to see which stars draw in the biggest audiences. From their lists it is possible to work out the most popular stars of all time.

MEN	WOMEN
John Wayne	Doris Day
Clint Eastwood	Betty Grable
Bing Crosby	Elizabeth Taylor
Gary Cooper	Shirley Temple
Burt Reynolds	Barbra Streisand
Bob Hope	Julie Andrews
Paul Newman	Jane Fonda
Rock Hudson	Ginger Rogers
Cary Grant	Julia Roberts
Tom Cruise	Greer Garson

To say that everyone was at it is hardly an exaggeration. Alan Selwyn, a writer who has a huge appetite for casting-couch stories, records that over at Keystone, Mack Sennett's door and fly were always open. No girl even got on the lot if she hadn't first been on his casting couch. Among the ones that didn't walk away (and there were probably hundreds of them) were Gloria Swanson, Mabel Normand, Norma Talmadge and her sister Natalie. At one of Fatty Arbuckle's orgies (this was before the super-scandal that ruined him) Adolph Zukor, eventually to survive as head of Paramount, was caught with his trousers down and had to pay off the police department. Chaplin had a penchant for under-age girls; he called them "The most beautiful form of human life - the very young girl just starting to bloom". His brother Sydney - whose appetite ran to four a day - was a direct influence on a young man called Darryl Zanuck. Chaplin advised him, "Pretty girls are out there for the taking. They're aching for it. Give it to them and then get out before they get their hooks into you. There's plenty more where they came from."

Marilyn Monroe started her Hollywood career on her knees. Ben Lyon, a casting director at Fox, liked her enough to give her a handful of sealed letters of recommendation which she duly presented to a handful of producers. Whatever their initial greeting, once the letter was open, the atmosphere in the office became perceptibly warmer. Ben Lyon had written, "This girl loves giving head." Marilyn herself said, "Hollywood is a place where they'll pay a thousand dollars for your body and fifty cents for your soul... I've slept with producers for work. I'd be a liar if I said I didn't."

Joan Crawford, when she was still Lucille LeSueur, made a pornographic short actually called *The Casting Couch* (1924); once established in mainstream Hollywood, she routinely offered herself to the producers she worked with. She was still doing it when, late in her

An innocent in Hollywood. Fatty Arbuckle, soon to be in real trouble.

career, she was offered a half-hour play in the television series, "Night Gallery". Fetchingly dishabille, she prepared to "discuss the script" with her new director. Sixty-five-year-old Joan Crawford opened the door to a terrified 25-year-old - Steven Spielberg.

Although not so well documented, casting-couch encounters were not exclusively heterosexual. One gay casting director at MGM took a fancy to the young man who every morning delivered rolls and croissants. "How'd you like to be a film star, son?" "I'd like it just fine, sir." The slogan on the side of the van read, "Hudson's Bakery Fresh Bread Daily", and that morning Rock Hudson was born.

Clara Bow, the "It" Girl of the Twenties, had a huge appetite for sex. Once, for a bet, she slept with an entire college football team called The Trojans. One member of the team pleased her so much that she got him a job at the studio as a prop man; and that's how John Wayne got started.

In the Thirties, Busby Berkeley was as renowned, in Hollywood, for his parties as for his choreography. Any of his chorus girls who refused to attend was considered to have resigned from the current Berkeley film. Betty Grable, who started in the chorus at 13, was a Berkeley girl: "Those parties were the pits. You'd come out in the early dawn feeling like a piece of meat dogs had been fighting over all night."

Betty Grable, a wartime pin-up star for millions; and her legs were insured for millions by Lloyds of London.

Sydney Chaplin's eager pupil, Darryl Zanuck, was making excellent post-graduate progress. At 20th Century-Fox, Zanuck had a regular tea-time treat. Every afternoon at four o'clock a contract star or starlet would come to his office. There she would be conducted into the "open secret" boudoir behind a bookcase. And for precisely half-an-hour the mogul's mind would be diverted from the cares of the day. Almost all of the Fox female stars - apart from Shirley Temple - knew

☞ page 146

FILM

SINGIN' IN THE RAIN

MGM 1952

Producer: Arthur Freed

Directors: Gene Kelly, Stanley Donen

Stars: Gene Kelley, Donald O'Connor, Debbie Reynolds, Jean Hagen and Cyd Charisse

Damp Squibs

Unquestionably one of the greatest film musicals of all time, *Singin' in the Rain*, started off life rather unpromisingly as a mixed bag of left-over song and dance numbers. These songs - originally written by Arthur Freed and Nacio Herb Brown in the Twenties and Thirties for other movies - were sold to MGM in 1950. After a long, hot summer locked away in a room on the MGM lot, screenwriters Betty Comden and Adolph Green worked the 30-year-old melodies into the story of Twenties Hollywood that we know as *Singin' in the Rain*.

Released a year after the box-office hit *An American in Paris* (1951) - which had won Gene Kelly an Oscar - *Singin' in the Rain* didn't have the best of starts but, nevertheless, turned popular with audiences and made a healthy $7.7 million. It was one of the last written-for-the-screen musicals.

Debbie Reynolds on her role: "In my opinion I was being thrown to the lions".

Gene Kelly on Debbie Reynolds: "Strong as an ox".

A year and a half after completing work on the film, Gene Kelly was in London for the Coronation. As he was watching the procession from a window, a loud speaker suddenly came on and a voice announced "...I'd like you all to join Gene Kelly"; "....thousands of lovely, cold, wet, shivering English men and women started to sing", recalls Kelly: "It was the biggest thrill of my life."

Left: Gene Kelly and Debbie Reynolds are all smiles in this studio picture, but on the set he was a tyrant. Right: Donald O'Connor, Madge Blake, Kelly and Jean Hagen.

Left: Cyd Charisse in the final ballet. Below right: "The Moses Supposes" routine.

SET SECRETS

Gene Kelly was known as a monster on the set. He was often cruel to the young Debbie Reynolds, but more likely to shout at her co-star Donald O'Connor. At least Donald didn't cry and ruin his makeup.

Debbie Reynolds was thrilled to be hired for the film, but couldn't sing or dance. "I was totally untrained", admitted Debbie, "but too stupid to be intimidated by the thought of dancing with Kelly and O'Connor". One day she danced so hard that the blood vessels in her foot burst and she fainted plain away.

Donald O'Connor needed three days in bed after dancing his solo, "Make 'em Laugh". The fact that he smoked four packs of cigarettes a day didn't help.

Cyd Charisse wore a brilliant white outfit in her famous dance sequence with the scarf. Disguising the star's bikini-line became the costume designer's major preoccupation.

The payments given to the three stars varied dramatically: Debbie Reynolds was on $300 a week, Donald O'Connor was on loan from Universal for a fee of $50,000 and Gene Kelly was making $2,500 a week.... a fee that was doubled after the first few weeks.

SET PIECE

Although it became the title song, "Singin' in the Rain" was in fact slotted into the film as a last-minute thought. As originally choreographed, it was not as a solo for Kelly but as a number for all three stars: Kelly, Reynolds and O'Connor were to come dancing out of the restaurant

together and make their way down the street.

Filmed on MGM's East Side Street, technicians had to pipe water over from two city blocks in Culver City. A tarpaulin was pulled over the set to make it look like night, and holes were dug in the pavement where Kelly could slosh about in the

puddles.

Unfortunately for Kelly, the Californian heat soon turned the rain into steam, and, soaked to the skin in a heavy tweed suit, he caught a heavy cold. His apparent childish exuberance in this scene is even more remarkable.

the secret of the bookcase. It became such a part of studio routine that films were scheduled to allow for a 30-minute break at 4pm. What was good enough for the boss was good enough for the hundreds of writers, directors, producers and technicians. This was a fine example of "cascading executive-stress relief".

Billy Wilder once had an appointment to see Ernst Lubitsch. When he arrived at Lubitsch's office he heard faint calls of distress. Wilder hesitated - Ernst's habit of taking a little sexual relaxation with some passing starlet was well-known. Discreetly pushing the door open an inch or two, Wilder saw a plaintively moaning blonde pinned to the couch by the hefty Lubitsch. Moaning was okay, of course, and Wilder was about to shut the door, when the girl screamed, "He's dead!" Wilder got her out from under, gave her the cab fare home and tidied up a bit before the ambulance arrived. Lubitsch, the man who made sex funny, had given his life for it.

Howard Hughes was a Texas boy who, at 18, inherited his father's millions, designed and flew record-breaking aeroplanes and started his own airline. He then bought himself a new toy - RKO Studios - and proceeded to break it. Hughes regarded his female contract artists as bedroom toys, available round the clock. Back in the Fifties, when Stewart Granger was married to Jean Simmons, Rank sold the fag-end of Simmons's contract to Hughes, who then demanded that she sign on for another seven years. When she refused, he notified all the Hollywood studios that if they gave her any work he would sue them. In his book, *Sparks Fly Upwards*, Stewart Granger says to Jean: "That monster is going to ruin our marriage, ruin your career, ruin our lives. I'll have to kill him." The plan was to invite Hughes round, get him out on the balcony... and tip him over. Simmons robbed us of a Made-For-TV True Story when she talked her husband out of it. The Grangers took Hughes to court instead - and won.

Shirley Temple, too young for Zanuck, left 20th Century-Fox at the age of 12 to go to MGM where she would be looked after like a favourite daughter. In a pleasantly furnished office she found herself sitting opposite producer Arthur Freed. Casually, he stood up and showed the little girl his penis. Shirley, who might very well have been Dorothy in *The Wizard of Oz*, reacted much as Dorothy did when confronted by the Cowardly Lion; she laughed. Freed was incensed. "Get out! Go on, get out!" Even as she shut the door behind her, Louis B. Mayer was making a pass at Shirley's mum.

That Shirley Temple adventure, expressed as a film, would never have got past the censor; but in the Fifties, the first cracks had already appeared in the Hays Code, partly brought about by a 1953 Otto Preminger film called *The Moon Is Blue*. This comedy contained not one ridiculed clergyman, not a whiff of nudity, miscegenation or drug addiction. Preminger's sin was to refuse to cut words, not images. Objected to were "virgin, pregnant, mistress and seduction." Preminger released the film without a Seal of Approval; and the sky did not fall.

An even more direct challenge to censorship came in 1965 with *The Pawnbroker*, in which nudity - a powerfully dramatic moment in which woman was seen naked to the waist - was brought back to the screen for the first time in 30 years. Sidney Lumet's film was passed uncut on the grounds that the scene was an essential element in the narrative. This decision opened the way for artistically valid scenes of nudity and sexual explicitness. It also hastened the end of the Production Code Administration, since a more liberal attitude towards

Alan Bates and June Ritchie in *A Kind of Loving.* The British censor, John Trevelyan, told director John Schlesinger, "We're paid to have dirty minds."

sex on screen was difficult to accommodate within a code of prohibitions, and a ratings system was adopted instead.

As a matter of record, nudity returned to British cinema screens earlier than in America. The year was 1951 and the British Board of Film Censors passed, uncut, a Swedish import called *One Summer of Happiness*. Home-grown product was treated more harshly. It is difficult today to see why the censor was so concerned about *A Kind of Loving*. Made in 1962 it starred Alan Bates and June Ritchie as a young working class couple trapped in the social and sexual conventions of the time. John Schlesinger, who directed the film, remembers that, when the screenplay was submitted to the British Board of Film Censors, John Trevelyan, who was the British Hays figure at the time, demanded over 30 cuts. ("Can't have this, can't have that... disgusting..... Yes, very likely, old man, but we're paid to have dirty minds.") Schlesinger and his producer went for Trevelyan's Achilles heel. They asked for his advice - oh and, er, could he possibly visit them on set so that they could show him exactly what they meant? And didn't he - once he was sitting in his own canvas chair and hob-nobbing with the likes of Alan Bates and Thora Hird - didn't he perhaps feel that it was all a question of how it was done? "Ah well now, see what you mean. Quite... Morning, Thora! ...Mmmm.... Maybe we should be a little more lenient." The strategy worked. Apart from one scene, Trevelyan passed everything.

Sheer cheek will do it, too. In 1976 Derek Jarman had to explain to the censor - by now, James Ferman - why full

Director Derek Jarman often had to economise. The cast of *Sebastiane* stoically made do with one pair of period sandals per couple.

THE RANK ORGANISATION presents
A PETER ROGERS' PRODUCTION
SIDNEY JAMES · KENNETH WILLIAMS
CHARLES HAWTREY · JIM DALE · JOAN SIMS
BARBARA WINDSOR · HATTIE JACQUES
in " **CARRY ON AGAIN, DOCTOR** "
In Colour
Screenplay by Talbot Rothwell
Produced by Peter Rogers
Directed by Gerald Thomas

frontals should be allowed in *Sebastiane*. With a perfectly straight face, he claimed that his budget wouldn't run to the expense of period costumes. "Passed. Next!"

There was one sad casualty in the censorship peace - the "Carry On" series. These screen versions of the saucy seaside postcard had flourished for years on good clean smut. But good clean sex robbed them of their impact and the "Carry On" films became impotent. Worse still, everything they said or did was politically incorrect, as when Kenneth Williams, a limp-wristed Caesar in *Carry On Cleo* (1964), full of the 'flu and with his aching feet in a bowl of hot water, looked into camera to say, "Oooo I do feel queer!"

Like Derek Jarman's *Sebastiane*, *Carry On Doctor* was subjected to severe costume cuts. With Barbara Windsor, Jim Dale and Hattie Jaques.

Natalie Wood
and Warren
Beatty saving
money on the
water bill in
*Splendour in
the Grass.*

If homosexuality became an unacceptable gag in the later "Carry
On" films, it was no joke at all in the days of strict censorship. Male
and female homosexuality had been hinted at in films from the earliest days - and spoken about, but only in the context of disapproval,
as in the 1962 film, *Advise and Consent*.

The first film in Britain to challenge the prejudices of a heterosexual society was *Victim*. Dirk Bogarde recalls that when they were
shooting it in 1961, everyone was very solemn, never cracked a smile,
still less a joke, about the subject of the film. They were instructed to
use only the word "invert" when discussing a scene or planning the
next day's schedule; perhaps this is why everyone in the film mispro-
nounces the word "homosexual" throughout. From the start of filming, director, cast and technicians were walking on eggs, fearful of
saying the wrong thing - until one of the electricians brought laughter
and relief to the set when he yelled, "Watch it, mate - don't bend
over!" The film's attitudes and language seem almost quaint today,
but the fact remains that this decent and honourable film helped to

change the law; and without *Victim* the acceptance of male and female homosexuality as a fit subject for the screen would have been considerably delayed.

But whatever happens, so long as it sells movies, the cinema will continue to use sex of all persuasions as persuasively as it knows how. Attitudes change all the time and some kinds of film would be unlikely to find favour now. For example, with the advancing tide of political correctness, feminism and concern about Aids, producers might well think twice before making a sex comedy about light-hearted promiscuity. But in the end, the real controls in film are commercial, not artistic or sociological. Studios want that all-important family certificate to get more bottoms on seats. On the other hand, there's the Devil's Alliance between cinema and television. There are the soft-porn channels in the USA; and Red Hot Dutch, a channel showing movies far more hard than soft, arrived in the UK not so long ago - so perhaps there is a new cinema audience growing up to reject anything they consider tame.

In any case, sex is joyful, life-affirming and funny, something to be celebrated, not censored. And sex belongs to us - not to the porn merchants, who give sex a bad name and haven't even got a name for eroticism. Warren Beatty used to talk about making a movie (starring him) with explicit sex as a natural part of the story. If he leaves it much longer he'll have to use a body double.

Explicit screen sex, then, is not a comparatively new development but an enormous pendulum which swung from a period of no censorship in the 1890s, through a period of rigid control in the Thirties and Forties, and then back, from the Sixties onwards, to the almost anything goes of today.

Soft porn pays. Russ Meyer's *Super Vixens* was the 1975 sequel to his first skin-flick, *Vixen!*, in 1968.

CHAPTER 5

The Sound of Music

Throughout the history of cinema, music and movies have been partners in a relationship that, when it's perfect, is a marriage made in heaven. Louis B. Mayer's right-hand-man, Irving Thalberg, said:"Without music there wouldn't have been a movie industry at all."

Even before the cinema found its voice in the late Twenties, there was music - silent films were never really silent. However humble the cinema, it usually had a pianist playing mood music that was more or less appropriate to the pictures on the screen. In the big theatres, there was often an orchestra; and for special occasions, like premieres, even a symphony orchestra. There was also music played during the shooting of a film, just out of camera range, to help the actors get into the right mood. On a John Ford pre-sound set, for instance, a brother of the director Frank Borzage sat nearby playing "Red River Valley" on the accordion.

The earliest films shown by means of the Lumière Cinématographe in Paris were accompanied by a saxophone quartet - and within 20 years, film studios began providing specially composed scores to accompany the films they released.

Gaylord Carter was 16 when he became a cinema pianist. It was a way of getting in free to see the silent films; and he got paid as well. When a print arrived at the cinema it usually came with a "filmatic cue sheet" with a few bars of sample music for each sequence (drama, comedy, military, Indian and so on.) But Gaylord had a few musical ideas of his own. When he was 21 he was spotted by Harold Lloyd, who was tickled to death when he heard Gaylord playing "Time on My Hands" to the shots of Lloyd cliff-hanging from the big hand of the clock in *Safety Last* (1923). Lloyd immediately recommended the young pianist to the manager of the prestigious Million Dollar Theatre in Los Angeles. One of his first jobs, on a salary that had jumped to a

AS TIME GOES BY

WORDS and MUSIC BY HERMAN HUPFELD

FROM

"CASABLANCA"

STARRING

HUMPHREY BOGART
INGRID BERGMAN AND
PAUL HENREID

DIRECTED BY
MICHAEL CURTIZ
A WARNER BROS. PICTURE

1/-

CHAPPELL & CO. LTD.
50 NEW BOND ST., LONDON, W.1
and SYDNEY
HARMS INC., NEW YORK
1467

Get out the handkerchiefs — zing went the strings of my heart, again!

WHITE CHRISTMAS

Words and Music by IRVING BERLIN

FROM THE PARAMOUNT PICTURE
IRVING BERLIN'S

"HOLIDAY INN"

FEATURING
BING CROSBY AND **FRED ASTAIRE** WITH
MARJORIE REYNOLDS, VIRGINIA DALE, WALTER ABEL and LOUISE BEAVERS

A MARK SANDRICH PRODUCTION

PRICE 1/- NET

THE VICTORIA MUSIC PUBLISHING COMPANY LTD.
52 MADDOX STREET, LONDON, W.1
IRVING BERLIN INC., NEW YORK
Authorised for sale only in the British Empire (except Canada, Newfoundland, Australia and New Zealand)
MADE IN ENGLAND

Silent film,
*Mabel's
Dramatic
Career*, given an
extra dimension by
the cinema pianist.

dizzy $125 a week, was playing the cinema organ - with a 35-piece symphony orchestra in the pit - to accompany Greta Garbo in her second American film, *The Temptress* (1926), a full-blooded melodrama enhanced by full-blooded music. Gaylord also played an organ solo (popping up like toothpaste from the tube) during the interval; and (sucked down again) brightened up the newsreels with his selection of mood music; Gaylord was never at a loss, and never out of work.

The big movie theatres in Gaylord's day were like cathedrals or palaces. Most of them were open from eleven in the morning to eleven at night, the programmes running continuously and with people coming and going all the time. Patrons certainly got their moneysworth. Gaylord remembers that, in 1926, Paul Whiteman and his orchestra introduced George Gershwin's symphony, *Rhapsody in Blue*, to Los Angeles; and when *Ben Hur*, starring Ramon Novarro, was premiered in 1925, Frank Newman, cinema manager and occasional poet, said "Gaylord, it's gonna take a while to get everybody in, so instead of playing marches and things, I want you to... *perfume the air with music*." So, while the seats were gradually filling up, Gaylord's charming arpeggios wafted over the audience. When it came to *Ben Hur* itself, which, after its premiere, ran for an unprecedented six months to packed houses, Gaylord worked punctiliously to a score supplied by MGM. Within two weeks, he had memorised it so that he could keep his eyes always on the screen, never missing a cue, free to interpret but never taking liberties with holy writ. Gaylord Carter still has his copy of that 1925 MGM *Ben Hur* score - the only one in existence.

The arrival of sound in 1927 soon put an end to the job of film accompanist. Indeed, for many this great watershed in cinema's history seemed to spell the end of the art of film-making which, after 32 years, was at its most sophisticated.. The silent film was so advanced both technically and artistically that it had a fluidity and range unequalled in any other medium. Editing - exemplified by the work of Griffith, Gance, and Eisenstein, not to mention that of the comic geniuses, Keaton, Chaplin and Harold Lloyd - was limited only by the film-maker's imagination. With sound, editing became a nightmare, films could only be made indoors, shot with imprisoned cameras that had less mobility than shackled elephants.

Ernest Torrence, Percy Marmont and Clara Bow are being put in the mood by off-camera musicians for *Mantrap* (1926), being directed by Victor Fleming.

Freddie Young, the distinguished cinematographer whose contribution to much of David Lean's later work is incalculable, was in at the start of sound in Britain, which arrived a little later than in America. He was then in his twenties, already a skilled cameraman, and not much impressed by the new development: "The sound people were a damn nuisance." Most of the trouble came from the microphone at the end of a long boom which dangled over the head of the actor who was speaking, only to swing to whoever spoke next, and back again. Lighting became a nightmare, the huge microphone throwing shadows on the walls and across the actors' faces. "The poor old cameraman had a hell of a time lighting for long shots and close-ups and medium shots - all with this damn mike floating about all over the place." Because of motor noise - only one among noises which were as plentiful and difficult to locate as fleas on a dog - the cameras were shut away in airtight booths in which the cameraman sat for a thousand feet of film, gasping for air. Eventually Freddie and his colleagues made, in the studio workshops, blimps which would muffle the noise of the camera. But these were very heavy, being lined with lead and cotton wool. Gradually the cameras were fitted with quieter motors; but, even then, they were cumbersome - and several were needed for every scene. Freddie Young remembers working on one of the Aldwych farces with Tom Walls and Ralph Lynn. There were five cameras, one in the middle and the others flanking it; there was a camera dedicated to Tom Walls's close-up, another to Ralph Lynn's, "And you'd have to light for all this on one sound track."

Another British veteran, director Ronald Neame, also remembers the coming of sound. Starting as a messenger boy at Elstree Studios, Borehamwood, at the age of 15, young Ronnie eventually became a cameraman, learning, as Freddie Young had, how to turn the handle of the silent camera at the correct speed of 16 pictures every second (two pictures for every turn of the handle). It may sound primitive but, at the end of a minute, Neame, Young and any of their fellow professionals anywhere in the world, would be accurate to a split second. They were also masters of under and over-cranking, for speeded up punches and "smoothing out the love scenes".

A picture of what it was like to work in a studio at that time gives some idea of how brutal the sound revolution really was. The grandly termed "studio" at Elstree was a large shed divided into two, with a roof of corrugated iron; when it rained the noise was deafening, but

CINEMA'S LANDMARKS

Since Hollywood experimented with wide-screen in the Fifties, there have been no revolutionary advances, and it is astonishing how much film-making in the Nineties still resembles the early Thirties.

1889: George Eastman invents perforated celluloid film.

1889: Thomas Edison's assistant William Dickson starts development on the Kinetoscope - a machine to show moving pictures in amusement arcades.

1891: The Kinetoscope is demonstrated in Edison's laboratories in New Jersey. It uses Eastman's celluloid film in a format based on Edison's specifications - 35mm in width, each frame nearly ¾in in height and bordered by 4 perforations. It remains the standard to this day.

1894: A "Kinetoscope Parlour" opens on Oxford Street, London.

1894: Colour films begin to appear, the pictures hand-tinted. By 1910 this is common place.

1895: On March 10th, French engineering brothers Auguste and Louis Lumière, using their newly invented Cinématographe, project moving pictures on to a big screen.

1895: Nine months later, on December 28th 1895, at the Grand Café on the Boulevard des Capucines in Paris, history's first paying audience watches a selection of one-minute films shot by the two brothers.

1896: First screening of a film in Britain is organised by Birt Acres at the Royal Photographic Society in London.

1899: Georges Méliès' film *Cinderella* demonstrates the possibilities of merging one-shot scenes.

1900: Cineorama, the world's first multiscreen system using 10 synchronised projectors, takes place in Paris. The crowds are so big, the police close it down after three performances.

1906: The world's first feature film, *The Story of the Kelly Gang*, is premiered in Australia. It makes £25,000.

1911: George Smith and Charles Urban produce the first major colour film, *The Durbar at Delhi*. It is a two-colour system, called Kinemacolor.

1914: On April 9th, *The World, the Flesh and the Devil*, the first feature film in colour, is screened in London.

1915: W. Griffith's *The Birth of a Nation* popularises new camera techniques, including the "close-up".

1917: *The Gulf Between*, the first Technicolor film , and America's first colour feature, is screened in New York.

1927: French director Abel Gance uses Polyvision to project his film *Napoléon* on three screens.

1927 October 7, *The Jazz Singer*, the first talking feature film (only partly talking), on the Vitaphone system, opens in New York. The sound comes from discs synchronised with the picture.

1928: *Lights of New York*, the first all-talking film is screened, still on Vitaphone.

1929: *In Old Arizona*, the first film using the Movietone sound-on-film process, is released. It spells the end of Vitaphone and other sound systems.

1932: The first film in Technicolor three-colour system is Walt Disney's "Silly Symphony" cartoon, *Flowers and Trees*.

1934: The short feature *La Cucaracha* is the first live-action film in the new Technicolor process

1935: MGM's *Becky Sharp* is the first feature film in three-colour Technicolor.

1952: The move to modern wide-screen systems begins with *This is Cinerama*, which uses three cameras and three projectors to record and project a single image. Its spectacular effects cause a sensation.

1953: *The Robe*, the first film shot in CinemaScope, opens. Other systems follow, such as Panavision, VistaVision and Todd-AO.

this had no effect on the busy filming going on underneath. One rain-free day in 1928, there were four productions on the floor, a small orchestra playing soft music for one of them, as a very young Madeleine Carroll took a bath in *The Guns of Loos*. Ronnie remembers the music, always a sign that the production was an important one, but was unable to see Miss Carroll, who was discreetly hidden by wooden flats. A few yards away, a second film was being made, *A Little Bit of Fluff*, starring Betty Balfour; a third was called *Toni*, with Jack Buchanan playing two roles - hero and villain (split screen, no less.) The remaining stage - or rather, the other half of the divided shed - was being used for only one film, *The Farmer's Wife*, directed by a plump young man called Alfred Hitchcock. All four directors were free to speak, shout or whisper instructions to their actors, and nobody worried about the noise of carpenters sawing and hammering. All the sets, or groups of sets, were bathed in green mercury lighting which gave a weird, overall illumination, while huge arc lights provided highlights and shadows.

In the USA, Anthony Quinn worked as an extra in several silent films. He was open-mouthed (but not so on screen) to find that the stars used to make up their own dialogue; he distinctly remembers that, "Ramon Novarro spoke Spanish. It sounded like gibberish."

Mix back to Elstree in 1929, and Ronnie Neame was now working for Hitchcock as assistant cameraman and focus-puller on another silent film, *Blackmail*. In the middle of shooting, the American revolution reached Borehamwood at last, so Hitchcock, undismayed, made the film again - this time in sound. Like Freddie Young, Neame found himself in a huge box with a glass window at the front, able to pan just a little; "But if we wanted to track, the whole booth had to go forward on rails". The camera booth was big enough for the whole crew; they even made tea in there. The feud that sprang up between the sound and camera people was in no way helped by the fact that the sound crew had their own wooden box and tea-making facilities: "The sound department thought they were the elite - this being the first sound film ever made in Europe." The battle went on for weeks, no doubt to Hitchcock's amusement, until compromises over lighting and mike shadows and the need for quiet were finally made.

But the biggest challenge came from Hitchcock's leading lady in *Blackmail*, Anny Ondra, a young Czech actress. She was supposed to be a London girl, but spoke with a thick foreign accent. This had mat-

tered not at all when *Blackmail* was silent, but now, "We couldn't re-cast her", says Neame, "because we were using three-quarters of the silent film, all the action stuff." Hitchcock notched up his second First when he engaged another actress, Joan Barry, who stood at the side of the set speaking the lines into a separate microphone while Anny mimed to them on the set. "And that", Neame recalls, "was the first-ever dubbing. It was very difficult, but it worked splendidly."

In Hollywood, in 1929, *The Jazz Singer* took a special Oscar, but the winner of the first Academy Award for Best Film was a silent pic-ture called *Wings*, made in 1927 by William Wellman, but with excel-lent sound effects for the air battles. Its stars were Clara Bow, Richard Arlen, Gary Cooper and a young country boy from Kansas, Charles "Buddy" Rogers, who became a big star and married an even bigger one, Mary Pickford. Buddy, now in his 90s, was then, like most of the actors in Hollywood, terrified of sound's arrival. Hobgoblin rumour of the year was that only one voice in a thousand would make it. Not sur-prisingly, Buddy and his pals - Richard Arlen, Jack Oakie and Gary Cooper - were in a state of near panic, Gary Cooper blurting out, "Buddy, I ain't got no voice, have you?"

Blackmail **(1929) turned into a sound film half-way through, giving Hitchcock a big headache: a leading lady (Anny Ondra) with a strong foreign accent playing a London girl.**

Before he could answer, Jack Oakie said, "I can sing, I can dance, I do everything, but I bet I don't have a voice." So the four friends shook hands on a solemn promise that, "If one of the four of us don't have a voice that records, we're going to give part of our salary to the boy that has no voice."

None of the four had to pay out, of course; nevertheless, a great many silent stars were destroyed, but by no means always because their voices didn't fit. The "Great Lover" of the silent era, John Gilbert, is supposed to have been laughed off the screen in a 1929 talkie, *His Glorious Night*, because he had a high-pitched voice. In fact, his pleasant light baritone offended nobody; what audiences laughed at - and it was the laughter of embarrassment - was the overblown dialogue in a story (perfectly acceptable as a plot for a silent film) about a princess who falls in love with a commoner. The excruciating scene that destroyed John Gilbert had the hitherto silent hero declaiming, over and over again, "I love you!" Twenty-three years later, the unfortunate actor was maligned again in the musical, *Singin' in the Rain*. In this 1952 comedy about Hollywood's awkward transition to sound, almost all of the scenes in the films within the film are based on period sequences, and the attempts to overcome technical difficulties by hiding microphones in vases and bosoms. Parody is no respector of fact, and in one scene, Don Lockwood repeats the words "I love you" over and over again... in a high pitched voice.

"I love you!"
***His Glorious Night*, the film that destroyed John Gilbert's career.**

Although he might have shrugged helplessly, Gilbert would not have spun in his grave in 1952; he had long before been devastated by the public's reaction to *His Glorious Night*. According to novelist and screenwriter Budd Schulberg, whose family knew John Gilbert well, "Jack locked himself away in his mansion and slowly drank himself to death. Basically, although he went on working for a few more years, he went from being the biggest star, one of the handful at the very top, to disappearing out of sight."

Douglas Fairbanks Jnr agrees that many silent stars fell by the wayside, sometimes because their voices weren't suitable but more often because so many of them had never been actors in the first place and they now had no idea how to act with sound: "It was the survival of the fittest." For some stars, like little Clara Bow, with her thick Bronx accent, to speak at all was to be betrayed. Many voice coaches were imported to Hollywood, one of them the fruity-voiced Mrs Patrick Campbell, appropriately the original Eliza in *Pygmalion*, who taught Hollywood stars How To Talk Proper In The Kinema. If she had taken the "It" Girl in hand, one wonders what kind of accent Clara Bow would have ended up with.

Many of the silent movie stars, such as Vilma Banky and Pola Negri, were European with little command of English. They had also become very expensive and, in this time of change, they were, with certain exceptions, expendable. Hollywood set out to find new performers, and for many of them they looked to the theatre. It is an extraordinary fact that, in 1930 and 1931, just about everybody we revere today - from Bette Davis to Ginger Rogers to Clark Gable to Jimmy Stewart to Henry Fonda and Katharine Hepburn - arrived in Hollywood at the same time. They must have been tripping over each other at the train station. Screenwriter Ron Base believes that they saved the movie industry. "They were unique beings, and they were that way by accident. There was no grand design on Hollywood's part, they were merely looking for people who could speak; and yet they found this incredible army of performers. I don't think we've ever quite recovered from that first group who arrived in Los Angeles. Their movie stardom has never been quite equalled."

The arrival of sound on picture created at least one new job - the film composer. At first the music used on film was arrangements of existing compositions. Then composers began to write original music for films, though still only to fill the background or set a mood. Finally as film-makers and musicians came to terms with the new art, music became an integral part of the film and the composer an essential member of the production team.

When Elmer Bernstein, one of Hollywood's most distinguished composers, began in films in the late Forties, the studios still had large music departments. He was at Columbia Pictures for a while. There were other composers along the corridor from his office. Copyists and orchestrators were on tap - and of course an in-house orchestra. Bernstein struggled for some years but got his big break composing for Cecil B. DeMille on *The Ten Commandments* (1956). He went before the legendary director who asked him: "Mr Bernstein, do you think you could do for ancient Egyptian music what Puccini did for Japanese music and *Madame Butterfly?* I gulped. Fortunately I gave the right answer. I said 'Well, I don't know, but I'd sure like to try.' I'm sure if I had said 'Yes', I'd have been out of there in two minutes."

Bernstein began by writing chants and pieces for the harpists to play during the shooting. Then when Victor Young, DeMille's original choice of composer for the film's music was too ill to write the score, the director asked Bernstein to come up with some themes ".... for Moses, for Nephretiri, for Ramases, themes for good and evil and all that kind of thing. And finally I had a test. DeMille appeared one day with two secretaries and said, 'Play the theme'. So I played him the big Moses theme; and he said 'How would you play that when he was a baby floating down the Nile in a basket?' So I had to sort of improvise. Finally instead of saying anything to me DeMille turned to his two secretaries he always had with him and said, 'What do you think?', and the secretaries, god bless them, both applauded. That's how I got the job."

He went on to write some of the most memorable film scores in the last four decades - including the music for *The Man with the Golden Arm* (1956), *Walk on the Wild Side* (1962), *The Age of Innocence* (1993) and the instantly recognisable theme of *The Magnificent Seven* (1960).

Bernstein has been in Hollywood for almost 50 years and writes his music on a piano. Hans Zimmer has been there less than ten years and writes his on a computer - in fact, on a whole battery of computers. He is only 37, but he is almost a throwback to the film composers of the Thirties and Forties, such people as Dimitri Tiomkin, who came out of a European tradition to make it big in Hollywood. Zimmer, born in Germany, was a member of the British pop group The Buggles, who had a big hit with "Video Killed the Radio Star". He explains how a composer works on a film: "What I really try to do is have as many dinners and lunches and whatever with the director. For instance, with Ridley Scott it works great, because you say: 'Well, what's this about?', and he'll tell you the story. And so suddenly you get the emphasis the director is putting on the scenes, the things that are important to him within the script. So you instantly get a much clearer picture. And then you go through this process where you sit there watching the first cut and you go: 'Oh my God! I have no idea what to do here'. Every start is the same, you sit there and you say, 'I don't know what to do. I can't write, I have no idea, I'm a failure, I should phone them up right now and tell them to get a real composer and fire me...'" He generally seems to get over his panic, because he has written some great scores, including the music for 1994's most successful picture *The Lion King*.

Director Nicolas Roeg has worked with Hans Zimmer. Some composers see their role as separate from, if not superior to, that of the director; they want to take over the movie and make it theirs because they love music - their music. This is understandable, but not what Nic Roeg wants or is prepared to accept. To hand over his baby to someone else, to give his film up to another artist's interpretation is unthinkable. Nic Roeg's relationship with Zimmer works because the composer, like all the composers Roeg has worked with, "...loves film more than he loves music". When Roeg is editing his film, "I lay on scratch tracks while I'm cutting with the editor. The music is a guide, it's not cast in stone. I've been very lucky, I've had a wonderful relationship with my composers, people like Stanley Myers, for example, and of course Hans Zimmer." It is perhaps significant that Zimmer collaborated with Myers on several films before his first solo score for *A World Apart* (1988).

Some films have been ruined by music that swamps the story, telling the audience what to feel, when it is the film that should do that. John Schlesinger, having directed opera on stage, has a good musical background, and is able more easily than some directors, perhaps, to communicate what he wants from his composer. "Sometimes, if the cue isn't working, you have to ask them to totally re-score it." *Far From the Madding Crowd* is a case in point. Sergeant Troy (Terence Stamp) executes a sword dance for Bathsheba (Julie Christie) as she fantasises about him. It is really a symbolic rape; he cuts off a lock of her hair, impales a caterpillar on her breast. But, "The scene wasn't working. Richard Rodney Bennett, who did the score, came up with something which still didn't answer it. I am constantly amazed that composers - good ones, anyway - never seem to get impatient with directors, are always ready to listen and act upon

☞ page 166

Walt Disney

Walter Elias Disney, animator, producer, executive: born Chicago, 5 December ,1901; died 15 December,1966.

AMERICAN TALE

Walt Disney's life reads like the classic American rags- to-riches tale. Born into a dour family in the mid-West, Walt found his bit of colour at the age of 14 when he signed up at the Kansas City Art School. Later he joined a local commercial art studio where he became friends with another young draftsman, Ub Iwerks. Together they formed their own company and promptly went bankrupt. In 1923, and taking Walt's brother Roy with them, they set out off to Hollywood to make their fortunes. Walt Disney died 40 years later, the undisputed King of Family Entertainment, with 29 Ocars and a theme park to his name.

Walt Disney in the Thirties when his cartoon empire took off.

THE MOUSE THAT ROARED

When Disney set up in Hollywood in 1923, animation was a competitive field. The Disney brothers' business sense and Iwerk's creation of such characters as Oswald the Lucky Rabbit — who delighted audiences with his stretchable arms and expandable car — soon put the Walt Disney Company well ahead of the game. But it was Mickey Mouse, born on 18 November, 1928, with the release of the cartoon *Steamboat Willie*, who secured their success. The mouse, drawn by Iwerks, not by Disney as it's sometimes claimed (though he did have Disney's voice), was soon receiving more fan mail than any other star in Hollywood. Most of the 119 Mickey Mouse cartoons were made during the next ten years.

THE SINGING MENAGERIE

Disney took full advantage of the coming of sound. *Steamboat Willie* was his first talkie, followed by the "Silly Symphony" series. This series exploited the notion that it was easier to draw cartoons to complement the beat of a prerecorded sound track, rather than the other way round, and resulted in such classic cartoons as *The Skeleton Dance* (1929) and *The Three Little Pigs* (1933) - and its hit song, "Who's Afraid of the Big Bad Wolf?". Goofy, Pluto and Donald Duck soon appeared to add their voices to the hullabaloo.

DISNEY HITS

By the late Thirties, Disney wanted to try his hand at making a full-length cartoon feature. The introduction of three-strip colour and the use of new multi-plane cameras meant that such an ambitious project was possible. Risking everything he had on the new venture, Disney started work on *Snow White and the Seven Dwarfs* (1937). The gamble paid off. On general release from February 1938, *Snow White* broke records all over the world, and its two songs "Whistle While You Work" and "Heigh Ho!" became instant hits. *Snow White* grossed more than $8 million on its first release (The Wizard of Oz only made $2 million). *Snow White* was quickly followed by *Pinocchio* (1940), *Fantasia* (1940), *The Reluctant Dragon* (1941), *Dumbo* (1941) and *Bambi* (1942).

TV AND THEME PARKS

In the Fifties, Disney diversified into film and made a series of nature documentaries, many

of which won him Oscars. He also formed a subsidiary company, Buena Vista, to distribute them. And, with the same innovation that he had brought to capitalising on the advent of sound, Disney was quick to embrace the possibilities of television. In 1954 he launched a weekly series, originally known as "Disneyland". It ran in one form or another until 1990.

Disneyland, the first of the theme parks, opened in 1955 in California. It became one of the world's greatest tourist attractions. Florida's Disney World came next. France's Euro-Disney is not yet in profit.

WHAT'S IN A NAME

Goofy was originally known as Dippy Dawg and planned to be a composite of "an everlasting optimist, a gullible Good Samartian, a half-wit... and a hick." The Seven Dwarfs were nearly named Blabby, Hotsy, Biggy-Wiggy, Biggo-Ego, Weepy, Jaunty and Awful. We nearly didn't have a Dopey - there were fears that the name would be associated with drug-taking.

Top left: *Snow White and the Seven Dwarfs*, Disney's first full-length animated feature. Above: *The Lion King*, 1994's cartoon blockbuster. Left: *The Jungle Book* (1967), one of the all-time great box-office hits.

suggestions. I asked Richard to re-score it again - and suddenly the scene was wonderful."

For Robert Zemeckis, who directed all three of the *Back to the Future* movies, choosing the right composer is as important as finding a marriage partner. Someone who has the talent and empathy to complement the director's screen images is so rare that Zemeckis regards Al Silvestri as his musical soul mate. Ever since 1984, when he made *Romancing the Stone*, he has worked exclusively with Silvestri. Music can sometimes become a vulgar manipulator, but Zemeckis sees music as another member of the cast, an important extra character who gives the audience emotional signals. Zemeckis and Silvestri are always in harmony; for example, "Al won't write music where he doesn't feel it should be, and silence is also very much part of the composition of music. For a composer to understand silence as well as music is very rare."

Richard Fleischer, veteran director of nearly 50 films, enjoys the distinction of having used no music at all in three of them. In his classic 1952 thriller, *The Narrow Margin*, the action takes place in sleeping compartments, corridors and a restaurant car of a train. "The sound of the train was music to me, and I used it as music." *Compulsion*, made in 1959, and based on the Leopold-Loeb murder case, was set mainly in the courtroom. The overall tone of unsentimental, intellectual compassion would, in Fleischer's view, have been hurt by the use of music; and in 1968, when he made *The Boston Strangler*, there was not one melodramatic chord to be heard.

But of course, not every director has the confidence of a Richard Fleischer; and when "incidental" music is brilliantly conceived, it can make the work of a run-of-the-mill director seem polished. Where music is composed in the service of a genius like Hitchcock, the composer has to be the master's equal. Bernard Herrmann's best work is found in fifties and Sixties Hitchcock. It is interesting that for the unforgettable shower scene Hitchcock didn't want to use music at all. Fortunately, he listened to Bernard Herrmann - and when *we* listen to him, we hardly need to see the film images to have them dancing before our inner eye. Perhaps that's why Hitch didn't want any music.

The arrival of sound, of course, brought more than just background music to films. It created a new film genre. As sound was perfected, and cameras were at last released from their prison walls, words were joined by music - music that was now free in ways it had never been free before, both technically and artistically. Such composers as Irving Berlin, George and Ira Gershwin, Jerome Kern, Irving Berlin, and Cole Porter sat up, took notice and started writing directly for the screen - and in particular, for the Hollywood musical.

After the success of *The Jazz Singer*, too many musicals had been churned out, most of them recycling the back-stage musical plot that was the romantic spine of the 1929 film, *Broadway Melody*. This was MGM's first talking picture, and the world's very first musical. Although it was technically primitive, it took the Oscar for Best Film. As a result of the rush to make musicals, audiences suffered a severe attack of indigestion. But fast-acting relief came from a man who was entirely ignorant of the mechanics of film, a theatre director called Busby Berkeley.

The vaudeville star, Eddie Cantor, was touring in a stage musical called *Whoopee!* and Sam Goldwyn wanted to put it on the screen.

Broadway Melody, MGM's first talking picture, with Mary Doran, Anita Page and Bessie Love. The film was re-made in 1944 as *Two Girls and a Sailor*, with June Allyson, Gloria DeHaven and Van Johnson.

392-89

Busby Berkeley. Sam Goldwyn was reluctant to hire him, but Eddie Cantor, star of the hit show, *Whoopee!,* knew the stage choreographer was a genius.

Cantor persuaded Goldwyn (who wasn't too keen because he had heard that the choreographer had a drink problem) to take on Berkeley as dance director for the film. A. Scott Berg, in his book, *Goldwyn,* tells us that the night *Whoopee!* closed in Cleveland, Eddie Cantor and Berkeley went to a restaurant, where the choreographer sketched designs for the major dance numbers on the back of a menu. The next day, they boarded a train for Hollywood, where Berkeley was, in Cantor's words, 'to revolutionise the making of musical films'. They talked their way across the country, 'for there were many changes to be made in transposing *Whoopee!* to the screen'. Berkeley already had in mind several techniques that were to become his trademarks, including the use of chorus girls making kaleidoscopic patterns when filmed from overhead. He had also dreamed up an ingeniously simple way of showing off the beauty of his dancing girls in their opening Stetson-hat number; the camera would hold on just one of them in close-up, and she would fall away, revealing another pretty girl, and so on down the line. This captivated audiences when, in 1930, the film *Whoopee* opened. Berkeley, in well over 50 films, worked his magic in Hollywood for the next 32 years.

Although the screen musical had its roots in the stage operetta and musical comedy, it was a totally new animal, recognised as such largely because of the talents of producers and directors such as Arthur Freed, Busby Berkeley, Vincente Minnelli, Ernst Lubitsch and Rouben Mamoulian. But the actual *making* of a musical was probably the most specialised, the most difficult, the most exacting, in the whole movie business.

Gene Kelly, in the foreword to Clive Hirschhorn's book, *The Hollywood Musical*, says, "The members of the group at MGM during

A Berkeley trademark from *Footlight Parade* (1933).

my tenure there were very serious about musicals. That is not to say that we didn't make them to entertain and uplift the spirit, but we thought that to do this effectively they had to be superbly crafted; and that meant the closest kind of collaboration among the choreographers, directors, producers, musicians, conductors, musical arrangers, designers, costumiers - the list is endless. There were probably more assembled talents in this field at Metro than anywhere else at any other time."

An example of just how fiendishly complicated shooting a musical sequence can be is the scarf number with Gene Kelly and Cyd Charisse from *Singin' in the Rain* (1952). It sounds wonderful and looks effortless, the art that conceals art; in fact, it concealed a good deal more than that. Cyd Charisse's scarf was endlessly long, and it looked as if the only way to make her ethereal partner dance was to use a wind machine. Unfortunately, this good old studio standby just wasn't up to the job, so co-directors Kelly and Stanley Donen sent out for two enormous aeroplane engines, and bolted them to the floor. The result was an unstable mixture of aerodynamics, choreography, and fingers crossed in case Cyd got blown out of her knickers. Still - one might think - the music must have been a help. In fact, the dancers couldn't hear it. They were desperately counting the beats.

Over at RKO, in 1933, almost ten years before Kelly arrived at MGM, Fred and Ginger started their unique partnership which was to last for seven years and nine films - with a reunion in 1949 when they made *The Barkleys of Broadway*. Ginger was sexy, street-wise and fun; Fred was classy and debonair, the elegant opposite of Gene Kelly's burly muscularity. To watch Astaire today, dancing alongside any of his contemporary male hoofers, be it George Murphy or even the man Fred most admired, Jack Buchanan, one's eyes are drawn irresistibly to Astaire; the magic is forever captured on film.

Warner Brothers were making musicals too, of course. While Fred and Ginger were *Flying Down to Rio* (1933), Warners made *Footlight Parade* (1933) and *42nd Street* (1933) - Warner Baxter to Ruby Keeler: "You're going out a youngster but you've got to come back a star!" - and rustled up their yearly "Gold Digger" film, starring the likes of James Cagney, Joan Blondell and Dick Powell. Paramount had Ernst Lubitsch and Rouben Mamoulian - *The Love Parade* (1929), *One Hour With You* (1932), and *Love Me Tonight* (1932) - all with Paramount's star, Maurice Chevalier.)

Their fourth movie together. Fred Astaire and Ginger Rogers in 1935 in the comedy musical, *Top Hat*.

Rita Hayworth, the one-time Spanish dancer, in *Gilda*. The woman who married, among others, Orson Welles, said, "Every man I've known has fallen in love with Gilda and woken up with me." She meant Rita Cansino.

The Hollywood musical also created a new kind of performer - the teenage musical star. Judy Garland and Mickey Rooney at MGM - all eyes and teeth in *Babes in Arms* (1939) and *Strike Up the Band* (1940); and, over at Universal, the classy girl next door, Deanna Durbin, and her occasional rival, Gloria Jean. Then with the outbreak of war, musicals, always escapist, were given a new rationale for their escapism - boosting morale with Rita Hayworth and Betty Grable pin-ups for the boys overseas.

Within the genre of the musical there was an interesting sub-division - the musical biopic - everything from James Stewart in *The Glenn Miller Story* (1953), Tyrone Power as Irving Berlin in *Alexander's Ragtime Band* (1938), Cary Grant pretending to be Cole Porter in *Night and Day* (1946); to biographies of such classical composers and musicians as Grieg in *Song of Norway* (1970), Johann Strauss Jnr in *The Great Waltz* (1938 and again in 1972) and Rimsky-Korsakov in *Song of Scheherezade* (1947). Rather unfairly, Beethoven has starred in only three biopics, while the more flashy Schubert was immortalised seven times.

With honourable exceptions, film biographies of the great have little to do with reality; and there is a further sub-division which might be called Blood on the Keys, derived from *A Song to Remember* (1945) with Cornel Wilde as Copin. This is the kind of film in which, if the central character sneezes, or stumbles, or gives a discreet cough - accompanied by a brave smile or a shifty look, - we know that in about 20 minutes' time he'll drop off the twig .

The big technical difficulty, of course, was how to make matinee idols look convincing as musicians. In *The Magic Bow*, Stewart Granger, as Paganini, was known in the trade, and behind his back, as Old Banana Fingers. If they'd sat him down in front of a piano next to Cornel Wilde and cast him as Chopin's twin brother, it would have been impossible for him to hit less than two keys at a time.

172

The Magic Bow was made in 1946, but mainstream musicals in Britain had done rather well in the Thirties - with stars like Jack Buchanan, Jessie Matthews, Gracie Fields, Anna Neagle and George Formby. In fact, Jessie Matthews was very nearly the successor to Ginger Rogers. Fred Astaire greatly admired Miss Matthews' work in *The Midshipmaid* (1932) and *Evergreen* (1934) and wanted her to be his partner after Ginger moved on. Contractual difficulties prevented this which was a bitter disappointment for Jessie Matthews, whose musical career never really got going again after the war.

In such a specialised field as musicals, it is extraordinary that Robert Wise, a director who had never made a musical before, came up with two Academy Award-winners which were also hugely successful at the box office, *West Side Story* in 1961 and - four years later - *The Sound of Music*.

West Side Story, as with any musical, required the pre-scoring of all the music and lyrics ready for playback on the set or on location,

When Fred and Ginger broke up, Astaire wanted British dancer Jessie Matthews to take her place. Sadly, the partnership never happened. In this scene from *Evergreen*, Jessie is on the right.

The hills are alive with the sound of Julie Andrews.

and months of rehearsals with the dancers; in other words, planning, preparation and pre-production. Post-production also included the superb special effect lap dissolve from the dress shop to the opening of the gym number which was achieved by the optical effects supervisor, Linwood Dunn, only after he'd tried eight or ten versions. All of this, not forgetting the screenplay and its rewrites, took up almost two years of Robert Wise's life.

In 1965, he made *The Sound of Music*. Like John Ford, whose fresh film techniques became the clichés of his imitators, Robert Wise, master editor that he is, performed some cunning sleight of hand with the songs, jump-cutting between locations, a technique which later became standard. To start with, though, Robert Wise's problem was how to get rid of the schmaltz. In fact, although Christopher Plummer moaned in later years, "It's very sad to be remembered for something as lightweight as The Sound of Mucus", the director and his writer Ernest Lehman, with the perhaps surprising, but wholehearted support of Julie Andrews, succeeded in stripping the story of much of its sentimentality. It seems unfair, to say the least, that the star's perceived image - the strapping, no-nonsense head girl with a heart and voice of gold - has militated against her over the years.

When Robert Wise first met Julie Andrews, *Mary Poppins* (1965) had not yet been released. The director was charmed, impressed, charmed again and remains to this day her greatest admirer, in particular for her work - and help - on the film. With Julie it was "Rehearse, rehearse, rehearse, can't do it too well. I'd say 'Print that' and she'd ask, 'Can I do it once more? I think I can get it a little better.' You've just got to love someone like that." She was also Ms Nice Guy, unfailingly polite and considerate to everyone, wonderful with the children in the film, keeping them happy, laughing and joking with them, generally taking them under her wing like (oh *dear*)... Mary Poppins.

Mr Not So Nice Guy, on the other hand, has an equally undeserved image as a good-humoured, likeable, modest, totally professional star. Rex Harrison possessed just one of those qualities. When Richard Fleischer directed him in *Dr Doolittle* (1967), Harrison, unlike most performers, refused to mime to his own playback on the set. He preferred to "speak-sing" live to the animals, treating them like actors - probably because he treated his fellow-actors like animals. He announced that he could relate to parrot, chicken, monkey or pig only if they had eye contact with him. The star would sometimes stop in the middle of a thus-far perfect take to complain to Fleischer, "It isn't *looking* at me!" All eventually went well, and in post-production, there were only one or two bits of *Doolittle* to be re-recorded; but Harrison announced that he wasn't satisfied with the way he had sung *all seven of his songs*. When Lionel Newman, the flamboyant, profanity-prone head of Fox's music department, heard what Rex wanted to do, he exploded. "There's no way it can be done. Harrison may be a f——— genius, but that much of a genius he ain't!" Harrison was attempting to stay on key, keep in tempo, change the way he had originally sung or spoken certain words, and do it all in perfect synchronisation. Lionel whispered to Dick Fleischer, "If he can do that, I'll kiss his ass in Macy's window on Christmas Eve." After two rehearsals Rex was ready for a take. The playback was perfect. Fleischer says today, "Rex was a pain in the neck. But he was a genius."

From Dickens to Lionel Bart to Carol Reed. *Oliver!* **had Mark Lester as Oliver Twist and Jack Wild as the Artful Dodger.**

Today, the musical proper is in limbo. Disney's 1992 attempt, called *Newsies* (UK: *The News Boys*), with Bill Pullman and Ann-Margret, was a flop, as was Fox's Bette Midler vehicle, *For The Boys* (1991). Back in the Sixties, very few original Hollywood musicals were made, other than *Mary Poppins*, *Thoroughly Modern Millie* (1968), *Bedknobs and Broomsticks* (1971) and the conveyor-belt Presley films. Fail-safe Broadway hits were still produced - *Pal Joey* (1957), *Oklahoma!* (1955), *South Pacific* (1958), *The*

TOP OF THE POPS

*B*eing a pop star is never quite enough. Being a pop star AND a movie star is where it's at; and, to their credit, most of the following crooners didn't do too badly when they transferred their talents to the big screen.

POP STARS WHO HAVE ACTED IN NON-MUSICAL ROLES

John Lennon	*How I Won the War* (1967)
Marianne Faithfull	*Girl on a Motocycle* (1968)
Glenn Campbell	*True Grit* (1969)
Arlo Guthrie	*Alice's Restaurant* (1969)
Mick Jagger	*Performance* (1970)
Art Garfunkel	*Carnal Knowledge* (1971)
Bob Dylan	*Pat Garrett and Billy the Kid* (1973)
Diana Ross	*Mahogany* (1975)
David Bowie	*The Man Who Fell to Earth* (1976)
Tom Waits	*Down By Law* (1986)
Deborah Harry	*Union City* (1980)
Sting	*Brimstone and Treacle* (1982)
Madonna	*Desperately Seeking Susan* (1985)
Tina Turner	*Mad Max Beyond Thunderdome* (1985)
Roland Gift	*Sammy and Rosie Get Laid* (1987)
Sonny Bono	*Hairspray* (1988)
Phil Collins	*Buster* (1988)
Cher	*Mermaids* (1990)
k.d. Lang	*Salmonberries* (1992)
Janet Jackson	*Poetic Justice* (1994)

King and I (1956), *Fiddler on the Roof* (1967), *My Fair Lady* (1964)... and, of course, *West Side Story* and *The Sound of Music*; but Hollywood stopped making them in the end. Ironically the last musical to win the Oscar for Best Picture was *Oliver!* in 1968 - and that was British.

The days when MGM was at its prodigious best, with so many music professionals, composers and lyricists under contract, together with a wealth of in-house facilities, are long gone; but ask Robert Wise if he thinks the age of the musical is over, and he says, "No. I think they run, like other things to do with the film business, in cycles. We seem to be in a kind of non-musical cycle right now, but I'm sure they'll be coming back."

Musicals may have disappeared from our screens, but songs are as important to films now as they were when *The Jazz Singer* gave movies its first voice - in some ways even more important. In recent years music has almost taken the movie industry prisoner - a willing prisoner - because today, it is quite possible for a film's songs to make more money than the film itself. That's what happened with *The Bodyguard* (1992). Whitney Houston's album of the songs she sang in the movie grossed more than the picture.

Money Money Money and *The Bodyguard*. Whitney Houston's best-seller topped the film it was in.

Film music that takes off on its own isn't a new phenomenon, of course. Twenty-six years ago, in 1969, a song that had nothing whatever to do with the movie it was in, is still popular today; and although it was in one sense bolted on to the story, "Raindrops Keep Falling on my Head" nevertheless perfectly characterised the spirit of *Butch Cassidy and the Sundance Kid* (1969), out-buddying its own buddy movie.

The popular success of simple melodies can be enormous but impossible to predict, of course. There are any number of songs, for example, which have been popular for a week or two and then totally forgotten... until suddenly, for one reason or another, typically with the added luck of perfect timing, they resurface to become hits, and sometimes standards. Take a little number called "As Time Goes By". It was already in decline when Max Steiner tried to remove it from *Casablanca* (1942) because, not unreasonably, he wanted all the music in the film to be his; but Warners told him he was stuck with it, because the film - and with it the song - had already been shot. Steiner was puzzled; composers nearly always composed to a completed film, so the offending scenes could be reshot, surely? In the name of continuity, absolutely not - Ingrid Bergman had just had her hair cut short for her next film, *For Whom The Bell Tolls* (1943). And so a song that had almost been forgotten bounced back with a little help from a piano player called Sam.

The same year that *Casablanca* came out, Bing Crosby and Fred Astaire appeared together in a musical called *Holiday Inn* (1942). The hit of the show was Irving Berlin's "White Christmas", sung, of course, by Bing Crosby. It turned up again almost immediately in another movie called *Blue Skies* (1946), and then twelve years later, Danny Kaye, Rosemary Clooney, Vera-Ellen - and Crosby - sang it together in a musical that was called *White Christmas* (1954). But it had always been Bing's song, really, and his solo recording of it eventually went to 25 million copies.

Even the professionals - perhaps especially the professionals - can't always spot a potential hit. After the first sneak preview of a 1939 MGM Technicolor musical, one of the numbers was very nearly cut, and only grudgingly left where it was; the song that almost got away was "Over the Rainbow".

On stage Ethel Merman belted out "There's No Business Like Show Business" well over a thousand times. It entered both the vocabulary and the list of all-time musical hits. So as a show-stopper, it could hardly be equalled. But creative inspiration blossoms under pressure; when Fred Astaire was making *The Band Wagon* in 1953 with Jack Buchanan, he asked songwriters Arthur Schwartz and Howard Dietz if they could possibly come up with a number that had the same kind of feel, the same kind of pezazz, the same kind of authentic showbiz feel as "There's No Business....." Schwartz and Dietz went away - and came back, less than an hour later, with "That's Entertainment".

The history of the cinema is littered with Firsts. One of them came in the 1952 classic western, *High Noon*, in which, for the first time, a narrative song was used to give us the plot in an easy-to-carry-tune:

High Noon, starring Gary Cooper, a Western full of Firsts and Best Evers, including an Oscar-winning song.

composer Dimitri Tiomkin won an Oscar for "Do Not Forsake Me Oh My Darlin".

And, of course, Walt Disney not only made the first ever feature-length cartoon, he also made sure that *Snow White and the Seven Dwarfs* (1937) - almost 60 years before *The Lion King* did exactly the same thing - had plenty of hummable tunes in it.

It was appropriately in the Sixties that the use of songs in movies took a new and revolutionary direction. And what better to launch the revolution than the music of the Beatles, those icons of a swinging decade. The man responsible was Richard Lester, the director of their first two films, *A Hard Day's Night* (1964) and *Help!* (1965). His freewheeling, anarchic way of shooting and editing their songs in those films kick-started a trend that would lead to today's pop video. Lester is modest about his achievement. He explains: "MTV very kindly sent me a piece of paper saying that I was the father of the music clip and, therefore, of MTV. But I have asked for a blood test. I don't think anybody ever sets out saying I'm going to do something revolutionary. I think you set out to say what are you trying to achieve at this point. I just managed to take what I felt was necessary to show the Beatles' personalities and their sense of energy and their sense of fun. Take the sequence in *Help!*, "Ticket to Ride". They're in the Alps and the first thing we felt was, let's put them on skis, because they've never been on skis before. So we got two cameras, went out in the snow, put the skis on and said, down that mountain, off you go, and anything that happened we filmed. We brought it back, laid up the track of "Ticket To Ride" and the editor, John Victor-Smith, started putting the images together. And in the first go, it was practically flawless."

☛ page 182

FILM

LAWRENCE OF ARABIA

COLUMBIA 1962

Producer: Sam Spiegel

Director: David Lean

Stars: Peter O'Toole, Omar Sharif, Alec Guinness, Arthur Kennedy, Anthony Quayle, Claude Rains, Jack Hawkins, Anthony Quinn

OSCARS

BEST PICTURE, DIRECTOR, CINEMATOGRAPHY, EDITING, ART DIRECTION, SOUND AND SCORE (ORIGINAL)

A.W. Lawrence, on hearing that Marlon Brando was to be considered for the part of his brother, commented: "I think it will inevitably mean that the film will be a flop, in this country at least."

Epic Plans

David Lean and the American producer Sam Spiegel, following their success with the stirring (and lucrative) drama *Bridge on the River Kwai* (1957), decided to collaborate again on another big picture. A film based the life of Ghandi was their first thought, but their nerve failed them at the last moment, and instead they paid out £20,000 for the memoirs of the desert hero, T.E. Lawrence.

Telling Tales

It was directed from a script by Robert Bolt which did not much resemble T.E. Lawrence's *The Seven Pillars of Wisdom*, and Lawrence's brother, A.W. Lawrence, refused to let Spiegel use the book's title. But although the resulting film may not have been true to Lawrence, it turned out to be one of the most exciting and beautiful productions of the decade.

Right: The film catapulted the little-known Peter O'Toole to instant stardom, and it was a good career move for Omar Sharif. Below: Director David Lean, the ultimate perfectionist, examining Anthony Quinn's make-up.

Left: The famous charge on Aqaba, filmed in Southern Spain, was captured in one remarkable tracking shot.

THE MAIN MAN

Marlon Brando was Lean's first choice to play the enigmatic Lawrence, but the actor was more tempted by an offer to film *Mutiny on the Bounty* (1962) in the South Pacific. Montgomery Clift was interested, as was Richard Burton; but it was Albert Finney who was actually screen-tested for the part (at the cost of £100,000), but who turned it down on the grounds that he hated being committed to a girl, a film producer or "a certain kind of big-screen image". A nose-job and eye operation later, it was the relatively unknown Peter O'Toole who was flown out to the desert to start filming.

PRODUCTION VALUES

Spiegel spent $13 million filming in Jordan, Morocco, Spain and Britain, slightly over-stepping the original budget of $2.5 million. The original plan was to spend only four months in the desert, but the crew was there for a good part of 1960, being maintained at a cost of $50,000 a week. Anthony Nutting, an ex-foreign office man, Arabist, and friend of King Hussein of Jordan, saved Spiegel money when he persuaded the King to hire out his army for £150,000. The King had originally suggested that £1,000,000 would be appropriate. O'Toole was given a deck chair to sit on in between takes, while Alec Guinness retired to a de-luxe caravan. In time, O'Toole was granted a hut for his deck chair - unfortunately it blew away.

ACCIDENTIAL HERO

O'Toole did most of his own stunts and, in the course of filming, managed to crack his skull, tear his groin, and strain most of his muscles. A camel bite left him without the use of two fingers, and he suffered third-degree sunburn. He drowned his sorrows by disappearing for all-night drinking sessions with Omar Sharif. It took 19 takes before David Lean was satisfied with his shot of Lawrence facing the sandstorms of Sinai. O'Toole had to keep his eyes open everytime.

EPILOGUE

David Lean's film not only took a long time to shoot, it was a long film. Spiegel forced Lean to wrap up the shooting by booking *Lawrence* for the 1962 Royal Command Performance. The audience that night sat through 3 hours and 45 minutes. Thereafter, 25 minutes were cut. But in 1989, David Lean, with the help of a rough-cut from Martin Scorsese, was able to reassemble his original film from scratch.

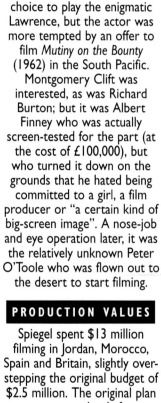

Then, a few years later, another kind of tradition was born. The music wasn't created for the film - it came from outside. *American Graffiti*, made in 1973, celebrated the early Sixties - and the music drove the film. It cost $750,000 to make and took $55 million at the box office. *American Graffiti* started the trend of a soundtrack based on pop and rock music. The idea soon spread as *Saturday Night Fever* (1977), *Grease* (1978), *Fame* (1980) *The Blues Brothers* (1980) and *Purple Rain* (1984) followed.

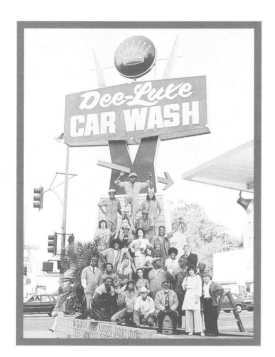

A genuine musical eccentric hit the screens in 1976, a film called *Car Wash*, produced by Art Linson, with a music score by Norman Whitfield. Linson's partner-to-be, Gary Stromberg, turned up at The Troubadour Club dressed in full African Dashiki day-wear, and wrote the story on a paper napkin with titles for songs (examples - "Niggers and Jews Have the Right to The Blues", "You Gotta Believe, I Used to Hate it Till I Ate It", "Hog Man", and the one about a guy who drives a caddy and washes cars with his body. Art Linson said, "Great idea."

Car Wash became one of the first big movies to use music to sell itself. When the film opened Art Linson was in Chicago and the song, "Car Wash" was already at number one: "So the kids were outside the the-

"A film called *Car Wash* about a car wash... set to *music?* You've got to be joking..."

atre waiting to get in, dancing to the hit record." The picture cost $1.8 million and made all the money back the first weekend it was released. It was a hit. Joel Schumacher, the writer who turned Gary Stromberg's paper napkin into a screenplay, is a self-confessed pop-culture sponge; he was delighted when film critic Vincent Canby said, "*Car Wash* is not about pop culture. It *is* pop culture."

The year 1994 saw the feel-good gumping of America. For Paramount Studios, *Forrest Gump* felt rather better than good, because in three months it grossed over $300 million. In the same period, one-and-a-half million copies of the soundtrack album were sold, a shrewdly packed time capsule containing 40 years of nostalgia - a misty-eyed wallow for every member of the family. So today, music is not just important for our enjoyment of a movie - it is part of the financial package. And when music is already in the public mind, film companies can find themselves in mega-buck heaven.

It's interesting that while the big escapist musicals were still being made in the Fifties we were still getting over the war years. In the relaxed Sixties and hopeful Seventies when unemployment was still something that happened to other people, we didn't mind our musicals having a hard edge to them - *West Side Story* with its New York street gangs, *Oh What a Lovely War!* (1969), Ken Russell's dark musical, *Tommy* (1975), about a deaf, dumb and blind boy who becomes a rock star.

But in the present climate, where are the escapist musicals? In a sense they're back, in the shape of *The Little Mermaid* (1989), *Beauty and the Beast* (1991), *Aladdin* (1992) and *The Lion King* (1994) which have brought back the musical in a new form.

The Golden Age of the musical may have gone, but fortunately for us - and for our children - Hollywood has left us a rich legacy of the very best in this tradition. Musicals that will never die because they have become legend.

Gene Kelly in the Oscar-winning *An American in Paris*.

CHAPTER 6

The Grand Illusion

In the cinema, nothing is what it seems. Real movie-makers, with the blood of Griffith and Gance and Hitchcock in their veins, love special effects, from the most elaborate down to the smallest. Francois Truffaut adored them and, in 1973, celebrated every last one, it seemed, in his film, *Day for Night*. The title is industry jargon meaning that a location scene is shot in broad daylight but with a blue filter on the camera lens to give the illusion of night. Film-makers can make their own weather, too, from a gentle drizzle to snow; from a slight breeze to stir the heroine's curls to a raging typhoon.

Special effects involve all kinds of separate elements coming together on screen - optical tricks, painting on glass, the use of models, miniatures, the matte (where part of the picture is masked off so that the film can be rewound and a second image added to replace the

Georges Méliès made *A Trip to the Moon* in 1902. From *Metropolis* to *Forrest Gump*, it all goes back to Méliès.

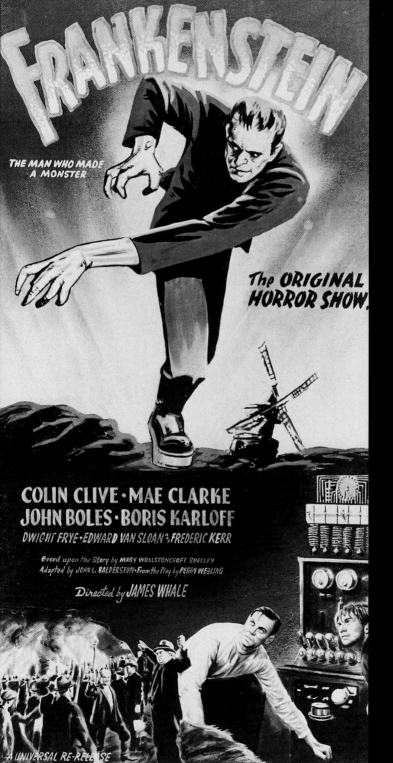

Boris Karloff poster advertising the James Whale classic. Would audiences have been quite so terrified if the actor playing the monster had been billed as William Henry Pratt?

masked-off portion), animation, all the way through to the computerised magic of morphing and laser-painting. So it's not surprising
that we tend to think of special effects as, well, special, inhabiting the
world of horror films and science fiction, turning Jekylls into Hydes,
melting monsters and morphing men; but the fact is that special
effects are not special in the sense of being unique to cinema fantasy,
because *there is no such thing as a film without special effects.*

Film itself is an illusion, relying on a specific human frailty - our
inability to separate still images when they follow one another at
speed, the physical handicap known as persistence of vision. Once its
immutable law was understood, endless subtleties followed. Close-ups
focus our attention on what the director wants us to see, editing
manipulates time and space, actors are sentenced to death on the cutting room floor; lighting, gauze and make-up can turn attractive
women into great beauties, while men become romantic, heroic or
designer-rugged.

Simple tricks can change an actor's vital statistics. There is a triv-
ially pursued claim that Alan Ladd was 5ft 0in. He was actually 5ft
7in, but still a bit on the short side for a hero; and yet, is there anyone taller in the saddle than *Shane* (1952)? Director George Stevens
made sure that his star was rarely seen in long shot, and then only
when alone or on his horse.

It's all a matter of getting things in perspective, although quite
often the perspective is false; or psychological. Humphrey Bogart, as
Casablanca Rick, found Ingrid Bergman's Ilsa infinitely desirable,
utterly adorable, and more than a trifle lofty. But who cares today how
tall Bogart or Bergman were? They are the stuff of legend; and the
hero of *Casablanca* (1942) has inspired small men everywhere, as
Woody Allen triumphantly showed us in *Play It Again Sam*, when he
delivered Bogie's farewell speech to a 1972 Ilsa.

Like gods, film-makers can give their performers gifts they never
had. In *Deception* (1946), a follow-up film exploiting the success of
Bette Davis and Paul Henreid in *Now, Voyager* (1942), Henreid is a
cellist - and the film climaxes with his virtuoso performance playing
in a concert. But because the actor could not play the cello, the hands
we see on screen are those of a professional cellist. Henreid's arms are
tied behind his back.

Film editing works its own magic; and some editors are very
resourceful, especially when there's an unforeseen shortage of materi-

al. Director Billy Wilder is quoted by Tony Curtis in his autobiography: at the first preview of *Some Like It Hot* (1959), Wilder found that the audience started to laugh as soon as they saw the legs of two "women" hurrying to catch their train. Then, as the camera revealed Jack Lemmon and Tony Curtis in drag, the laughter became a roar, and Wilder decided to provide more of the same by re-editing the sequence; to do it he had to use every single take of the actors walking past the same three cars. "They go by the same cars five times, but people don't know it", says Wilder. "That's when film-making gets to be fun."

A small effect was used by Alfred Hitchcock in his 1941 thriller, *Suspicion*. Roughly two-thirds of the way through, we see Cary Grant climbing the stairs to say goodnight to his rich wife, Joan Fontaine. By this time, cast against type, Grant has lost something of his country-house-cred, having, for all we and Joan Fontaine know, done the sort of things that Basil Rathbone would take in his everyday stride. Is it really possible that Cary murdered his bumbling old pal, Nigel Bruce? Is he, even as we watch his steady progress upwards, planning to smother Joan Fontaine with a pillow? Will he reveal himself as his identical twin from the bin? Or... *has he put something a bit stronger than milk in her milk?* Hitchcock, eschewing a vulgar close-up, concentrates our minds and our eyes wonderfully; in the glass that Grant carries, he has put a tiny light.

There is a marvellously funny scene in Buster Keaton's film *The Boat* (1921). As the boat leaves the jetty with Buster standing to attention on deck, it sinks. But getting it to sink caused Buster and his crew enormous problems. They tried everything from from loading it with pig iron to filling it with holes. In fact - in the shot it isn't actually sinking, it's being pulled down by a winch from a tug just out of camera shot.

Curtis and Lemmon. Two worn-out pairs of legs in *Some Like It Hot*.

Nothing in films is what it seems. A simple gag in *Young Sherlock Holmes* (1985) was not at all simple in its execution. Ash falls from the cigar of an old man asleep in a chair at his club; it is caught by a waiter with an ashtray. It looks simple enough. But to achieve the effect a fake cigar had to be made with a magnet, a mechanism and a wire which led to an assistant who could press a button to make the ash fall off just at the right moment!

Not just what, but where a film is shot is more often than not an illusion. Milford Junction - where, in *Brief Encounter* (1945), Celia Johnson and Trevor Howard fanned the flames of a hopeless passion, was, in reality, Carnforth Station, at the foot of the Lake District. In the Spaghetti Westerns, Spain doubled as the Wild West; Francis Coppola turned the Philippines into Vietnam for *Apocalypse Now* (1979); and in *Full Metal Jacket* (1987), Stanley Kubrick shot in East London at Beckton Gas Works. So in the world of special effects the end justifies the means.

In the early days of cinema, before special effects became a separate profession, visual deceits were the responsibility, indeed the prerogative of the cameraman. Freddie Young, the distinguished cinematographer, now in his nineties, always regarded special effects as part of his job. For David Lean's *Dr Zhivago* (1965), Spain had become Russia and, for part of the film, the unit was shooting in northern Spain where a certain amount of snow had fallen; unfortu-

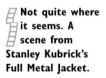

Not quite where it seems. A scene from Stanley Kubrick's Full Metal Jacket.

nately, there wasn't nearly enough of it to suit David Lean. The art department set to work to build a house which was covered in candle -grease icicles, and the trees were skillfully sprayed with whitewash; but through the thin carpet of snow on the field, the furrows were still visible. Freddie arranged for a nearby marble factory to deliver hundreds of tons of marble dust - to thicken the snow. It wouldn't have done for the actors, of course - they received a light dusting of rock salt over their hats and shoulders, while shaving soap provided the "frost" on their moustaches.

Another Freddie Young special was the famous scene in *Lawrence of Arabia* (1962) when Omar Sharif, mirage-like, endlessly approaches the camera. Just before Freddie went to Hollywood to sort out his equipment, director David Lean asked him to think about how the "mirage" might be shot. As he was strolling round the Panavision Cameras factory, an Aladdin snapping up metal-and-glass treasures, Freddie chanced upon a very long lens for which, he was informed, there was little demand. "It was 470mm or something, and it gave me

Dr Zhivago. All that glisters is not cold. The snow here is marble dust.

Anthony Quinn
as Barabbas
in Richard
Fleischer's epic.

an idea." It sounded good to Lean who, on the day of the shoot, pointed Omar Sharif and his camel in the direction of the horizon. Sharif kept going until he was little more than a pinpoint in the distance. "So we shot about a thousand feet with this tiny little figure coming towards the camera." The sequence is, of course, one of the most memorable in the film.

Some special effects are physically big and correspondingly expensive; but *Barabbas*, made in 1962, contained an effect that was God-given. Richard Fleischer's art director had discovered, quite by chance, that a total eclipse of the sun was due. Fleischer decided to shoot the opening sequence just before, and during the eclipse. At considerable expense, a hill was constructed outside Rome, the three crosses required for the scene were erected; everything was made ready in time for the eclipse. Meanwhile, many local people, hearing that something unusual was going on, had gathered to watch and, as the eclipse began, they fell to their knees and prayed. The filming was a gamble because the cameraman was afraid that flares from the sun would ruin the shot. When Fleischer ran the processed film, there was indeed a flare; it was immediately above the central cross - and it was in the *shape* of a cross. Fleischer says, "I tell you, when we saw that, we said it was the hand of God. We've often been accused of doctoring the film but we never touched it. It's one of the greatest special effects of all time, and it had nothing to do with computers or anything else."

In the field of special effects, as with most aspects of the cinema, it is difficult, if not impossible, to pin down who did or made or devised something first. So many people were working all over the world at the same time that overlaps and simultaneous cries of "Eureka!" were bound to occur. The story of special effects, therefore, is the continuing story of development, every generation building on the work of the last.

At the start of the century, a genius who was a writer, director, technician, designer and an actor, produced a cornucopia of visual effects which has never been replaced. Improved upon, yes, but there is nothing in the cinema today that does not owe a debt to Georges Méliès, whose most famous "enchantment" fantasy, *A Trip to the Moon*, was made in 1902. Working alone in a small room just outside Paris, he made magic that astonished the world; but he in turn owed a debt to the theatre, where trapdoors, mir-

rors and gadgets were the stage magician's stock in trade - and Méliès was originally a stage magician. But there is nothing that we see today, be it superimposition, dissolves, the use of models and miniatures, even morphing and digital effects, that is not in some way based on Méliès' pioneering work.

D.W. Griffith is credited with the first use of creative lighting. In *A Drunkard's Reformation* (1909) he used artificial lighting to create a "fireside glow", then the sunlight effect in *Pippa Passes* (1909) and the dim, religious light in *Threads of Destiny* (1910). Griffith's cameraman, Billy Bitzer, pioneered many lighting effects. Some tricks were discovered, like so many others, by accident. The opening scene of *Enoch Arden* (1911) uses backlighting, a technique Billy Bitzer

All but forgotten by the start of the Twenties, Georges Méliès (1861-1938) ended up running a railway-station tobacco kiosk, and died in a home for cinema veterans.

stumbled on when he turned his camera on Mary Pickford and Owen Moore as they sat at a shiny-topped table with the sun behind them. Normally, cameras were never pointed at the sun, but instead of the actors appearing in silhouette as Bitzer expected, their faces were bathed in a magical radiance - the effect of the sun reflected in the table top. Bitzer went on to devise a system using mirrors. One mirror would reflect the sun into a second, and the sunlight could then be directed to the back of the actor's head.

In the Twenties and Thirties, German cinema was a big influence on Hollywood, particularly in the area of special effects, where the Expressionist movement, allied to a love of fairy tales, gave set designers and special effects men almost limitless opportunities to explore fantasy and illusion. *The Cabinet of Dr Caligari*, made by Robert Wiene in 1919, was a success with an American audience usually resistant to anything "arty". Many German directors and technicians started to gravitate to California, among them Fritz Lang, who arrived in 1934. Seven years earlier, in 1927, he had made *Metropolis*.

Director Lang was a painter who had also studied engineering, and the design of his futuristic city is very architect-based - not surprisingly because he employed two architects and an engineer to design it. Waving his special-effects wand, he also played on mankind's dream of flight. Defying the laws of aerodynamics, Lang's aeroplanes flew below the level of the buildings in his city; and from *Metropolis* to *Blade Runner* (1982) and beyond, film-makers have been doing the same thing ever since.

Like Maria in *Metropolis*, robots and monsters of all kinds have been created by effects and make-up experts. There are all the screen

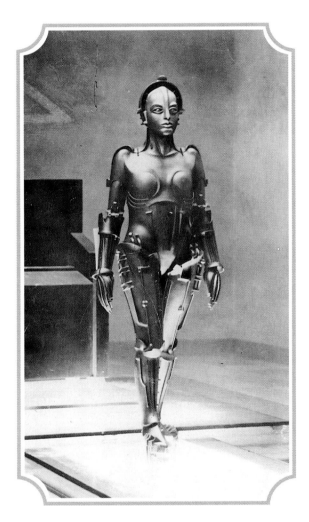

One of the sexiest robots of all time. Maria, created in 1927, is the star of Fritz Lang's *Metropolis*.

monsters of Frankenstein, the gunslingers and robot women in *Westworld* (1973), *Alien's* alien, Arnie's terminators and chrome men, and Maria's sexy robot descendant (Patricia Roc) in the 1949 film, *The Perfect Woman*. There have been Hydes galore, gremlins, were-wolves, vampires, the stand-up comic alien in top hat and tails from *Spaceballs* (1987), *King Kong* (1933 and 1976), *Mighty Joe Young* (1949), and a multitude of dinosaurs from *The Lost World* (1925) to *Jurassic Park* (1993). And throughout the cinema's hundred-year history, make-up and monsters have gone hand in hand, sometimes hand in glove puppet, occasionally *body* in puppet, as in *E.T. - The Extra-Terrestrial* (1982), when some of the several E.T.s made for the film were inhabited by small people, of whom the late Pat Billon (2ft 10in tall) is the best known. The Italian sculptor and inventor, Carlo Rambaldi, who had previously worked with Spielberg on *Close Encounters of the Third Kind* (1977), designed all the E.T. models, and won his third Oscar into the bargain.

A milestone in monster movies was the 1933 film, *King Kong*, made at RKO. Linwood Dunn, now in his 90s, was working there in the special-effects department, specialising in optical printing. The chief technician on *King Kong* was Willis O'Brien, a specialist in stop-action who, in 1924, had created the monster effects for *The Lost World* over at Warner Brothers. At RKO, Linwood wandered over to the separate stage which O'Brien and his crew used for their set-ups and animation. As he watched, he realised that some of the work could be done much more easily, faster and more efficiently by using an optical printer. He told them to shoot the animation, then give him the background and the animation and he would composite it on the optical printer. So very soon Linwood became part of the team, contributing notably to the famous scene in which Kong climbs the Empire State Building. The model of Kong was superimposed on what was in effect a silhouette of the building; then the optical printer was used to make the composite.

Ray Harryhausen, was 13 when he saw *King Kong* at his local cinema. As a young man, and as a direct result of seeing that film, he became a model maker, and later created the special effects for, among others, *Mighty Joe Young* (1949), *Jason and the Argonauts* (1963) and *The Golden Voyage of Sinbad* (1973.) "King Kong changed my life. It just struck a note in me than made me want to do this type of film-making - to put fantasy on the screen."

Today's special-effects maestro, Dennis Muren, who already has eight Oscars on his mantelpiece for visual effects, was influenced in his turn by Ray Harryhausen; in particular by his work on the 1953 film, *The Beast From 20,000 Fathoms*. Like the thirteen-year-old Harryhausen, Muren, at nine, was astonished by what he saw on the screen; scared, too, because he hid under the seat whenever the beast appeared. But as soon as he got home, he got out his still camera and photographed his collection of plastic dinosaurs in an attempt to reproduce what he'd seen.

Rick Baker, the make-up and special-effects artist who received an Oscar for his work on the 1981 film, *An American Werewolf in London*, worked on *Star Wars* (1977) and, more recently, did the make-up for *Wolf* (1994). Although only in his early 40s, Baker has always been impressed by the silent films of the actor, Lon Chaney Snr. Chaney was known as the Man of a Thousand Faces" because of his elaborate disguises in such films as *London After Midnight*, directed in 1927 by Tod Browning (but now lost), and Rupert Julian's 1925 version of *The Phantom of the Opera*. In those days, the raw materials for special make-ups were limited and, when creating one of his grotesques, Chaney had to make do with cotton, false teeth, nose putty and collodium - a highly inflammable liquid routinely used for making photographic plates, but pressed into service for make-up as a liquid plastic material, it was dangerous to use and uncomfortable on the skin. But Chaney's most reliable tools were his body and his face. Even before applying make-up, he could transform himself into Quasimodo, or indeed any living creature; a period joke was, "Don't step on that spider - it might be Lon Chaney." The make-up he first saw on TV and then in the cinema had a great impact on Baker. "I had a little make-up mirror I put in my bedroom, with little lights round it, and I would stand in front of it making all these faces. Sometimes I'd paint my face, and distort my mouth with this big set of false teeth." In *The Phantom of the Opera*, the cilmactic moment is the unmasking of the phantom. Rick often wishes he had been in the cinema when that moment was screened for the first time.

Another influence on him was the old Universal horror films, in particular James Whale's 1931 *Frankenstein* with Boris Karloff as the monster. Karloff's brow was built up over a period of six to eight hours by gluing cotton on his face and then painting it with the omnipresent collodium. "It's pretty horrible stuff, especially painted round your

eyes. When I'm working with an actor today and he complains about how uncomfortable it is - and remember, I'm using modern techniques and modern adhesives - I tell him it's nothing to what poor old Boris Karloff had to go through."

By the late Fifties, Ray Harryhausen had had his fill of monsters. Ever since *The Lost World* back in 1925, stop-motion animation had been identified with marauding dinosaurs or short-tempered monsters. In 1958, Harryhausen was ready for a change, and not simply the change into Technicolor for *The Seventh Voyage of Sinbad*. In the last few years, monsters had destroyed city after city - Rome, San Francisco, New York - and Ray wanted to use his skills with rather

☛ page 198

"Time we made a move, guys." Model supremo **Ray Harryhausen** with members of the cast of *The Seventh Voyage of Sinbad.*

★ 195 ★

GREAT MONSTER MAKE-UPS

*M*en - and very occasionally women - as, or turning into monsters - have been one of the enduring attractions of the cinema. Outlined Below are some of cinema's landmark monster creators "Which is he playing now?" - Somerset Maugham's famous put-down as he watched Spencer Tracy on the set in *Dr Jekyll and Mr Hyde* (1941).

1. Max Schreck as the first proper movie vampire in the surreal German masterpiece *Nosferatu, A Symphony of Terrors* (1922). A marvellously sinister-looking Count, called Orlok.

2. Lon Chaney Snr as *The Phantom of the Opera* (1925) - "The Man of a Thousand Faces". Famous for the unmasking scene when he reveals his grotesquely disfigured face.

3. Bela Lugosi as *Dracula* in the seminal 1931 film. The movie now creaks terribly, but we can forgive him anything the immortal lines "I... am Dracula. Welcome to my house" and "Children of the Night! What music they make!".

4. Boris Karloff as the creature in the 1931 horror masterpiece - *Frankenstein* The monster's mould-breaking make-up, designed by Jack Pierce, and Karloff's touching performance make this one of the all-time greats.

5. Boris Karloff, magnificent again, this time as the 4000-year-old corpse in *The Mummy* (1932). Two great make-ups by Jack Pierce: one a combination of linen, fuller's earth and clay that create the newly discovered mummy; the other, the wrinkled re-incarnated murderous creature inside the wrapping.

6. Charles Laughton as Quasimodo in *The Hunchback of Notre Dame* (1939). This is the best of several versions, thanks to the pathos of Laughton's brilliant performance and the make-up created from foam latex by George Bau.

7. Lon Chaney Jnr in the horror role he made his own - *The Wolf Man* (1941). Jack Pierce here created another eye-catching make-up - fangs, claws, a canine snout and lots of yak hair.

8. Christopher Lee in Hammer's genre-reviving version of *Dracula* (1958). Lee's stylish performance confirmed him as Karloff's successor to the monster crown. His The Mummy, a year later, which stayed wrapped up and used its eyes

9. David Naughton as *An American Werewolf in London* (1981). Rick Baker's Oscar-winning make-up and clever technology created one of the most stunning transformation scenes in horror films. A lycanthropic classic.

10. Jeff Goldblum as *The Fly* (1986). This is authentic modern horror, which shows Jeff gradually turn into a fly in all too realistic and stomach-churning detail. The make-up won Chris Walas and Stephan Dupuis an Oscar.

Stop action stopped. A moment from *Jason and the Argonauts*. Ray Harryhausen's skeleton warriors provided some of the most alarming screen images ever seen on screen.

more finesse. He was experimenting with a new character - a skeleton - but the right vehicle was not immediately to hand. So he ransacked the Arabian Nights stories until he found what he was looking for. The animated skeleton made its first appearance, fighting on a spiral stair-case, in *The Seventh Voyage of Sinbad*. One skeleton then became six in *Jason and the Argonauts* (1963), each one inhabited by a smaller brother inside, made of metal, with tiny ball and socket joints. "You could place it in any position and it would hold the pose beautifully." The basic principle of stop-animation is the same as that for a car-toon, where the image is drawn on a cell and then advanced. With model animation, the figure is advanced frame by frame, the problem - solved only by years of experience - being to make the figure move naturally, as if it were a live actor. Jason's fight with the skeletons was choreographed and then rehearsed by stunt men. By the time the sequence was finally put together, Ray Harryhausen had spent four and a half months on it. In another scene, a bronze statue comes to life. It was quite a small model, made to look 100ft high by shooting the actors at a distance and then combining the two pieces of film, using rear projection and split screen.

Harryhausen's *The Golden Voyage of Sinbad*, made in 1973, features Kali, an Indian goddess endowed with six arms. In rehearsal, three stunt men were strapped together, one behind the other, to show the positions for the six arms. In stop-animation, more often than not, the stunt man works with an invisible companion who will materialise only in the completed sequence. For the actor it is a question of choreography and becoming a human metronome, trying to remember the counts. "Half their training", says Ray, "is to imagine what they're looking at. Sometimes they have to make love to a teapot for a close-up because the leading lady has gone off to her dressing room. We had one actor, shadow boxing with an invisible opponent, who got into such a muddle trying to remember his counts, that he just sat down and started to cry."

The star of innumerable films is the werewolf. Until 1981, and *An American Werewolf in London*, these creatures were usually created by a series of lap dissolves, a little more make-up being applied at each stage. The problem with this method is that the register is never precise; eyes tend to dissolve a little higher or lower than the previous image. Working together, director John Landis and Rick Baker storyboarded each sequence. The actor was David Naughton, his transformation a mixture of additions to his body and prosthesis. Rick had been experimenting with a false head that had a full set of wolf (yak) hair. This he filmed, at the same time pulling all the hair back *into* the head through the material. When the film was reversed, the hair appeared to grow *out* with no need for complicated and less than efficient lap dissolves. For another part of the sequence, David's arm was held behind his back, a false arm having been attached to his elbow. So the stretching and changing of his hand was the product of mechanics. In the end, almost every part of David's body was duplicated - legs, arms, torso - with a whole set of heads in different stages of transformation.

One of David Naughton's wolf heads was full of mechanical tricks so that it could physically change. The teeth could be pushed forward, stretching the rubber jaws and distort-

Kali, star of *The Golden Voyage of Sinbad*, bringing a new meaning to the word swashbuckler.

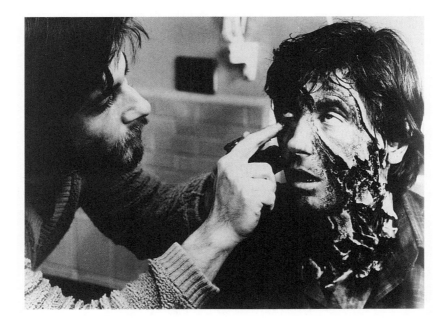

Werewolves can give you a nasty nip. Rick Baker applies make-up to Griffin Dunne, a decomposing victim in An American Werewolf in London.

ing the head. Rick Baker put little forms in the cheekbones to push them out, while other devices stretched the ears. In this way the transformation was accomplished without the use of optical effects. The sequence was shot on a set whose floorboards were built 5ft above the studio floor. David was then hidden under the boards with only his head and arms visible. The false wolf body was blended in with his shoulders, and other appliances attached to his hands and face. John Landis wanted David to be naked, so that his entire anatomy would seem to change. In the finished film, the audience sees David drop to his hands and knees from a standing position, and then fall to the ground. From that moment he was underneath the floorboards; with him were the technicians who operated the wolf's body above.

There are tricks within tricks. When Ridley Scott shot the famous exploding-stomach scene in *Alien* (1979), he did not rehearse it with the other actors. Instead, he brought them on set only for the actual take. When all the blood and slithery bits burst out of Hurt's "stomach", Sigourney Weaver and her fellow actors got splashed; and Scott got the reactions he wanted. "Why not try acting, dear boy?" as Olivier might have said, as indeed he did say to Dustin Hoffman when they were making *Marathon Man* (1976), and Hoffman insisted on running round the block in order to appear suitably breathless on set.

Roy Scheider *did* try acting, and very effectively, in *Jaws* (1975).

In the scene where he sees the shark for the first time, he was reacting not to Spielberg's rubber shark, not even to Richard Dreyfuss pulling a face. He was reacting to *nothing*. Spielberg made his actors do almost the same thing in *Jurassic Park* (1993). They reacted, open-mouthed, to state-of-the-art dinosaur faces held up on sticks.

Reacting to Orson Welles was best left to people who could hold their own. At RKO, Linwood Dunn, seven years on from his pioneering work on *King Kong*, was at the peak of his creative skills when Orson Welles and *Citizen Kane* arrived in 1940. Welles went post-production mad when he realised what Linwood's optical printer could do. As Linwood saw it, Orson was a One-Picture Wonder, and a pain in the neck, goading the old hand with an infuriating "What do you mean, it can't be done?" Linwood would explain, tartly, that the impossible takes time. "I'll get it." And money. "I'll get it," and Welles went straight to the front office and came back with both ingredients. "There was never a picture made in the history of the movie business that had more alterations and changes done in post-production than *Citizen Kane*." When Kane is found dead, holding a ball in his hand, Orson said, "I want to be inside that ball". Biting back the words, "It can't be done", Linwood said that one optical zoom on top of another would result in a loss of picture quality. "Try it, Lin." As Linwood had predicted, the picture quality was poor. Orson now suggested double exposing more snow in the ball - and, to Linwood's chagrin, it smoothed out the grain and the lack of resolution; furthermore, once the camera started to pull back - in other words, as soon as it was in motion - the problem was solved. Linwood still wasn't happy because, as the camera pulls back, the snow fills the whole frame as well as the ball; but Orson told him to leave it as it was. Today Linwood says - and whether it's praise or criticism is anybody's guess - "It was the kind of thing the man liked."

The film is full of sets and effects that were invented in post-production. In the scene in which Kane stands inside an enormous fire-place talking to Susan Alexander (Dorothy Comingore) there was no elaborate set on the stage. Susan is sitting on a couch, but the huge window above her was painted in afterwards. In another sequence, the camera appears to go over the roof of a night-club, through the sign and down into the night-club below. It is actually the marriage of two different shots. As the camera came over the roof it stopped at the skylight. Orson said, "No, I want to go right on through it." So

Linwood made an optical zoom into the skylight, added a couple of lightning flashes made on the optical printer, and made a reverse zoom on the inside shot. Then he put the two shots together. "I don't think its a great shot, but it's what he wanted."

Robert Wise, who was the editor on *Citizen Kane*, has been asked many times if he realised in 1940 that they were making what 50 years later would be considered one of the greatest films ever made. "I have to say no. Even Orson, who had a pretty good-sized ego, didn't feel that. But you couldn't see those rushes coming in every day and not realise you were getting something very special." And Welles' behaviour was often outrageous. "You wanted to tell him to shove it, and walk off... but before you could do it, he'd have an idea that was so brilliant you'd stand there with your mouth gaping open."

In 1968, Stanley Kubrick's *2001: A Space Odyssey* became the most believable science-fiction film ever made. Indeed, by comparison, the actual moon landing (a year later) looked like low-budget special effects. When, in Kubrick's film, we saw man and his ships in the black vastness of space, disbelief was suspended totally. The actors were suspended, too, in some of the scenes Keir Dullea, for example, dangled (like Harold Lloyd in the Twenties) from wires attached to the studio ceiling when he made his explosive re-entry through the airlock of the mother spaceship. The same piano-wire trick was used for the scene in which the uppity HAL gets his brains scrambled by a *very* cross Dullea.

Miniatures were used extensively in *2001*. These go back to Méliès, of course, but miniatures had never been used like this before. The models that had the freedom of Kubrick's universe were painstakingly constructed, photographed, and enhanced by Kubrick's sometimes

A spaceship from Stanley Kubrick's 2001: A Space Odyssey, the film that made the NASA moon landing look amateurish.

mischievous choice of music. *2001* overran its shooting schedule by over a year and the budget more than doubled to $10.5 million; but every dollar was put on the screen by a team of British and American effects experts under the supervision of Wally Veevers, Douglas Trumbull, Tom Howard and Con Pedersen. Wally Veevers, who had worked on *Things to Come* back in 1936 and, for Kubrick, on *Dr Strangelove* (1964), was now in charge of the model and matte work; Douglas Trumbull, who would later be Oscar-nominated for his work on *Close Encounters of the Third Kind, Star Trek - The Motion Picture* (1979) and *Blade Runner*, was a young American special-effects man responsible for the "stargate" sequence at the end of the film, using his so-called "slit-scan" system. Too complicated to be described in detail here, Trumbull says that, "It's like photographing car head-lights at night with the shutter open - you get streaks of light. If you had the cars blink their lights on and off you'd get streaky dots. My slit-scan device took that concept to a very complicated extreme. The whole thing shoots automatically, in total darkness. It runs itself up

The musical spaceship at the centre of Close Encounters of the Third Kind.

and down on tracks, opens and closes its shutters and cycles the optical matte, all automatically."

The "reality" of *2001* is so impressive that it is difficult to believe today that the film was based so firmly on miniatures and models. These were motorised, running on tracks to ensure perfect smoothness of motion. "Miniatures" and "models" are relative terms here because the spaceship "Discovery" was 54ft long, and moved along a 150ft track. It took four and a half hours to make the journey which, for matting purposes, had to be shot several times; and the space station was 9ft across and moved only ⅜in every minute as it rotated.

The crew of the spaceship are seen through various windows. Again, it was a combination of old and new. A shot of the model ship moving along its track was made, but with the windows blacked out. The film was rewound to the start and another identical shot made; but this time the model was covered in black velvet, and a scene of the interior action was front-projected onto a glossy white card which exactly filled the window area. The front projection was new, *2001* being the first feature film to use it, but the rest was a return to the matting techniques used by film cameramen in the silent era.

Some tricks weren't really tricks at all; rather, they were impressive and expensive feats of engineering. One was the centrifuge inside the Jupiter-mission spaceship, built rather like a ferris wheel. It was 38ft

Arthur C. Clarke's
FAVOURITE SCI-FI FILMS

1.
Metropolis (1926, Fritz Lang)

2.
Things to Come (1936, William Cameron Menzies)

3.
Frankenstein (1931, James Whale)

4.
King Kong
(1933, Merian C Cooper and Ernest B. Schoedsack)

5.
Forbidden Planet (1956, Fred McLeod Wilcox)

6.
The Thing From Another World (1951, Christian Nyby)

7.
The Day The Earth Stood Still (1951, Robert Wise)

8.
2001 - A Space Odyssey (1968, Stanley Kubrick)

9.
Close Encounters of the Third Kind: Special Edition
(1980, Steven Spielberg)

10.
Alien (1979, Ridley Scott)

11.
Blade Runner (1982, Ridley Scott)

(Source: *The Variety Book of Movie Lists*)

in diameter and rotated at three miles per hour. We see it first when one of the astronauts, Gary Lockwood, goes for his daily jog inside it. *Then* it becomes a trick, as he runs up one side and down the other. In reality, he trundled away like a hamster at the bottom of the wheel, as the cameraman, suspended in a seat mounted on gimbals, constantly adjusted the camera to keep Lockwood in frame.

Douglas Trumbull was 23 when he worked on *2001*. Apart from the "stargate" sequence, he was in charge of the animation of the stars and planets. He remembers the inventiveness of Geoffrey Unsworth, *2001*'s cinematographer. Some of the colour transparencies that were air-brushed to create the light and dark sides of the earth were photographed with a special gauze. "Geoffrey had found some pre-war black silk stockings that turned out to be really great flare filters. They gave a beautiful glow without de-sharpening the shots. So whenever you see the sun or the earth or Jupiter with a beautiful glow round it - that was all due to Geoffrey's black silk stockings."

The mixture of old and new techniques worked brilliantly; and once again, small is sometimes big. The swirling galaxies were not models; they were produced by photographing interacting chemicals trapped on 3in-diameter glass slides.

What made *2001* all the more remarkable was that it had been created by industry mavericks, not by a big studio's special-effects department. The disintegration of the studio system in the Fifties meant that all those in-house departments that made and stored period clothes, and employed highly paid artists and technicians to design and build sets which were constantly being recycled on the backlots of Hollywood, simply weren't needed any more. Among the casualties were the special-effects department at 20th Century-Fox, headed by L.B. Abbott, where Fred Sersen (who specialised in studio tank work) had provided the entire seascape set for Hitchcock's *Lifeboat* (1944); the RKO special-effects department (headed by Jack Cosgrove) where Linwood Dunn worked as head of photographic effects; and the special-effects department at Warner Brothers, with Byron Haskin in charge. A. Arnold Gillespie, who worked on both versions of *Ben Hur* (1925 and 1959) and of *Mutiny on the Bounty* (1935 and 1962), was at MGM, where Lee Leblanc headed the matte painting department; Stanley Horsley was head of effects at Universal; and two brothers, Howard and Theodore Lydecker, were resident effects men at Republic Studios. A few experts who worked as independents became legendary figures, such people as production-designer William Cameron Menzies, who was hired in 1923 by Douglas Fairbanks Snr to design the sets for *The Thief of Bagdad* (1925), but who is perhaps best known for directing (for Alexander Korda in Britain) the 1936, H.G. Wells-based, science-fiction film, *Things to Come*.

With no special-effects factories left, there was no recruitment - and during a 20-year hiatus, an entire generation of talent was lost. Then, in 1975, a miracle happened. In one corner of a California warehouse, down in the valley, a 15-minute drive from Hollywood, George Lucas (with Douglas Trumbull's assistant, John Dykstra) founded ILM - Industrial Light & Magic. Lucas and his partners assembled a small group of Sixties babies, rebels without a cause - until Lucas gave them one. When *Star Wars* opened in 1977 audiences saw a city-size spaceship progressing, in cosmic majesty, over their heads. It was a milestone in cinema history, one of those adrenaline-rush moments that turn up perhaps once in a decade; and the start of that film began something else. *Star Wars* gave the kiss of life to the dying industry of special effects.

It was not, however, immediately apparent. After *Star Wars*, the young model-makers and computer wizards and artists and designers flew the ILM coop to take long, lazy holidays, never expecting to see each other again. Sitting on the beach in Hawaii, twisting their ankles on the French Alps or pony-trekking in Wales, they certainly didn't expect to be recalled to ILM, nor did they suspect that ILM was to become the special-effects world leader.

Thomas G. Smith, who became general manager of ILM, says that most of the young people working there (a high percentage of them were under 20; very few were over 30) had little experience of working in feature films; but they were dedicated to their different tasks, working all hours of the day and night. The rather older film executives who came visiting the house of magic were sometimes alarmed. Tom Smith says, "They would find all kinds of shenanigans going on, people wearing costumes and bathing suits wandering around." Even George Lucas wasn't too pleased with the way the place was run. He had a sneaking feeling that things were not being done efficiently - until the results reassured him. Dennis Muren, visual-effects cameraman and later supervisor at ILM, says that George was still thinking in terms of throwing models past the camera or sliding them down wires. He was not, apparently, dying to get into the latest technology;

☞ page 210

S T A R   W A R S

2 0 T H   C E N T U R Y - F O X   1 9 7 7

Producer: Gary Kurtz

Director: George Lucas

Stars: Mark Hamill, Harrison Ford, Carrie Fisher, Alec Guinness, Peter Cushing.

O S C A R S

MUSIC (ORIGINAL SCORE),
EDITING, COSTUME DESIGN,
VISUAL EFFECTS, SOUND,
SOUND EFFECTS, ART DIRECTION

However alien Chewbacca may be, he clearly has a strain of orangutan in his lineage.

In the making

Star Wars (1977) was initially turned down by both Universal and United Artists. According to the film's producer, Gary Kurtz, there was trouble from the start over the film's title. And 20th Century-Fox, who took the film on, argued that neither the word "star" or "war" in a title ever spelled financial success. Nevertheless, *Star Wars* became one of the highest-grossing films of all time.

Secret of its success

A manufactured fairy tale, *Star Wars* worked. As Lucas and Kurtz admitted, it was "a real gee-whizz movie". The beguiling formula including a wealth of elements, such as T.H. White's Camelot stories, Thirties sci-fi creations (particularly *Flash Gordon*) and references to many other kinds of films. But, most of all, audiences were excited by the film's sophisticated special effects.

Luke Skywalker (Mark Hamill) wondering how to snatch Princess Leia (Carrie Fisher) away from the forces of evil.

Harrison Ford as cynical space pilot Hans Solo - the role that brought him to stardom.

Rebellious Princess Leia has decided to escape from her galaxy with the help of her robots.

A long time ago in a galaxy far away...

"

May the Force be with you...

THE STAR DESTROYER

This cost $100,000 to make. Painstakingly designed, the model had a quarter of a million port-holes.

ACADEMY AWARDS

The film was nominated for eleven Oscars, including Best Picture, but the seven it won were all "technical awards".

DARTH VADER

David Prowse played the man behind the mask, but his voice belonged to an uncredited James Earl Jones.

SET SECRETS

Sir Alec Guinness in this, his most lucrative film role, admitted to not knowing who he was playing. Nevertheless, he was Oscar-nominated for his Obiwan Kenobe.

DANGEROUS GAMES

When Luke and Princess Leia jumped over the chasm, there was a frighteningly real 30-foot drop beneath them. They only did the scene once.

GALAXY WARS

Star Wars was to have been part of a nine-part series. In fact, only two more – *The Empire Strikes Back* (1980) and *Return of the Jedi* (1983) – have so far been

Right: Sinister Darth Vader, he of the metal head and computer-voice, could be Luke's real father.

made, and these weren't directed by Lucas. There are reports that Lucas is now writing the stories of the first three in the series.

STAR BUCKS

Taking a modest up-front fee of $50,000 for the script, and $100,000 to direct, Lucas cannily went for 40% of the music and merchandising rights. Total sales from toys, souvenirs, clothes and comic books are now estimated at more than $2,500,000,000. The costumes looked great, but everyone had problems: Peter Mayhew suffered heatstroke inside his furry Chewbacca costume, and the headless Storm Troopers kept bumping into each other; one trooper was knocked out cold.

WHAT'S IN A NAME?

R2D2 is film editor's speak for Reel 2 Dialogue 2. And Luke Skywalker, Luke S........ of course.

but he was soon won over. The first thing that has to be understood about models and computers is that when a spaceship roars towards an audience, the model is actually motionless in front of a blue screen; the camera moves, a motor controlling its forward advance on a rail. Frame by frame, the camera is moved nearer. The reason for doing it frame by frame is that the model is small, and to keep it in focus the camera has to be stopped down because of the long (perhaps of a second's duration) exposures. During the second that the camera lens is open, the camera is moving slowly forwards. Everything - focus, movement, tilting and panning - is controlled by computer. A storyboard, approved by George Lucas, was always the master plan for the deployment of spaceships, planets, and heavenly bodies - both cosmic and human. Explosions were made to last longer by taking a shot running at 60, 90 or 200 frames and playing it back at 24; shades of the old silent days of over and under-cranking. *Star Wars* went one or a dozen better with explosions *within* explosions, all of them computer-generated.

ILM's first big venture in *digital* effects was not for a Lucas film but for *Star Trek II - The Wrath of Khan* (1982). There is one scene in which a spaceship flies over a cold and forbidding planet that metamorphoses to a lush home from home, full of green trees and blue waters. For its day, the effect is stunning; but there was no planet, no physical model in a studio with a camera approaching on a rail. The entire sequence was made in a computer. When Steven Spielberg saw it, he was so impressed that he said he wanted to make a whole movie that way; but that would be more than a decade later.

Industrial Light & Magic has become synonymous with state-of-the-art special effects. It has created effects for some of the most memorable films of all time, including the "Star Wars" trilogy, *Raiders of the Lost Ark* (1981), *Indiana Jones and The Temple of Doom* (1984), *E.T.* (1982), *Back to the Future* (1985), the "Star Trek" films, *Poltergeist* (1982), *Cocoon* (1985) and, of course, *Jurassic Park* (1993). As ILM grew, it attracted and trained new talent. It now juggles with several major film projects simultaneously. Like a successful film star, ILM is sought our by the major studios when effects work is called for. Special effects move so swiftly now that their pioneering use of digital images painted directly on the film by computer-controlled lasers may well have been overtaken by the time this book is published.

The first time Dennis Muren did anything directly with computer graphics was in 1985 for Barry Levinson's *Young Sherlock Holmes*. In it, a character steps out of a stained glass window to do battle. The sequence was shot in a church at night. Muren had considered stop-motion, using a rod puppet, but went instead for computer graphics. He worked with the computer experts at ILM to put together a sequence of seven shots that took six months to complete. "That's a long time. But what we got on screen was unique." *Young Sherlock Holmes* was, in fact, the first feature film whose effects were painted directly on film with a laser.

Three years later, in 1988, a George Lucas story, *Willow*, directed by Ron Howard, gave Dennis Muren the opportunity to use morphing. It sounds surprisingly like the sort of "impossible" thing Orson Welles demanded of Linwood Dunn nearly 50years earlier. Two pieces of film are shot and then blended together. "The sequence in *Willow* probably had five or six changes from one character to another." Muren again used morphing to create an alien water snake creature for a 1989 James Cameron film, *The Abyss*. This was an exciting time for Muren and his team because they were learning as they worked. Making the body of the creature was difficult enough, but the face on the head was even more so. "There were two faces, in fact, and it had to look like the actors in the film." In the end, the human faces were laser-scanned and the digital information fed into a computer. The results were astonishing. "I thought to myself, this is an incredible tool we've got here, and in five or ten years we're still going to be learning how to harness it."

Two years later, in 1991, Dennis Muren and his colleagues took a leap forward from what had been done on *The Abyss* with James Cameron's *Terminator 2: Judgement Day* (special effects by Fantasy II Film Effects and Industrial Light & Magic.). "*T2* had a lot of stuff that we had never done, didn't know if we could do." The chrome

"Funny, I keep thinking it's Thursday." **Aliens in Star Trek II: The Wrath of Khan.**

man, an android that reflects any environment that surrounds it, was a comparatively easy thing to construct with computer graphics. The real problem was that the android had to move and behave like a human, while changing effortlessly from one shape or form to another, and back again. "It took a lot of time to figure out how, mathematically, we could get the geometry to move around without it ripping itself apart." But, like all special effects, from Méliès on, the most effective tricks are achieved by a cunning mixture of reality and fantasy. Computer graphics allow the terminator's finger to flow like liquid chrome, extending to become a long metal spike; but when the terminator gets shot at the end by Arnold Schwarzenegger, he turns into a kind of pretzel man - and that was a prop. "And there's something very good about having a prop on the set, because the actors can work with it, relate to it. The director can direct, the cameraman can light it." The trick, in fact, is not to push one technology to do something it can't really do, but to use one or more technologies together, so that, like Sean Connery's wig, you can't see the join.

Rick Carter, the production designer for *Death Becomes Her* (1992) and *Forrest Gump* (1994), was also responsible for the design of *Jurassic Park*. When Steven Spielberg was planning the film, he wanted "a really big gate" for the park. Rick's first suggestion was a gate 25ft high, but Spielberg wanted it even bigger. It soon became clear that he saw it - and the film - as, in part, an homage to *King Kong*. Indeed, at first, Spielberg thought that a mechanical dinosaur could be made, rather like the huge King Kong in the Universal studio tour in Florida. He wanted the people at ILM to make one: "I want a full-size Tyrannosaurus Rex that I can direct."

Spielberg got his dinosaur - but not the one he expected. Down in the valley, Dennis Muren and the ILM experts constructed the skeleton of a T-Rex in the computer, and then moved it through a run cycle, to show Spielberg that dinosaurs could actually be made in the computer. The process was so new that as they got further into it, "We hit upon an arc of technological breakthroughs." And so the role of the computerised dinosaur in *Jurassic Park* grew and grew, with Muren leading the way. Almost every step brought a new discovery. One of the simplest things in computer graphics is that once a single model has been made, it can spawn endless clones - and that is where the idea for running herds of dinosaurs came from. Dennis Muren says, "The tests were just amazing, so they gave us more money to move ahead." In the meantime, a Tyrannosaurus Rex had been made, in the computer, by Steve Williams, and a test shot was done of the dinosaur walking past camera. "But I wanted to do it as if it was in the film, so we did it in broad daylight, with the T-Rex very close to the camera, looking right into the lens - and it came out great." When Spielberg saw the test he gave the go ahead for more money to be spent. In the finished *Jurassic Park*, over 50 sequences are made up of computer-graphic dinosaurs.

The possibilities offered by computer graphics seem endless. In *Forrest Gump*, Rick Carter worked closely with the director, Robert Zemeckis and Ken Rolstein, the effects supervisor. When the scene where Gump goes to Washington DC and addresses the peace rally was to be shot, there were about 750 extras there. By moving them around and feeding the information into the computer, less than 1000 people became a crowd of 300,000 The other computer miracle was its extraordinary ability to juggle with history (as Woody Allen had done in his 1983 film, *Zelig*), putting Forrest Gump into old news-reels, allowing him, for example, to exchange words with President

Jurassic Park. Computer magic that would have made Méliès' mouth water.

Kennedy. Ever since the cinema began, sound effects and dialogue have been added to film, and the dubbing (or looping) of dialogue has been routine for well over 50 years; so in a sense, "gumping" is no more than a step - albeit a giant one - forward. The film loop has been replaced by computer imaging, as Tom Hanks as Gump was required to move and speak as accurately as the person he was replacing.

Even though *Forrest Gump* is full of computer tricks (as were *Who Framed Roger Rabbit?* (1988) and the "Back to the Future" trilogy) its director, Robert Zemeckis, does not enjoy the process of special effects, which he finds time-consuming and boring. Not the results, of course, which are stunning. But, bringing us full circle, Zemeckis knows that cinema is all illusion. "Part of the fun that I have as a film-maker is being not only a story-teller but an illusionist as well. I like special effects simply because I enjoy showing people things they could never see in any other circumstances."

He is amused when actors talk about "playing the reality." When an actor plays an emotional scene in close-up, more often than not he is addressing a piece of sticky tape attached to the nearest piece of studio ironmongery roughly at his co-star's eye level. The latest criticism is that the images created in the computer aren't real images; but then what is a real image? An image exists only because light is focused through an optical system and recorded on something, be it film, video tape or in the brain of a computer,. It is all illusion, none of it exists in any kind of reality. The digital image is simply the extension of the lens, bending the light in a different way.

If President Kennedy can be made to talk to Forrest Gump, why not feed the necessary information about Bogart into the computer and give him a three-picture deal to star opposite Winona Ryder, Julia Roberts and Jodie Foster? Do the same for Fatty Arbuckle and we could give him back his lost career. Michael Caine might go back (in black and white) to play opposite a young Katharine Hepburn in *Bringing Up Baby*; and Mrs Miniver could go on the game to help the war effort.

Robert Zemeckis makes the prediction that film-makers will become image-makers, and that film will be replaced by computer graphics. It won't happen immediately, or even in the next few years, but eventually the only restriction will be the film-maker's imagination. Anything that can be imagined will be capable of realisation.

Méliès would have agreed with that.

FAMOUS DINOSAURS

Gorgo

1. ***Godzilla, King of the Monsters*** (1954): a fire-breathing tyrannosaurus and Japan's greatest box-office hit. Many sequels followed

2. ***Rodan*** (1956) introduced us to this breed of winged pterondactyl which hatches from eggs buried deep in a volcano and emerge to devastate Japan.

3. ***Reptilicus*** (1962): a dinosaur found in the bottom of an oil well who ultimately destroys Copenhagen.

4. ***Gorgo*** (1961): a 65ft baby dinosaur whose mother ends up trampling London underfoot on her way to rescue him from a circus.

5. ***The Giant Behemoth*** (1959) lives in the Thames and also ends up trampling London underfoot

6. ***The Ymir***: a reptilian from Venus who, in *20 Million Miles to Earth* (1957), destroys Rome.

7. ***The Beast From 20,000 Fathoms*** (1953): the only dinosaur to die with his head caught in a Coney Island roller coaster.

8. ***Prehistoric Fest:*** Rodan meets Godzilla meets Mothra (a giant moth) and Ghidrah (a three-headed dragon) in *Ghidrah, the Three-Headed Monster* (1965).

9. The worst dinosaurs ever filmed: ***King Dinosaur*** (1955)

10. The best dinosaurs ever filmed: ***Jurassic Park*** (1993).

Godzilla

Ready When You Are, Mr DeMille!

Anyone who stays for the credits at the end of a film knows that it takes scores of people to make a movie, from cameramen and composers to gaffers and grips. Freddie Young, for many years David Lean's cinematographer, says that the cameraman is next in importance to the director; some editors might claim that place, or even dispute the first. Composers of film music, choreographers of musicals and special-effects magicians have been known to *make* a film instead of simply making it. From start to finish, creating a story on film is an ensemble activity in a way that painting and writing normally isn't. But when all is said and done, no movie gets made without a producer to pitch and promote the idea, a writer to write the screenplay and a director to decide on what precisely will be committed to film. Of the three trades, the late Burt Lancaster said, "Directing is the best job in the picture business, because when you're director, you're God."

He was right, of course, but there was a time, back in the days of the great Hollywood dream factories, when directors were told what to direct, replaced if they didn't follow orders, and shunted off to their next assignment while the film they had just left was edited in the cutting room. Today the director may be God, but the pecking order has shifted more than once during the first hundred years of the cinema.

In the early days, anyone could become a director. DeMille became one after half a day's experience (see page 41). One silent star made a habit of shaking the hand of everyone he met, from streetcar conductor to the man on the studio gate, because, "Tomorrow, that guy may be my director." When Edison and Porter and Méliès and scores of others were making films, the producer was, more often than not, director, cameraman and special-effects man combined; and with no dialogue to be recorded, nobody cared much about the writer, if indeed, the film *had* one. Until sound arrived in 1927, the writer - the

Pioneer producer, director and autocrat, Cecil Blount DeMille (1881-1959).

"necessary evil" reluctantly hired by Irving Thalberg of MGM - knew his/her place and stayed at home and wrote books or plays... although these works were often the inspiration for a film, like the novel by the Reverend Thomas Dixon Jnr., *The Klansman*, which Griffith adapted to become *The Birth of a Nation* (1915).

Among the most important independent producers to work in Hollywood were Sam Goldwyn, David O. Selznick, Sam Spiegel, and the man who made Hollywood's first feature film, *The Squaw Man* (1913) - Cecil B. DeMille. DeMille was a force to be reckoned with in both silent and sound eras. He was of course, producer and director, a man in charge of everything. De Mille decided what book to adapt and which writer would be hired to do the job; he chose the cast, the composer and the technical crew; and he decided how his films would be publicised. In a superb trailer for *The Ten Commandments* (his 1956 version) he appeared on screen to declaim, "Note the striking resemblance between Charlton Heston and Michelangelo's statue of Moses."

Charlton Heston as Moses in DeMille's version of *The Ten Commandments*.

Sam Spiegel. Producer, friend of royalty and cheque-bouncer.

DeMille was a flamboyant actor who loved playing the part of the Hollywood producer, striding about in riding pants and laced-up boots that finished just below the knee. In theThirties, his resonant voice was known to all America because of the radio programme he hosted, the Lux Radio Theatre of the Air. At 18, Evelyn Keyes was taken by her agent to see DeMille in his bungalow on the Paramount lot. He looked her over, put her under contract, and sent her to acting school - also on the Paramount lot - where they would banish her Southern accent. "He lived like an emperor. He never walked alone. For instance, if he entered the commissary it was always with a retinue following him. *Nobody* walked alongside." She remembers, too, DeMille's son-in-law, who followed his employer around all day, carrying a tall stool. When DeMille wanted to sit down, the stool was there, every time, the descent of seat of pants to seat perfectly judged. DeMille never looked round first, never feared a pratfall; and never missed.

Stunt man Loren Janes worked on *The Ten Commandments* in 1956. When Moses comes down with the tablets to find his people worshipping the golden calf, the earth opens up, down go graven image - and three stunt men. The set was 40ft high and built on rollers. While Loren and his two colleagues were rehearsing this dangerous stunt, DeMille came over and peered down at the 40ft drop. "Mr DeMille," said Loren, "Do you have any direction for us?" "Just save your lives." said DeMille, and started to walk back to the camera. Then he paused for a moment: "And make it look good."

Anthony Quinn's first part was in a DeMille picture, *The Plainsman* (1936). He had heard that they wanted Indians. The casting director asked if he spoke Cheyenne. If Quinn had been asked if he could ride a unicycle, tame lions or fly an aeroplane, the answer would have been the same: "Yes, of course." He demonstrated with a

Young Anthony Quinn (left) and Jean Arthur in a scene from C.B. DeMille's *The Plainsman*. It was Quinn's first film role and almost almost his last.

little gibberish, which satisfied the casting director and delighted DeMille when it was tried on him, probably because he had been told that Quinn spoke no English. "And for Chrissakes don't let him know," said the casting director. The 20-year-old actor was given four pages of dialogue, to be delivered in "Cheyenne" and seated on a horse. He did ride, didn't he? - as well as speaking fluent Cheyenne? "Oh sure, of course. Well... not for a while, not, actually, since I left the reservation back in, er, the reservation." The casting director winked at him and sent him off for riding lessons. When he came back, "I knew the four pages by heart. I still known them. I use them for Arabs, I use them for Greeks, I use them for everything when I'm lost for dialogue."

It couldn't last; something had to give. DeMille was angry three times over, his anger rising exponentially, when Quinn (a) argued with him on a point of direction - (b) in English! - and (c) the star, Gary Cooper, backed him up. At about this time, Quinn asked Evelyn Keyes for a date. When DeMille heard about it, he shouted at his protégé, "Don't you dare go out with that half-breed again!" Appalled at the racist remark, Evelyn was delighted when Quinn later married one of DeMille's daughters - but *this* son-in-law never became a stoolie.

Famous for his biblical epics, DeMille made two versions of *The Ten Commandments* (1923 and 1956.) He followed the first one with *King of Kings* in 1927 and *The Sign of the Cross* in 1932. In case anyone should suspect that his work was tainted by commercial motives (the 1923 *The Ten Commandments* grossed $14 million), he started

C.B. DeMille working on *The Sign of the Cross* with Claudette Colbert.

each day's shooting with a religious service on the set; and after the filming of the crucifixion in *King of Kings*, the entire cast had to stand with heads bowed during five minutes of organ music.

Robert Parrish (actor, editor and, later, director) played a teenage rebel in a DeMille film called *This Day and Age*, made in 1933. Still pictures of action scenes were commonly made for the sales and distribution of a film. Parrish recalls how DeMille would stand in front of the whole company, acting out the scene for the stars. They would copy him, and when he saw the action or expression he wanted, he would yell "Still!" and everyone would freeze. If anyone moved, he made life uncomfortable for the culprit. On one occasion, DeMille yelled, "Still!", the photographer took the picture, and one of the extras moved slightly just as the picture was snapped. Through his megaphone DeMille yelled, "That boy in the sweater moved. No, not you, the boy at the end.," "I didn't move, Mr DeMille." The director made the entire cast and crew wait until the film was developed. Fifteen minutes later, looking at the still wet print, a triumphant DeMille saw the blurred face of the accused boy. He picked up his megaphone. "The still was spoiled because this young man didn't listen to directions. When I say 'Still' I expect everyone to remain perfectly still. Now we'll try it again." He turned to the unfortunate boy. "All right, son, you can go home. We won't need you any more."

Samuel, the Goldfish-turned-Goldwyn, was born in Poland, came to England as a child, and arrived in America at 15. He became a glove-maker before joining his brother-in-law, Jesse Lasky, and Cecil B. DeMille. Later, although he took no part in the MGM merger, his name remained sandwiched between Metro and Mayer. He founded his own studio, and became the most powerful producer in Hollywood, making family films of the highest quality. Most of his "Goldwynisms" may have been created by his publicity department; they certainly served to obscure his private eloquence when negotiating contracts or discussing career moves with actors. A manipulator with few equals, he made Sidney Poitier an offer he couldn't refuse. In 1958, Poitier turned down *Porgy and Bess* because he believed the story demeaned black Americans. Goldwyn, entertaining the actor in his baronial home, was civilised and sympathetic, wanting only what was best for Poitier - and not a Golwynism was heard in the mansion. The very same day, Stanley Kramer offered Poitier a role-to-kill-for in *The Defiant Ones* (1958). It soon became clear that Poitier would not

get the part unless he signed for *Porgy and Bess*. To this day, Poitier reckons, "I think I was manipulated. As smart as I thought I was, that time the white folks were smarter."

Sam Spiegel, occasionally calling himself S. P. Eagle, was born in Poland, and came to Hollywood in 1941. He produced *Tales of Manhattan* a year later, and was the driving force behind *The African Queen* (1951) of which his friend, Alexander Korda, said, "A story of two old people going up and down a river. You will be bankrupt." Then came *On the Waterfront* (1957), *The Bridge on the River Kwai* (1957) and *Lawrence of Arabia* (1962.)

Spiegel had style. In his book on Spiegel, Andrew Sinclair tells us that, in 1936, Spiegel was arrested for incurring debts by false pretences, obtaining money by means of worthless cheques and forging a guarantee. Released on bail, he was committed for trial at the Central Criminal Court at the Old Bailey on April 8th. Instead of going to court, he threw a lavish champagne and caviar party for his wealthier friends and associates at the Dorchester in London. Half way through, two police officers arrived to take him in charge. "Ladies and gentlemen" said Spiegel, "Please continue to be my guests. I am temporarily the guest of His Majesty's Government."

Ronald Neame, who started as a studio messenger boy, and became a cameraman, wanted to be a producer. He had worked as cinematographer with David Lean on *In Which We Serve* (1942), *This Happy Breed* (1944) and *Blythe Spirit* (1945). Then, just after the war, he was sent by J. Arthur Rank on a visit to all the Hollywood studios to find out as much as he could about what was needed back home to re-equip the Rank Organisation with cameras, lights, and indeed anything that would help to make film-making simpler and more efficient. When he returned, Ronnie went to see his boss with what appears to have been a casual request casually acceded to. "Arthur, would you let me produce a film?" "Oh, I don't see what not, Ronnie. What do you want to produce?" Well. I'm not sure, Arthur, but I do know it would be wonderful if David Lean could direct it." "Good. Go away and decide what you want to make and then come back and see me." Neame and Lean thought they would *quite* like to make *Great Expectations*. "And why not." said Uncle Arthur. "Off

An average day for *The Untouchables*. Early Kevin Costner with scene-and-picture-stealer Sean Connery.

you go, then. Don't spend more than you have to, and let me know when I can see it." *Great Expectations*, which came out in 1946, has become a classic, of course.

What does a producer do today? According to Art Linson, who made *The Untouchables* (1987), it is essential to know when to say nothing. When Ned Tanen was head of motion pictures at Universal, Linson and his partner Gary Stromberg went to see him with an idea for a film. The meeting was held on the top floor of the black tower at Universal, a building seemingly constructed entirely of windows, with views across the valley. Tanen said "OK, what do you have?" "Er, well, you see, um, er..." said Linson, starting as he did not intend to go on. He took a deep breath. "It's a day in the life of a car wash... put to music [*Car Wash*, 1976]." Tanen's jaw dropped, and a deep chasm of silence opened up, on the other side of which the head of motion pictures swivelled round in his chair to stare out into the valley. When he swivelled back, he looked ill. "That" he said at last, "is the worst idea I have ever..... let's make it into a movie. Let's go." Linson looked at Gary, grabbed his arm, hurried him out of the office and into the elevator. "In Hollywood you must take yes for an answer. *There is nothing else to say after yes.*"

Producers need directors. Where do - and did - directors come from? Apart from the first ten years or so of cinema's history, when almost anybody could became a director, and the last twenty or so when film schools have turned out trained directors every year (who might or might not make it in the industry), the road became difficult. Ronald Neame, promoted to producer by J. Arthur Rank, wasn't able to start directing until the late Forties, after which he made many films, among them *The Golden Salamander* (1950), *The Card* (1952), *The Man Who Never Was*, (1956), *Tunes of Glory* (1960), *The Prime of Miss Jean Brodie* (1969) and *The Odessa File* (1974). Freddie Young, more or less Neame's contemporary, chose not to rush things. He made his directorial debut when he felt he was ready for it - at the ripe age of 82.

Before they became directors, Joel Schumacher was an art director and Nic Roeg a cinematographer. Director Robert Parrish was previously an editor, and before that, growing up in Hollywood, it was comparatively easy to get work as a child actor. Parrish's school was only two blocks from Charlie Chaplin's studio, and one day Chaplin's assistant director visited the school looking for extras to appear in a new film called *City Lights* (1931). Bob Parrish and one of his friends were chosen. On the lot, Chaplin came over and asked, "Can either of you boys shoot peas through a peashooter?" "Yes, sir," said Parrish, "I can. I'll show you." "No you won't. I'll show you." Chaplin got a peashooter from the prop man and blew expertly, just as a small street urchin would blow down a peashooter; then he ran out into the middle of the street to pretend he'd been hit. "He liked to play all the parts, he hated giving up any of them to the other actors. He would have played the part of the blind girl [Virginia Cherrill] as well, if he could have got away with it." Years later, Parrish met Chaplin in Ireland. "Bob, we're very lucky, you and me." Parrish thought he was talking about the beauty of the Irish landscape. "No, no, no, not that. Our picture is being released in New York and we'll make a lot of money out of it." Parrish reflected that he had made $7.50 a day shooting peas at Chaplin, and Chaplin was making millions.

Robert Wise, like Bob Parrish, was an editor for many years before he became a director. He believes that research is a vital part of the director's job. In 1958 he made *I Want to Live*, a film based on the true story of a woman who went to the gas chamber in San Quentin in the mid- Fifties. Susan Hayward won an Oscar for her performance and Wise an Oscar nomination. In preparing the film, Wise and his art director went to San Quentin to see (and measure for the studio reproduction) the death cell where the woman spent her last night; and the gas chamber. Wise also asked to see an execution. "I felt like a ghoul in a sense, but I didn't want the critics to be able to say well, that's some Hollywood writer's version of what it's like to go to the gas chamber." A young man had been convicted two years earlier of killing two women in Oakland; now he was to be executed, and the warden arranged for Wise to be present. Fortunately - for Wise - it was an unemotional affair; the young man was very quiet, so the director was able to force himself to watch. Even though the director wanted to tell the truth, the whole truth and nothing but the truth, not all of it reached the screen. In the film, Susan Hayward is strapped into the chair, the fumes rise... and Wise cuts to her hands clenching a couple of times. The censor would never have allowed it, of course, but, "The truth is that the body in the chair writhes and twists and turns for about seven or eight minutes before it is declared dead."

Sean O'Fearna, aka John Ford, made over 125 feature films from 1917 onwards, many of them silent Westerns. His best films have influenced directors ever since. One of his greatest admirers, later a close friend, is Robert Parrish. When he was a child actor, the first part he ever had was in 1928 in a John Ford film, *Mother Machree*. He worked in several more Ford pictures. By 1935 working both as actor and apprentice film editor on *The Informer*, he knew he wanted to be a director; so he watched Ford at work whenever he could. On the first day of shooting, Ford introduced a short, red-faced man to the assembled cast and crew on the set. Pointing at his laboratory specimen, Ford said, "This is an associate producer. Take a good look at him because you will not see him again until the picture is finished shooting." Three weeks later, Ford was half-way though the last day's shooting when the associate producer walked on the set to congratulate Ford for finishing under schedule. Ford was chewing on his handkerchief, a sure sign that he was thinking, conniving or dreaming. Recklessly, the red-faced man approached him and said, "The rushes look great, Jack." Ford was silent for a long time, then he called for the second assistant, Eddie O'Fearna, Ford's brother. "Eddie - have we finished yet?" "Not yet, Jack. Half a day to go." "Then what's this front-office sonofabitch doing on the set?" While the red-faced associate producer turned puce, Ford called Joe August, the cameraman, over. "Joe, the front office likes the rushes, so there must be

The great John Ford on location.

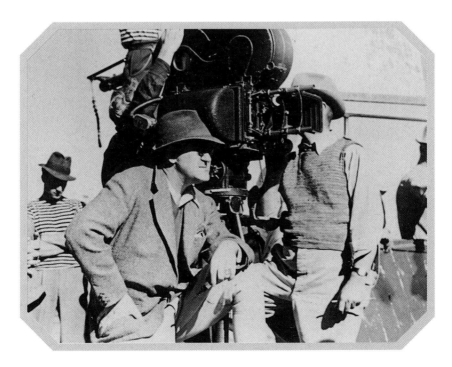

something wrong. We'll have to keep shooting until we find out what it is. We won't finish tonight after all." Ford shot, and re-shot, made extra close-ups and spent almost a full day shooting main title backgrounds. The associate producer's congratulations cost RKO about $25,000.

A few years later, when Parrish arrived on the set of *The Grapes of Wrath* (1940), cast and crew were standing around waiting for Ford to decide where to put the camera. He was alone in the middle of the set looking through the finder that had been removed from the camera. The finder matched the camera's own lenses, and in those days the director would often use it to find the right spot to shoot from. The instrument was over a foot long, five inches wide, encased in metal; it was also very heavy. Without turning round, Ford called Bob Parrish over. "Yes sir?" "Didn't you say", said Ford, picking up on a conversation they'd had five years earlier, "that you wanted to learn how to be a director? Well here's your first lesson. Stand close to me and listen carefully" He still held the finder in front of his face. "From time

The Grapes of Wrath, an American tragedy whose cast included Dorris Bowdon, Jane Darwell and Henry Fonda. One of John Ford's finest movies.

to time, when you come on the set in the morning, you'll find that you haven't got an idea in your head, that you just can't figure out how to stage a scene. When this happens you call for the finder immediately. Go to the center of the set as though you know exactly what you're doing. Put the finder to your eyes the way I'm doing and close your eyes. That's important. Nobody will disturb you because they think you're looking for a setup. After you've held this position for about 15 minutes and have just about got your problems worked out, a spy from the front office will arrive on set because the jungle telegraph has told the production office it's 9.30am and you haven't made a shot. This spy is called an associate producer, and it's a ten-to-one shot that he's yellow. He won't come right up to you and tell you to get off your ass. He'll slink up to you like a sidewinder to a position just about where you are now and say, 'How's it going, Jack?' or 'Darryl likes the rushes' or some such crap. Now listen carefully, Bob. *This is the important part.* As soon as the sonofabitch speaks, and you're sure he's in the right spot, you swing the finder like this." With that, Ford turned his head and the finder sharply to the left and cracked Bob Parrish on the forehead. Blood flowed and Ford kept on talking, never taking the finder from his eyes. "After you've been at it a few years, you'll discover that your aim will improve and you can knock off two or three associate producers a week. With your eyes closed. That's the end of the first lesson. You can go back to the cutting room now. I think I've got my setup."

Robert Parrish became a director at last, by a circuitous route. In 1935 he was a working as an extra on a film starring Dick Powell, *Shipmates Forever*. Powell remembered him because Bob threw up over his sailor suit. Twelve years later, Parrish, now an editor, had just won an Oscar for his work on *Body and Soul* (1947). Dick Powell rang to arrange lunch. "I'm planning a picture" he said, "and I want you to direct." Parrish was pleased, but puzzled. "How do you know I can direct" "Because" answered Powell, "anybody can direct." Powell might have directed the film himself, but he explained that he was too busy playing the stock market, and would rather leave it to someone else. *Cry Danger* (1951) starred Dick Powell and Rhonda Fleming, and it launched Robert Parrish on a long and satisfying directing career.

Ronald Neame worked with Alfred Hitchcock in Britain, notably on Hitchcock's first sound film, *Blackmail* (1927). [see page 232]

Neame was aware that, although Hitchcock was still only a young man, he was very sure of himself. He knew everything about the making of a film, "which, I have to regretfully tell you, doesn't apply to a lot of directors today; they have not learnt their craft." Hitchcock believed that the script was the film, and he used to say, having finished the screenplay with his writers, "Well, we've made the film, all we have to do now is shoot it."

Hitchcock had a reputation for being cruel, and Neame confirms that he used to play practical jokes on some members of the unit, jokes that were often less than kind. He could make actors of both sexes feel uncomfortable and insecure. What he

did to Cary Grant is something of a mystery, but he must have done something. At the end of a day's shooting on location for *North by Northwest* (1959), Hitch saw Grant getting into his Rolls, and asked him for a lift to his hotel. Grant shook his head and shut the door.

Pioneer British cinematographer and director, Ronald Neame.

In the days of the great Hollywood dream factories, the difference between producers and directors working in the studios and those working outside was marked. Julian Blaustein, now in his eighties, worked as a story editor, then as a producer - *Broken Arrow* (1950), *The Wreck of the Mary Deare* (1959), *Khartoum* (1966) - and became a vice-president at 20th Century-Fox. There were the seven major studios and a handful of important independents. "Ordinary" producers worked for the studios; even Hal Wallis was under contract at Warner Brothers. Studio output was enormous. 20thCentury-Fox and MGM, for example, were making over 50 films a year each, so every week they had a picture going out on release. Julian Blaustein, overseeing 26 pictures a year, saw his job as expediting the work of the producers working under him. Outside the system, Selznick hired top-flight producers and directors such as Dore Schary, Mervyn Le Roy, and Alfred Hitchcock, but he supervised their pictures so his output was comparatively small. Darryl Zanuck, head of 20th Century-Fox, delegated, as did Blaustein under him. He did not walk on to every set and check the set dressing, nor did he check wardrobe and make-up. Selznick did. When the composer of a score was about ready, he would assemble several musicians on a small sound stage so that Selznick could listen to the proposed score. Zanuck didn't have time for anything like that.

The producer working under contract was not concerned with financing. Once he had developed a project and the studio had decided to go ahead, the producer had nothing but the best at his disposal. The big studios like Fox and MGM had the finest collection of crafts people in the industry - the art department, wardrobe, hairdressers, special effects, camera department, sound department - all were facilities automatically available. Blaustein says, "I never had an assistant when I was a producer. I didn't need one." All the assistants - and assistance - he needed were on tap. One of the advantages of working for a big studio was the continuity of work. If a producer made a flop, he didn't have to go scratching around for a new project; the chances were that he was working on several pictures at once. One of the disadvantages was that the producer was first asked, then urged, and finally told to use a certain contract director. This was simply because, if the director didn't work, there would be no picture to which to assign his salary.

Directors working for the studios were not like today's

Director Richard Fleischer worked in the Hollywood studio system and even survived Howard Hughes' take-over of RKO.

directors. Richard Fleischer was 27 when he was put under contract at RKO, the smallest of the majors: "But it really had everybody there. the biggest stars, the biggest directors and a terrific talent roster of young directors. I was very fortunate to be part of that. Everybody knew their job - it really was a motion picture factory." Fleischer's boss was Sid Rogell, head of the B-picture department. Rogell took a liking to the young man and allowed him to attend all the production meetings to show him how the system worked; he was also given access to all the stages, even the closed sets.

Only people with talent were taken on by the studios. That being a *sine qua non*, they wanted people who knew what they were doing and could bring pictures in on time and on budget. "They were very strict about that, and they made life hell for you if you were behind your schedule by half a day" recalls Fleischer. He tells a story about Sid Rogell who, finding that one of his B-picture directors was two days behind, stormed down to the set. He picked up the script, grabbed a handful of pages at random and tore them out. Then he threw the script back at the producer and said, "Now you're two days ahead." The same story has been told of other people, notably John Ford, but given the structure of most B movies at that time, the legend is undeniably true in spirit. Looking back from the Nineties, rough justice like that has its appeal; more than one feature film today would have benefited from a little random page-plucking at the shooting script stage.

No director worked for a studio unless he (and occasionally she) was under contract, normally for seven years, in the same way that actors were put under contract. The studio told him what picture he was going to make, who was going to be in it, who was going to write the script, who was going to design it, photograph it and orchestrate it. On the other hand, as Blaustein had found, there was a department for everything, and everything was of the best, including, at RKO, a 100-piece orchestra.

Michael Curtiz, originally from Hungary, directed more than 60 films in Europe before settling in Hollywood where he made, for Warner Brothers, some of the finest spectacles and dramas of the pre-war and wartime periods. He will always be remembered, of course, along with everyone associated with it, for *Casablanca* (1942). He never managed to conquer the English language, and he became almost as well known for his fractured English as for his work. When,

☛ page 234

Alfred Hitchcock

BORN LONDON, 1899 - DIED LOS ANGELES, 1980

"Film is life with all the dull bits removed..."
Alfred Hitchcock once remarked, and what more appropriate a comment from the director who brought the psychological thriller to our screens. He was, moreover, the first director whose name on a film meant more to audiences than the stars listed over the title.

EAST-END BOY

Although Hitchcock always considered himself an American director, he spent the first 40 years of his life in England.

Born in 1899, the son of a poultry dealer and fruit importer, young Alfred grew up in Leytonstone, East London. At 11 he was sent to school, a strict Jesuit foundation. He later claimed that the brotherhood only taught him one thing - the meaning of fear. "The Jesuits used to terrify me to death..." he liked to say, "... but now I'm getting my own back by terrifying other people."

BRIGHT LIGHTS

Hitchcock's first break into the budding film industry came after reading in the paper that the American "Famous Players-Lasky" (later Paramount Pictures) were coming to town. He turned up at the company's Islington studios with illustrations for title credits and, at the age of 20, was taken on as the studio's title designer. His pluck paid off. Just two years later he was given his own film to direct. Unfortunately the aptly named *Number Thirteen* had to be abandoned due to lack of funds, but it was a start.

THE BEST OF BRITISH

It was in 1926 that he really made his mark with the silent thriller, *The Lodger*. It was also the first film in which he himself appeared as an extra, a trademark of many of his later films. That year also marked another first - his marriage to his script girl Alma Reville who was to collaborate on many of his later scripts.

By 1929, with the release of *Blackmail* - a superior thriller (and his first talkie) - Hitchcock had established himself as one of Britain's leading directors. It was a reputation he consolidated in the mid-Thirties when he rejoined Balcon at Gaumont-British to make the classics *The Man Who Knew Too Much* (1934), *The 39 Steps* (1935) and *The Lady Vanishes* (1938).

Hitchcock's cameo appearance in *Rebecca,* with George Sanders.

THE LAND OF OPPORTUNITY

The Lady Vanishes marked a turning point for Hitchcock and, in 1938, he made a lucrative deal with the Hollywood producer, David Selznick. Hitchcock's first film for the Americans was the very British *Rebecca* (1939). Based on Daphne du Maurier's novel, starring Joan Fontaine and Laurence Olivier, the film was a big hit, and the only Hitchcock film to win a Best Picture Oscar.

Throughout the Forties, while still contracted to Selznick, Hitchcock worked for several studios. In 1943 he attempted his first American subject, *Shadow of a Doubt*, - co-written by the playwright Thornton Wilder. It was one of Hitchcock's favourites.

The Ingrid Bergman films *Spellbound* (1945) and *Notorious* (1946) were made at this time. The latter won Claude Rains an Oscar nomination. There followed several less distinguished films, but he was back on form in 1951 with his adaptation of Patricia Highsmith's novel, *Strangers on a Train*.

Hitchcock was in his mid-50s and working as an independent producer-director at Paramount when he entered a highly creative stage of his career. Using his 15 years of experience in the ways of Hollywood he assembled a team of favourite stars, and technicians and kicked off with two

Grace Kelly films: *Rear Window* (1954) and *To Catch a Thief* (1955). These were rapidly followed by *The Man Who Knew Too Much* (1956 - a remake) and *The Wrong Man* (1956) starring Henry Fonda. *Vertigo* (his last film with James Stewart), and *North by Northwest* (his last film with Cary Grant) came out in 1958 and 1959.

Although the Sixties are not considered golden ones for Hitchcock, he did direct three last great pictures - *Psycho* (1960) - arguably the most popular film of his whole career - *The Birds* (1963) and *Marnie* (1964); work he wasn't able to match in later years. During this period he also found time to launch his own television series, "Alfred Hitchcock Presents".

Hitchcock once said that the most exquisite murders were domestic. And of all Hitchcock's strengths, perhaps the one that made him most popular with audiences, was his preoccupation with the trials of the ordinary man. Audiences felt that what was happening on screen, however horrible, could just as easily happen to them.

In addition to entertaining stories, his films were beautifully and carefully shot. From the beginning Hitchcock's work was described as "American" - meaning slick. He also worked with some of the greatest stars around. Although he was known to treat stars badly, Hitchcock knew how to use his actors. Ingrid Bergman, Cary Grant, James Stewart and Grace Kelly were given great roles, and often surprising ones: who else would have cast Cary Grant as a murderer or Janet Leigh as a thief?

Above: Hitchcock regarded the script as a film's most important ingredient. *Notorious* star Ingrid Bergman clearly agrees. Right: In *The Birds*, our feathered friends turn nasty, though the stuffed ones on the tree seem harmless enough.

in 1936, he directed Errol Flynn and David Niven in *The Charge of the Light Brigade*, he wore, like DeMille, riding breeches and riding boots. Niven took for the title of one of his books the order shouted by Curtiz to cue the arrival of a hundred head of riderless chargers. "Okay," he yelled into a megaphone, "Bring on the empty horses!" Niven and Flynn doubled up with laughter. "You lousy bums! You and your stinking language. You think I know fuck nothing. Well, let me tell you - I know fuck all!"

At the start of the Sixties Omar Sharif was a well-known young film actor in Egypt, but totally unknown to the rest of the world. Then he was asked to test for a part in *Lawrence of Arabia* (1962). Sharif was flown out to the desert in a small private plane. As they approached, he could see nothing but sand... and then a jeep swam into view, with a man standing beside it. " The plane stopped with the passenger door precisely next to the man, who had not even moved. The door opened. "Omar", said David Lean, "I'm delighted that you could come."

Omar Sharif didn't have a moustache at that time, but Lean thought he ought to have one for the test. Afterwards, the actor flew back to Cairo. Ten days later he heard that he'd got the role, a small part that quickly grew until it was practically second lead to Peter O'Toole. Like Sharif, O'Toole was an unknown at that time; in fact the big names - Jack Hawkins, Alec Guinness, Anthony Quinn,

Donald Wolfit, Claude Rains, Anthony Quayle, Jose Ferrer - were in supporting roles. Although the principal actors and film crew stayed in the desert for nearly a year, 300 miles from the nearest road, they lived like kings. A famous chef was flown in from London, as was a fine selection of wines. One of the few drawbacks was that no women were allowed to stay or visit, in case the desert-crazy, albeit gourmet-fed men, misbehaved. "It might also have created bad blood." This seems unlikely, since they worked non-stop for three weeks and were then given three days off. Omar Sharif and Peter O'Toole used to fly to Beirut. "We would get off the plane and dig into the whisky and the champagne and the girls."

The two men became close friends; indeed, the desert-stranded company was like a large family, or perhaps a community of families. After a day's shooting, O'Toole, Sharif and a few others would sit at a table outside the tent, talking and watching the sunset. But not Lean. "He used to stay all by himself always. He didn't look for the warmth of company. Every morning, he used to go out there before everybody and put his chair in the middle of the desert and sit there looking at... nothing. He was burning it all into his brain, his eyes, his imagination. He was very hard on himself, you know."

Sometimes, Lean would be flown out very early for the first shot of the day. Flown because, from horizon to horizon, there must be no marks in the sand. Like characters in a nursery rhyme, there were Three hundred men/ With three hundred brooms/ To brush the land-scape smooth/ For take two. When the actors arrived (often, like Lean, flown there) they would have to wait until their director was ready. Round about mid-morning, he might call them into his cara-van to have more of the endless tea, and to discuss the scene. "Omar... Peter... I have no idea how to shoot this. What do you think?" Whether his request was genuine or simply a way of getting them even more involved in their characters is difficult to say. The fact remains that it always took a long time to get started, but once Lean had made up his mind he was actually a very fast director. "You did one take - two takes maximum, because we had rehearsed so thoroughly. During these rehearsals, stopwatch in hand, he would repeatedly tell us to act in half the time. It's a great piece of advice. Most actors tend to be slow if they're not told."

Lean was an imposing figure on set or location, seemingly aloof and austere, and for the most part silent. That distinguished actor,

Anthony Quinn, only eight years younger than Lean, was nevertheless a little in awe of him. "I had this scene with Peter O'Toole who asked me to attack Aqaba, and in the script I was supposed to reply, 'Tomorrow we attack Aqaba'." Quinn played the scene, Lean said "Cut" and then noticed that Quinn was looking unhappy. "What's the matter, Tony?" Reluctantly, Quinn said, "Lawrence is asking me to attack Aqaba with my 5,000 men, and I know all the Turks are there and I've got no chance of beating them... I think I'd go off somewhere and *think* about it before saying yes" "My gosh, Tony, you're right! Now then... where would you go?" Quinn pointed to a large rock. "I think I'd go back there and hunch down and think about it, how it means I'm gonna endanger my men... and then make up my mind.

Spectacle: David Lean's *Lawrence of Arabia*.

Oh, I don't say any of this, of course, but I think to myself there's probably gold there and I'll tell my men we'll all be rich if we attack Aqaba. Then I get up and go back to where Peter is and I say 'Tomorrow we attack Aqaba'... but with a different feeling." Lean nodded thoughtfully, drawing on his cigarette - "He smoked a cigarette upside down, by the way - kind of hidden in his hand, I mean" - and he said, "Fine. Now of course, if you walk over to that rock, that means... I have to move all the camels over, and all the horses, yes... Yes. Well, it'll take about five hours to do that. Fine, we'll do it your way." Quinn was deeply embarrassed, especially when Peter O'Toole, who had been hovering in the background, asked him what was happening, and he had to explain.

Five hours later, everything was ready. Peter asked his question, Quinn went over to his rock, had a think, came back and said, "Tomorrow we attack Aqaba". Lean said, "Fine, we haven't got time for another take, the sun's just gone down behind the mountains." And he started to get into his Rolls Royce. Quinn stopped him and said, "David, I apologise, I'm so sorry, I don't know what happened to me. I should've kept my mouth shut." Lean almost put a hand on his shoulder. "Tony, it was a better scene. You must never hesitate to tell me when a scene is wrong." And then came the Only From Lean pay-off. "I am not that insecure."

Aloof? Austere? Some people allege, too, that Lean was without humour. After shooting one particular scene between Robert Mitchum and Sarah Miles in *Ryan's Daughter* (1970), Lean was so moved that he could barely whisper, "Cut". Mitchum, who likes to pretend that he simply stands where he's told, says the lines and tries not to knock anything over, started to walk past the camera. Lean gave him pause with, "Bob... that was... beautiful." Mitchum said, "You didn't think it was too Jewish?" Lean stared at him... then smiled uncertainly, an earnest professor of humour greeting an impenetrable one-liner.

What does it feel like to know that for the first time in your life, you are going to direct a film? On the first morning of the first day of his first feature film, Robert Zemeckis wanted to be the first person there. He was happy with the location, happy about what he was about to do... until he saw the giant convoy of trucks pulling in to line the streets and fill the parking lot. "That was when the panic set in. I thought, My God, I'm responsible. There was something about the image of these giant 40ft trailer tractors that scared the hell out of me." If it had been D. W. Griffith's first day on a trip back to the future, there would have been, Zemeckis thinks, a lot of things he would have recognised as being much the same as when he made *The Birth of a Nation*. On any Nineties film he would feel comfortable, understand completely what was happening, although, of course, some of the equipment and technical things would look very different.

Ron Howard, an alumnus of Roger Corman's unofficial film school, made the transition from cute actor to incisive director with *Grand Theft Auto* (1977). Everybody was waiting at the location, the interior of a house, where the first scene would be shot. Everyone was wondering how this new young director would operate on his first day. Howard walked in with total confidence. Unhurriedly, he made clear his intentions. "[The actress] will come through that door over there; she walks over there, sits down in this chair here, picks up the phone. The camera will be on the door; it will dolly and pan with her here. When she picks up the phone, we'll cut to a close-up. Right. That's your shot, I'm gonna have some coffee, tell me when you're lit." Everybody was impressed. Hey, the kid knows what he's doing, he's given us the movements for the actress, he's given us the movements for the camera. Corman joined his ex-pupil for coffee and congratulated him. As he suspected, the young man had been rehearsing the opening shot of The Ron Howard Story all weekend.

John Schlesinger's first day illustrious as feature film director came with *A Kind of Loving* in 1962, on location on the outskirts of Manchester. It was a scene with Alan Bates and June Ritchie coming back from their honeymoon, with Thora Hird, as the dragon of a mother-in-law, leaning out of a window talking to them. "I'll never forget driving up in the car to this location and thinking, 'Oh God, I wish I could turn round and go away.' It's good to be on your toes but

☛ page 242

"The censor's paying us a visit today, so no lower than this, OK?" John Schlesinger directs *A Kind of Loving.*, his first feature film, from the stalls. With June Ritchie and Alan Bates.

ANIMAL
PASSIONS

A nimals have done the cinema proud - even providing the occasional star. Dogs have probably earned the most. Rin Tin Tin used to get thousands of fan-letters, had a valet, a personal chef, his own limousine and a chauffeur to drive him - but then he was credited with saving Warner Bros. from bankruptcy. Of course acting with animals is tough on humans. Hooch, for instance, (in *Turner and Hooch*) was an exceptionally slobbery beast and could drench Turner's (Tom Hanks) clean shirt in 10 minutes flat. Here are some of the animals that hit the big time.

Rin Tin Tin

A German Shepherd discovered as a pup in the trenches by a Col Lee Duncan, Rin Tin Tin was taken back to the USA and groomed for greater things. He appeared in many silent features and several serials in the Twenties, before making a successful transition to sound. At the height of his success he was earning more than $1,000 a week. After Rin Tin Tin's death in 1932 there was a whole dynasty of Rinties to follow in his paw-prints: the most illustrious being his great grandson, Rinty IV. Born in an air-conditioned kennel, he starred in his own series, "The Adventures of Rin Tin Tin", and was insured for $250,000.

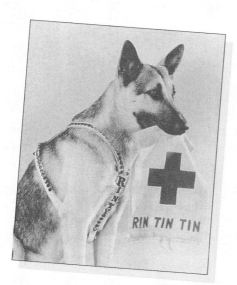

Benji

B enji was plucked from canine obscurity - or more accurately from the Burbank Animal Shelter. Trained up by Frank Inn, he appeared on CBS's TV series "Petticoat Junction" (1963-1970), and starred in the 1974 box-office hit, *Benji*. Too old for the film's sequel, *For the Love of Benji* (1977), Benji II took over - in a big way. He charged $7,500 for personal appearances, only travelled First Class and was fed on cubes of filet mignon. The sequel was popular enough to pave the way for further follow-ups: *Oh, Heavenly Dog* (1980) and *Benji the Hunted* (1987)

Lassie

H ollywood's most famous doggie. Six collies have played the faithful hound since *Lassie Come Home* was released in 1943 - all of them male. Only the very first Lassie was female because, during filming (which took place in the summer), she shed her coat - as female collies do.

Strongheart

C inema's first canine super-star, Strongheart, started life as a Red Cross dog serving in World War I. Cast as half-dog half-wolf in *The Silent Call* (1921), he was an immediate celebrity — even publishing his own book: *Letters to Strongheart*.

Beethoven
➤

Just shows you — dog stars never die. This huge, shaggy, cuddly St Bernard took $50 million at the box office in 1992.

Cheetah the Chimpanzee
➤

Cheetah was an essential cast member of any *Tarzan* film. He could play, turn somersaults, carry messages and give cuddles. The original Cheetah, who played opposite Tarzan in 1918, eventually grew too big and was sold to a circus. The very last Cheetah had a more tragic fate, in 1957. Breaking out of his cage, he attacked his owner and was shot by a sheriff's deputy.

Trigger
➤

The world's smartest horse, this golden palamino appeared in 87 movies - including *The Adventures of Robin Hood* (1938), where he was Maid Marion's mount - as well as more than 100 episodes of Roy Roger's Fifties television series. Rogers always claimed that stand-ins were never used in the *Trigger* films, and fondly remembered in this steed's obituary that "we had to do more retakes for human actors than for Trigger." Trigger is now stuffed and on display at the Roy Rogers-Dale Evans Musuem, Victorville, California.

Flipper
➤

The film *Flipper* (1963) was such a success that it was turned into a TV series. Mitzi was the 300lb female dolphin lead and was, as her owner said, "a ham from the word go." She died of a heart attack in 1971.

Clyde
➤

Clint Eastwood's side-kick in *Every Which Way But Loose* (1978) was Clyde the orang-utan. Just like his boss, he could fall down dead when someone shouted "Bang!" Clyde and Clint teamed up again for *Any Which Way You Can* (1980)

TIPS FROM TRAINERS

To get a wasp to crawl across a window pane, chill it first

To get a cat to rub past your legs cover them in liver pate.

I was really terrified when I saw the whole unit and the lights and everything else getting rigged and got out of vans." He is still nervous occasionally but, in the end, the adventure consumes him. He enjoys taking a whole group of people with him on the adventure of making a film. "The director is a mixture of many things, part artist, answerable to the money, a public relations man dealing with the press, dealing with actors and crew, all of whom need handling in different ways. He tries to give actors space to give of their best, allowing them to give the performance he wants." Schlesinger's years as an actor were useful because he knows what it feels like to walk on to a set at eight in the morning; and playing a love scene at that hour is daunting. Like Lean, Schlesinger is secure enough to use other people's ideas. "Provided you acknowledge it and say 'Top of the class, good idea, thank you.' It's when you don't do that, when people pretend a brilliant idea is their own, that it's unacceptable."

Producers and directors need writers; they needed them desperately after 1927. Once sound was tamed, the old spontaneity of the silents returned to the cinema, enhanced by totally new dramatic possibilities which were nourished by playwrights and novelists. As a rule, however, even the most distinguished of these were not regarded much more highly than the humble dialogue writers who were incarcerated in the writers' buildings to be found at every major studio. Crouched over their typewriters, they worked like battery hens, laying their daily quota of scrambled dialogue.

Novelist and screenwriter Budd Schulberg remembers that sound made Hollywood a much more intellectual place because of the influx of playwrights and novelists. Anthony Quinn says, "Suddenly this new breed came in. You saw F. Scott Fitzgerald, Faulkener, Steinbeck, Thomas Mann - but they had to go back to school and learn how to write motion picture scripts." Everybody was competing to hire the best. One day an agent came to Warner Bros. promoting a writer called Jacob Wasserman, who had just written *The Life of the Ant and The Life of the Bee*. Warner Brothers signed him. Anthony Quinn was under contract there at that time, "Nineteen-forty-one, I think it was, and Jacob Wasserman was terribly impressed with the Hollywood stars walking down the street; and Jack Warner was impressed with Jacob. 'Write anything you want. Just write any motion picture you want and we'll make it, because we know you're a great writer.' A year later, Wasserman came in with his script. 'Terrific. It just so happens',

Jack Warner said, 'that I've just had a call from Louis B. Mayer offering to loan me one of his big stars. Tell me, Jake, is there a part for Greta Garbo in your script?' And Jacob Wasserman said, 'I don't know. Would she play an ant?' "

Budd Schulberg's father, B.P. Schulberg, who eventually became general manager of Paramount studios, started in the business by writing what were then called photoplays. He wrote two a week for Edwin Porter; they were turned into very short films, of course. Budd Schulberg is always irritated when pictures are announced at festivals as the film of the director concerned. "Somebody wrote those characters, somebody put those words into their mouths, some of them were outstanding writers - and nobody mentions their names. 'Directed by'! - as if they made it up." Schulberg is probably the only writer in the world who was on the council of the Screen Writers Guild in the Thirties and is still on the council today in New York. "And we're still hearing the same thing there on the agenda, the same things we were talking about 50 years ago." Still... is he pleased about the financial success of writers like Joe Eszterhas? "The money is fine. It would please me more if it came to writers of more serious subjects."

Producer Art Linson says, "You're not allowed too many failures before you have a damn hard time getting your calls returned. You can't even get writers to want to work with you." It's that "even" that gets under the skin. Most writers and all screenwriters are paranoid, which is not to say that producers and directors and stars aren't out to abuse them. Screenwriters everywhere may take some comfort in what Robert Parrish has to say: "When I was a film editor I always said what all film editors said, that the film is made in the cutting room. I was wrong; the film is made in the script. Whatever you start with, that's what's made. Everyone else concerned - director, editor, actors, cameraman - can hurt it, or they can make it a little better, but they can't make it."

One of the most financially successful writers in Hollywood was Ben Hecht who, in the Twenties, had co-written with Charles MacArthur the hit stage plays *Twentieth Century* and *The Front Page*. His friend, Herman Mankiewicz, sent him a telegram urging him to come to Hollywood. It read:

> ..."MILLIONS ARE TO BE GRABBED OUT HERE
> AND YOUR ONLY COMPETITION IS IDIOTS"...

Hecht was only too pleased to do a bit of intellectual slumming in Hollywood. He spent a week writing a script called *Underworld* (1927), for which Paramount paid him $10,000. He stayed in Hollywood to write nearly 60 more scripts, at least 30 of which, he later claimed, took no more than two weeks to write. At one time he was paid $10,000 a week. From Howard Hughes, he demanded and got one thousand dollars a day, payable at 6 pm of each day he worked. David Selznick paid him $3000 to re-write *Gone With the Wind* after filming had started.

Billy Wilder, an Austro-Hungarian, had been a writer and co-writer of other people's films in Europe before coming to Hollywood to do the same thing there. He had directed one film in France in 1933, *Mauvaise Graine*, but as an American he had to wait until 1942 to direct *The Major and the Minor* (with a non-dancing, non-singing Ginger Rogers.) From then on, he always wrote what he directed and wrote always in collaboration, most happily with I.A.L Diamond.

But in 1944, according to Otto Friedrich, author of *City of Nets*, he wanted to make a film of James M. Caine's *Double Indemnity*. Starring Fred MacMurray and Barbara Stanwyck, the film is a classic *film noir*, with an incisive, pared-down, totally unsentimental script. Paramount bought the book for Wilder - James Cain got $15,000 for it - but the author was unavailable as co-writer because he was under contract to Fox. Someone Wilder had never heard of - Raymond Chandler - was recommended to him. When he read *The Big Sleep*, Wilder wanted to work with him, and a meeting was arranged. It was mutual suspicion on sight, Chandler, then in his 50s (Wilder was not yet 40) and smoking a pipe, wore a shirt and tie under a tweed jacket with leather-patched elbows. Wilder, who

Classic Billy Wilder, whose uncomfortable collaboration with Raymond Chandler worked beautifully. *Double Indemnity* starred Fred MacMurray and Barbara Stanwyck.

had had a decade in which to assume his American persona, wore a baseball cap and waved a riding crop when he spoke.

Chandler had never written for the movies and thought the work might take up two or three weeks he could ill afford to spend. He was not pleased when Wilder told him, "We are going to write this picture *together*. We are going to lock ourselves in this room and write a screenplay. It is going to take us a long time. You will be on salary even if it takes a year to write this picture."

Thoughtful and considerate flat-sharers know how difficult it is to live in harmony; here, two large egos were trapped in a shotgun marriage. It was torture. Wilder respected Chandler's talent, but Chandler scorned Wilder's and Wilder himself, even though - perhaps because - the director was the one who knew how to write movies. Chandler said later, "Working with Wilder was an agonising experience and has probably shortened my life." Wilder was no less bitter. "He gave me more aggravation than any writer I ever worked with." They laboured together for months, hating the collaboration, hating each other. Wilder went often to the bathroom, just to escape from his fellow prisoner. Alone, Chandler drank bourbon and filled the room with pipe smoke, so that when Wilder returned, he would cry out, "For Chrissakes, Ray, open a window." little knowing how much the oft-repeated appeal fuelled Chandler's slow fire of resentment.

One day, when the sun poured through the venetian blinds, Billy Wilder said, mildly enough, "Go and fix that, will you, Ray?" It was one order too many, and Chandler walked out of the office, walked out of Paramount, and went home. Three days later, armed with a typed list of grievances, all written out in quiet fury on yellow paper, he turned up in the office of Joe Sistrom, Wilder's producer at Paramount. Chandler's list went into considerable detail. "Mr Wilder is at no time to swish under Mr Chandler's nose or to point in his direction the thin, leather-handled malacca cane which Mr Wilder is in the habit of waving around while they work. Mr Wilder is not to give Mr Chandler orders of an arbitrary or personal nature such as , 'Ray, will you open the window?' or 'Ray, will you shut that door, please?' Mr Wilder frequently interrupts our work to take phone calls from women. I can't work with a man who wears a hat in the office; I feel he is about to leave momentarily." Sistrom sent for Wilder, who apologised, and somehow the two men worked together for another six months - with Chandler repeatedly threatening to resign, and

Wilder cajoling him into continuing. At last the work was finished, and Wilder could get on with making the film of *Double Indemnity*.

Except that nobody wanted to be in it. Alan Ladd turned it down, so (of course) did George Raft. Fred MacMurray wasn't keen on playing the part, either, later saying, "I never dreamed it would be the best picture I ever made." Barbara Stanwyck had to be bullied into playing a cold-blooded killer. "What are you?" the director demanded, "a mouse or an actress?"

All things considered, Wilder comes out of this story rather well. However, he went to the Academy Awards ceremony, certain that he would win an Oscar. When it went instead to Leo McCarey for *Going My Way* (1944). When McCarey was also named best director, Wilder could not bear it. As McCarey marched down the aisle to receive his award, Wilder stuck out a foot and tripped him.

In the early Forties the German playwright, Bertholt Brecht, his wife and two children, reached America largely on funds solicited by Fritz Lang. The "enemy alien", subject to an 8pm curfew, forbidden to travel more than five miles from home without special permission, wanted very much to write for the movies. He wrote several scenarios, one based on an episode in the life of his fellow-exile Peter Lorre. It was Fritz Lang, once again, who came to his rescue by suggesting a film based on the true story of the killing, in 1942, by two Czech guerrillas, of Reinhard Heydrich, deputy chief of the Gestapo. Lang and Brecht produced a treatment which Lang sold to an independent producer, Arnold Pressburger. Lang then hired John Wexley - who had written *Angels With Dirty Faces* (1938) and *Confessions of a Nazi Spy* (1939) - as Brecht's collaborator. The playwright thought of Wexley as a jobbing writer whose task was to serve Brecht's genius; Wexley's view was different, and he made sure that every page of the script had his name on it. Brecht merely had notes to support his later claim to a shared screen credit. He had hoped that, "Credit for the film would possibly put me in a position to get a film job if the water gets up to my neck." The Screenwriters Guild, in spite of Lang's support for Brecht, ruled that the full screen credit would go to Wexley, not because he had written the whole script, but because Brecht was a German who would someday go back to Germany, whereas Wexley would remain in America, and therefore the screen credit was more important to him, an American, than to the refugee from Nazism that was the basic subject of the movie.

Fighting over screen credits has long been endemic in Hollywood. When Orson Welles and Herman J. Mankiewicz collaborated on *Citizen Kane* (1940), it was hard to separate one author's contribution from the other's. Mankiewicz had long wanted to write a story about the newspaper magnate, William Randolph Hearst, and, incidentally, his mistress Marion Davies. Welles liked Mankiewicz's script but thought it too wordy and slow, so he cut out whole scenes and subplots and wrote in his own. The two writers revised each other's drafts, and Mankiewicz slyly used Welles as the model for Kane's furniture-smashing tantrum. When the script was at last finished, Welles claimed that it was entirely his work; Mankiewicz appealed to the Screen Writers Guild, saying that he was the original author. He later claimed that Welles offered him a bonus of $10,000 to let Welles take full credit. Mankiewicz asked Ben Hecht what he should do. Hecht gave him a characteristic answer: "Take the ten grand and double-cross the son of a bitch." The Screen Writers Guild eventually decreed a joint credit, with Mankiewicz's name first.

Writers for the movies, right from the start, could never be sure of a sole credit, co-writing credit or any credit at all. *Everybody Comes to Rick's*, an unproduced stage play by Murray Burnett and Joan Alison, was the starting point for *Casablanca* (1942). As is Hollywood's way with writers of novels and plays, Murray and Alison were not asked to write the screenplay. In the end several writers were paid to work on the project; only three credited. In her book, *Round Up The Usual Suspects*, Aljean Harmetz tells us that producer Hal Wallis engaged his brother-in-law, Wally Kline, and Kline's partner, Aeneas MacKenzie, to work on the script, which they did for seven weeks; none of their work was used. A small contribution was made later by Hal Wallis's favourite writer, Casey Robinson, who laboured for three weeks; but most of the *Casablanca* screenplay was written by the Epstein brothers and Howard Koch. Julius and Philip Epstein were identical twins with identical tastes in practical jokes, and an almost identical approach - both witty and cynical - to the work in hand. Jack Warner caught the Epsteins slinking into the studio at lunch-time one day, and read the riot act. "Railroad presidents get in at nine o'clock; bank presidents get in at nine o'clock. Read your contract. You're coming in at nine." Dissolve to Warner at his desk some time later, the twins sitting meekly opposite. Throwing down several pages of script, he said, "This is the worst scene I ever read in my life."

☞ page 250

FILM

E.T. – THE EXTRA-TERRESTRIAL

UNIVERSAL 1982

Producers: Steven Spielberg,
Kathleen Kennedy

Director: Steven Spielberg

Stars: Henry Thomas,
Dee Wallace, Peter Coyote,
Robert MacNaughton, Drew Barrymore

O S C A R S

**BEST SOUND EFFECTS EDITING,
VISUAL EFFECTS, MUSICAL SCORE**

Martin Amis' reaction to *E.T.*: "I felt like I had lived out a one-year love affair - complete with desire and despair, passion and prostration - in the space of 120 minutes."

Steven Spielberg: "I always considered it a love story, even before the script was written. That was going to be my love story."

Love Affair

Spielberg wanted *E.T.* to be the next *The Wizard of Oz* (1939). Whether or not he succeeded, this magical tale of a fatherless 10-year-old boy and his love for a 900-year-old alien, certainly enchanted moviegoers the world over. More than 240 million people went to see the film, making *E.T.* one of the highest-grossing films of the century.

The Child in Me

Steven Spielberg was just 34 when he made *E.T.* Based on a plot originally called "Growing Up", Melissa Mathison's script, was heavily modelled on Spielberg's own childhood memories. "I think I'm Peter Pan — I really do!" the director is supposed to have declared.

Below: Spielberg liked this image so much, he used it as the logo for his production company, Amblin'.

FILM Facts

LOW BUDGET

The film cost just $10.3 million to make, and 10% of this went on building and designing E.T. the creature - cheaper, as Spielberg pointed out, than a cameo appearance by Marlon Brando.

BABY FACES

Spielberg came up with a picture of how he wanted E.T. to look by super-imposing Einstein's eyes over the photograph of new-born child. It was decided that the alien's neck should be extendable so that people would know it was more than a midget in a suit; and E.T.'s long arms and short legs were meant to give the impression of friendliness - as was his Donald Duck behind.

TALKING HEADS

Bringing E.T. alive was the responsibility of special-effects man Carlo Rambaldi. His success was such that "E.T. could have sung arias if he'd wanted to." E.T.'s head alone was capable of 35 individual movements: including frowning eyebrows, smiling lips, pulsating veins and a whole range of muscle movements, all coordinated by electronic cables and elaborate hand-controls. E.T.'s eyes even dilated in the light - though Spielberg was disappointed that they didn't look a little wetter than they did.

HUMAN ATTRIBUTES

Despite sophisticated electronics, whenever E.T. walks, there is actually someone inside his latex suit. The kitchen scenes were played by a little boy called Matthew de Merritt, who, born without legs, was an expert at walking on his hands. Most of the others shots were played by 2ft 10in Pat Bilon, who died shortly after filming.
E.T.'s hands came courtesty of mime artist Caprice Rothe, who answered Spielberg's ad for someone with "long, graceful fingers."

SILVER TONGUED

E.T.'s voice belonged to a retired teacher hired for the part when she was overheard ordering in a local supermarket. The extra-wheeze factor was added in the sound studios, with Debra Winger's voice mixed in for luck.

FLIGHTS OF FANTASY

The flying BMX bikes were models, convincingly filmed by George Lucas' special-effects firm, Industrial Light & Magic.

RICH PICKINGS

Universal, in gratitude, gave Spielberg his own headquarters on the lot. The adobe-style building was packed with electronic games.

The bikes are still on the ground, but the magic of special effects is about to get them airborne.

Phil instantly became deadpan Rick in *Casablanca*. "How is that possible? It was written at nine o'clock."

Oddly enough, the very last line in *Casablanca* - "Louis, I think this is the beginning of a beautiful friendship" - was supplied not by a writer, but by producer Hall Wallis. All thought is suspended during *Casablanca* - one never questions the idea of exit visas that cannot be rescinded, we find nothing odd in a refugee pimpernel being sought here, there and everywhere in his flashing neon sign of a white suit - and Ingrid Bergman is so beautiful that she can make us swallow the one ludicrous line in one of the greatest movies ever made. As we hear distant artillery, she says to Bogie, "Was that canon-fire, or is it my heart pounding?" What? Who wrote that? Not the Epsteins, surely, unless they enlisted the help of the fat man to play one of their practical jokes. That must be it - an ad lib mischievously tossed in from the sidelines - "Try this, my dear!" - by Sydney Greenstreet, his shoulders heaving with barely repressed laughter.

It is difficult to believe that playwrite/screenwriter Alan Bennett would allow anyone to tamper with his work, but in the case of the 1995 film version of his play, *The Madness of George III*, he did. The title was changed to *The Madness of King George*, because, it was put to Bennett, audiences might well think they had missed *The Madness of George* and *The Madness of George II*.

Which makes one wonder, mused Bennett, writing in the *London Review of Books*, where this leaves *The Third Man* and *The Second Mrs Tanqueray*. Bennett was more fortunate than most writers, it might be argued, because his screenplay was not taken apart by script doctors and other writers. Nevertheless, like a parent with a houseful of noisy children, one can be worn down, nagged into giving in to compromise. Bennett says, "Had Nicholas Hytner [the director] at the outset suggested bringing the King from Kew to Westminster to confront the MPs I would have been outraged. By the time I was plodding through the third draft I would have taken the King to Blackpool if I thought it would have helped."

Robert Zemeckis and his partner Bob Gale wrote the screenplay of *Back to the Future* (1985). It took them several years to sell it. They took the script to every studio and production company or production entity in town. Although films are "green lighted" on the strength of a screenplay, "You have to understand that it is not the finished form, the screenplay is the blueprint for a movie", says Zemeckis. His career

Romancing the Stone starring picaresque Michael Douglas and Kathleen Turner. Douglas also produced.

started with two films that did not make money, although they were critically acclaimed. In Hollywood, if a director's films don't make money, he is deemed to be unlucky. Fortunately for Zemeckis, Michael Douglas, wearing his producer's hat, thought the director's work was excellent, and asked him to direct *Romancing the Stone* (1984). Initially, there was resistance to this, but Douglas backed Zemeckis all the way. *Romancing the Stone* was a box-office success - and then everybody wanted Zemeckis to make films for them. But he went back to the only man who had had any faith in *Back to the Future* - Steven Spielberg. From the time that film was made, Zemeckis has never stopped working.

Hollywood screenwriters today can make vast sums of money. William Goldman, David Mamet, Michael Crichton, Quentin Tarantino, are all millionaires; and Joe Eszterhas, who got $3 million for writing *Basic Instinct* (1992), puts Ben Hecht in the shade. Not too long ago, he sold a synopsis for a thriller, *One Night Stand*, for $2.5 million. More recently, Paramount offered him $3.4 million to write *Reliable Sources*. Paramount's Sherry Lancing was so taken by Eszterhas's idea that the deal was completed in seven minutes.

Perhaps, like Art Linson, Eszterhas said nothing after "Yes".

Page numbers in *italic* refer to the illustrations

GENERAL ACKNOWLEDGEMENTS:

This book, more than most, is a collaborative effort. In particular, the authors would like to thank James Smith, who found the pictures, Emma Hagestadt who researched the features and Ann Lloyd who subedited the text. The book, of course, is based on the ITV television series *Lights, Camera, Action!* (co-produced by John Gau Productions and LWTP). So we owe a large debt to Frank Simmonds, the series director, and his hard-working team of Sally Brien, Ian Brown, Ann Munyard and Amanda Murphy, who gathered a lot of the material we use in the book .

As far as quotations in the text are concerned, where individuals are quoted the excerpts are for the most part taken from the many interviews filmed for the television series. Excerpts from books are generally speaking acknowledged where they are used.

However, short or passing references have not been mentioned in the text as the constant reference to authors and titles would be tedious. These, and other sources that have been most valuable as background reading in the preparation of this book, are gratefully acknowledged below:-

Bacall, Lauren. *By Myself* (Jonathan Cape Ltd, 1978) • Bach, Stephen. *Final Cut* (Jonathan Cape, 1985) • Bart, Peter; Suares, J.-C; Beck, J. Spencer. *Variety History of Show Business* (Hamlyn, 1993) • Bart, Peter. *Fade Out* (Simon & Schuster, 1990) • Base, Ron. *Starring Roles* (Little, Brown and Company, 1994) • Behlmer, Rudy, ed. *Memo From David O. Selznick* (Samuel French, 1989) • Bennett, Alan (article by). "King of America"(*The Guardian Weekend*, 25 February, 1995. The article first appeared in *The London Review of Books*) • Berg, A. Scott. *Goldwyn* (Hamish Hamilton, 1989) • Blum, Daniel. *A Pictorial History of the Silent Screen* (Spring Books, 1962) • Brosnan, John. *Movie Magic* (MacDonald & Jane's, 1974) • Brownlow, Kevin. *The Parade's Gone By* (Secker and Warburg, 1968) • Brown, Karl. *Adventures With D.W. Griffith* (Secker and Warburg, 1973) • Curtis, Tony. *Tony Curtis - the autobiography* (William Heinemann, 1994) • Edwards, Anne. *Judy Garland* (Constable and Company, 1975) • Edwards, Anne. *The DeMilles* (Harry N. Abrams, 1988) • Etherington-Smith, Meredith; Pilcher, Jeremy. *The IT Girls* (Hamish Hamilton, 1986) • Fleischer, Richard. *Just Tell Me When to Cry* (Souvenir Press, 1993) • Flynn, Errol. *My Wicked Wicked Ways* (William Heinemann, 1960) • Ford, Selwyn. *The Casting Couch* (Grafton Books, 1990) • French, Philip. *The Movie Moguls* (Weidenfeld and Nicolson, 1969) • Friedrich, Otto. *City of Nets* (Headline Book Publishing, 1987) • Gabler, Neal. *An Empire of Their Own* (W.H. Allen, 1989) • Goldman, William. *Adventures in the Screen Trade* (Macdonald & Co, 1985) • Granger, Stewart. *Sparks Fly Upwards* (Granada, 1981) • Halliwell, Leslie; Walker, John, ed. *Halliwell's Film Guide* (Grafton Books, 1994) • Halliwell, Leslie; Walker, John ed. *Halliwell's Filmgoer's Companion* (HarperCollins, 1993) • Harmetz, Aljean. *Round Up the Usual Suspects* (Weidenfeld and Nicolson, 1993) • Higham, Charles. *Merchant of Dreams* (Pan Books, 1993) • Higham, Charles; Greenberg, Joel. *The Celluloid Muse* (Angus & Robertson, 1969) • Hillier, Jim. *The New Hollywood* (Studio Vista, 1993) • Hirschhorn, Clive. *The Hollywood Musical* (Octopus Books, 1981) • Hirschhorn, Clive. *The Warner Bros. Story* (Octopus Books, 1979) • Hosodo, Craig. *The Bare Facts Video Guide* (The Bare Facts, 1993) • Huston, John. *An Open Book* (Macmillan, 1981) • Katz, Ephraim. *The Film Encyclopedia* (HarperPerennial/HarperCollins, 1994) • Linson, Art. *A Pound of Flesh* (Andre Deutsch, 1994) • Lisa, Philip and Pfeiffer, Lee. *The Incredible World of 007* (Boxtree, 1992) • Manvell, Dr. Roger. *The International Encyclopaedia of Film* (Rainbird Reference Books, 1972) • Marx, Samuel. *Mayer and Thalberg* (W.H. Allen, 1976) • Niven, David. *Bring on the Empty Horses* (Hamish Hamilton, 1975) • O'Donnell, Pierce; McDougal, Dennis. *Fatal Subtraction* (Doubleday, 1992) • Parrish, Robert. *Growing Up in Hollywood* (Little, Brown, 1976) • Perry, George. *Forever Ealing* (Pavilion Books, 1981) • Poitier, Sidney. *This Life* (Hodder and Stoughton, 1980) • Pollock, Dale. *Skywalking* (Samuel French, 1990) • Pyle, Michael and Myles, Lynda. *The Movie Brats* (Faber and Faber, 1979) • Robertson, Patrick. *The Guinness Book of Movie Facts & Feats* (Guinness Publishing, 1991) • Richards, Jeffrey. *The Age of the Dream Palace* (Routledge & Kegan Paul, 1984) • Shipman, David. *Cinema - The First Hundred Years* (Weidenfeld and Nicolson, 1993) • Sinclair, Andrew. *Spiegel* (Weidenfeld and Nicolson, 1987) • Smith, Thomas G. *Industrial Light & Magic* (Virgin Publishing, 1991) • Stine, Whitney. *Mother Goddam* (Fletcher & Son, 1974) • Swanson, Gloria. *Swanson on Swanson* (Michael Joseph, 1981) • Taylor, John Russell. *Hitch* (Faber and Faber, 1978) • Taylor, Philip M. *Steven Spielberg* (Butler & Tanner, 1992) • Walker, Alexander (and MGM). *Garbo* (Weidenfeld and Nicolson, 1980)

PICTURE ACKNOWLEDGEMENTS:

The publishers would like to thank all the film production and distribution companies both past and present whose publicity photographs appear in this book. Every effort has been made to trace and acknowledge holders of copyright, although in a few cases this has proved impossible. We apologise in advance for any unintentional omissions, and would be pleased to insert the appropriate acknowledgement in any subsequent editions of this publication.

Kobal Collection, courtesy of: (cover, clockwise) Famous Players/Paramount, RKO, United Artists, Orion/Hemdale (front cover), Universal (back cover), Embassy, Warner Bros., Paramount, RKO and Columbia (front cover), RKO only (back cover), Warner Bros, Mirisch Seven-Arts/United Artists • (book) Amblin - 33 top, Amblin/Universal - 213, Chaplin/UA - 100, Columbia - 32 lower left, 53 top right, 99, 101 lower right, 117 upper left, 118, page 132 middle left, 181,190, 204, Embassy - 86, Goldwyn - 53 bottom right, Guild/Carolco - 119, King Bros - 215 middle left, Stanley Kramer/UA - 179, London Films - 52 right, LucasFilm Ltd./Twentieth Century Fox - 208 bottom left, 209 bottom right, MGM - 53 top left,101 middle left,124,144,155, 167,183,189, 202, 203, 241 middle right, New World - 215 lower right, Paramount - 70, 77, 211, 218, 223, 241 top left, 244, LucasFilm Ltd/Paramount - 32 mid right, 109, Rank - 149, Selznick - 14, Selznick/MGM - 9,15,16, 93, Touchstone - 117 bottom left, Triancra/Orphee - 135, Twentieth Century Fox - 53 bottom left, 101 bottom centre, 114,132 centre, 174,197 bottom right, 251, United Artists - 129,187, 222, Universal - 29,182,197 middle left, 248,249, Universal/LucasFilm - 75, Warner Bros - 33 bottom, 52 right, 96, 101,112,113,133 lower left, 150,169,188, 241 lower mid right, Warner Bros/Regency Ent. VOB/Canal+ - 177

BFI Stills Posters and Designs, Pages: 12,36,37,38,39,44,45,47,54,82,97,120,121, 131,136,154,226,230 and courtesy of: AMPAS - 96*, Anglo-Amalgamated - 147, 239, Biograph - 80, B.I.P. - 48,49, Chaplin/UA - 5, 20, 21, Columbia - 34,35,138,172,180 bottom left and right,181 bottom, 218 bottom left, 236, 237, Columbia/Sir John Woolf/Romulus - 175, Eon Productions/United Artists - 26, 27, Famous Players/Lasky - 42, Hammer Films - 197 middle right, LucasFilm/Twentieth Century Fox - 208 right, 209 top left, middle left, Megalovision - 148, Melies - 184,191, MGM - 8, 55, 62,160, Paramount - 219, 220, Polygram Filmed Ent. - 197 bottom left, 200, Prana - 192, 196, Rank - 173, 229, RKO - 72, 73,116,169,171,197 top right, 233 bottom left, Twentieth Century Fox - 227, UFA - 78, United Press - 97 bottom, Universal - 106,185, 196 bottom left, top right, 196 bottom right,197 top left, Universal Elektra - 131, Warner Bros - 137,168, 234, 240,
* *"Academy Awards", "Oscar", and the Oscar statuette are trademarks of the Academy of Motion Picture Arts and Sciences. The statuette is also its copyrighted property.*

A.P. Wideworld - page 66

Disney Video - 165, top & bottom

Walt Disney Pictures - 164, 165 middle

Joel Finler Collection, courtesy of: Associated British Pictures - 159, MGM - 64 bottom left, Paramount - 57 top middle, 155, 64 top, Rebel Films - 151, RKO - 125, 65 top left, Selznick/United Artists - 232, Twentieth Century Fox - 81, Universal - 233 bottom right, Warner Bros - 65 middle right

Ray Harryhausen, courtesy of: Columbia/Charles H. Schneer - 193, 198, 199

James Smith, courtesy of: Twentieth Century Fox - 122, United Artists - 116, Warner Bros - 107, Warner/Chappell Music - 153